THE
FOREST OF DEAN
BRANCH

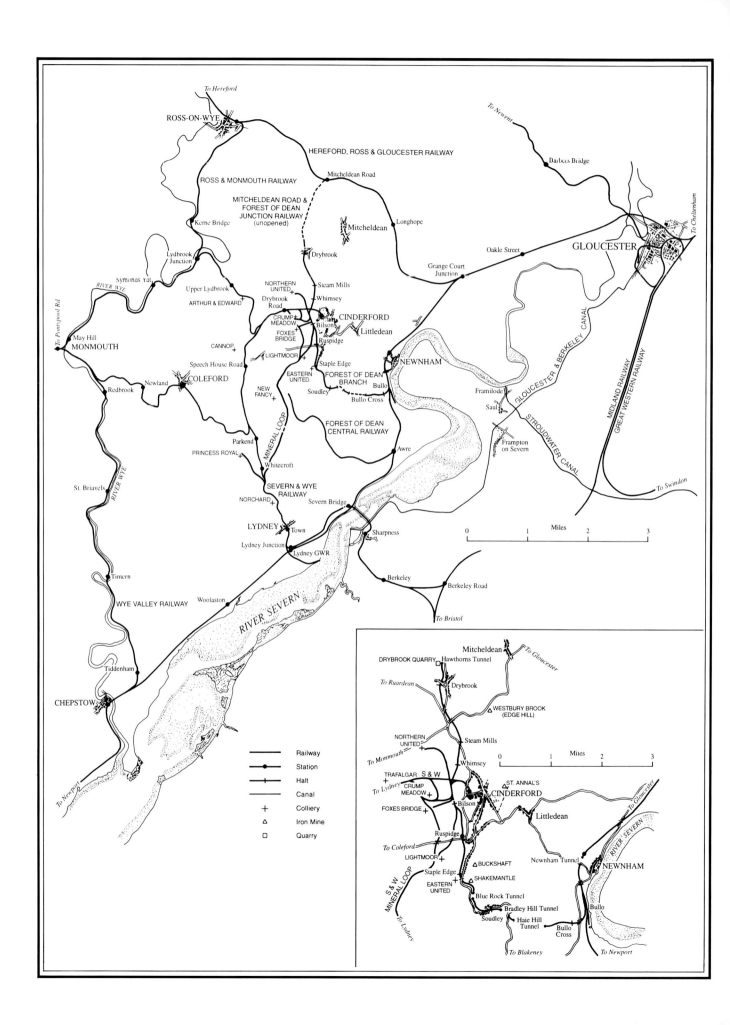

THE
FOREST OF DEAN
BRANCH

by
IAN POPE & PAUL KARAU

Volume One
NEWNHAM TO CINDERFORD

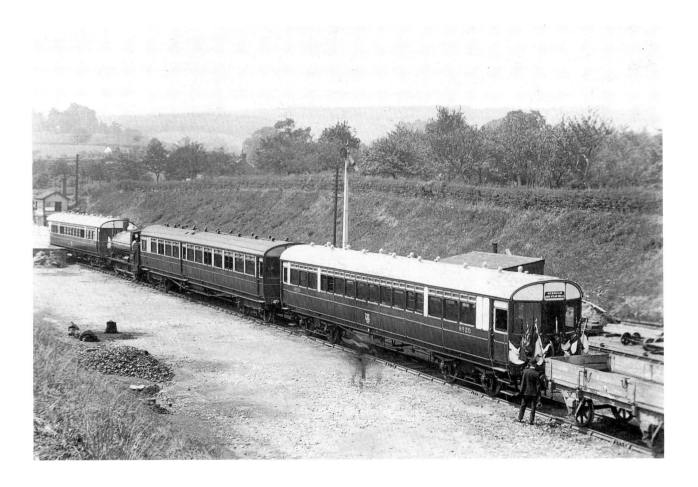

WILD SWAN PUBLICATIONS

Above: A panoramic view of Upper Soudley from the woods above the village. An enlargement of the coal train is reproduced on pages 22/23.

Collection R. How, cty. Elsie Ibbotson

Title page: The first extended working to Drybrook Halt in Newnham yard prior to departure on 4th November 1907. The formation consists of Diagram J1 trailer No. 20, a Diagram L trailer, a '2021' saddle tank, and another Diagram J trailer.

Collection J. E. Kite

FOR
BOB AND HARRY TRIGG

© Wild Swan Publications Ltd
and Ian Pope & Paul Karau 1992
ISBN 1 874103 05 4

Designed by Paul Karau
Printed by Amadeus Press, Huddersfield

Published by
WILD SWAN PUBLICATIONS LTD.
1-3 Hagbourne Road, Didcot, Oxon, OX11 8DP

ACKNOWLEDGEMENTS

When so many people have helped in our research over the years, it is difficult to believe that some have not escaped our memory while actually compiling this list. We hope anyone not included will forgive any such failing on our part. First and foremost we would like to pay particular thanks to Bob and Harry Trigg, not just for their hospitality and patience while answering our questions, but for giving us such an intimate mental picture of the line. We returned from each interview with quite a different perspective on the pictures we had collected and thought we knew.

We would also like to thank Bob How for help in many directions, not least for casting such an astute eye on the manuscript and page proofs. He also relayed some wonderful material from Elsie Ibbotson who, amongst other things, was kind enough to share her memories of a happy childhood in the Forest. David Bick gave generous access to material vital in piecing together the history of Eastern United Colliery, and without Peter Copeland's unique and splendid photographic surveys, not only would this volume be far poorer, but we might not have had the inspiration to tackle it at all. In addition to his own photographs of the line, Alec Pope came up with some real historical treasures and, as usual, was only too keen to help.

We would also like to thank: Keith Allford, Ralph Anstis, Mabel and Ken Beech, Maurice Bent, Daphne Booth, Maurice Buffery, Roger Carpenter, Mike Christensen, Don Gardiner, Cecil Hawden, John Hodges, Ken James, Vern Jordan, John Mann, Bob Marrows, John Norris, Margery Oakey, Harry Paar, Neil Parkhouse, Pete Skelton, Ian Standing, David Tipper and Chris Turner. The following organizations also provided invaluable assistance: The Public Records Office at Kew, Gloucestershire County Records, Gloucester Reference Library, Dean Heritage Museum and ARC Southern.

UDLEY.

CONTENTS

SOUDLEY VALLEY.

The ageless charm of the Soudley Valley, a natural route into the eastern side of the Forest of Dean. It is difficult to associate this picture of bucolic tranquillity with the clatter and grime of industry, but in fact Soudley was an iron-making centre as long ago as the early 13th century. This, together with the associated iron ore and coal mining industries, grew to maturity in the early 19th century, providing the stimulus for a tramroad to carry the 'superabundant produce' of the area to the tiny port at Bullo Pill on the Severn. This so encouraged trade that the tramroad was soon replaced by a branch of the Great Western's broad gauge South Wales Railway, the woodland echoing to the sound of locos working hard on the steeply graded line.

Collection R. How

AN OUTLINE HISTORY

THE Royal Forest of Dean has long been a source of mineral wealth for those enterprising enough to dig beneath the oak and beechwood. The mining and smelting of iron ore was carried out by the Romans, and continued successfully after the last legions departed for strife-torn Rome, whilst the extensive coal deposits were worked for both domestic and industrial use. Stone was also quarried for building purposes, and limestone for use in iron-making and agriculture.

The dawn of the Industrial Revolution brought increased demands for coal and iron ore, driven in part by improved methods of converting the ore into a usable form. This was not achieved overnight, nor did the improvements always receive immediate commercial success. Nevertheless during the latter part of the 18th century a pattern of gradually increasing production emerged. At the same time the Crown was increasing the felling of timber for commercial gain, and to build the fine ships of the King's Navy.

A major obstacle to exploiting the expanding production was the inability of the primitive roads and pack horse transportation of the period to carry the increasing loads to market, such roads as existed being described, no doubt accurately, as 'execrable', and impassable in winter. This was, of course, a problem of national proportions, not limited to the leafy confines of the Forest. In other areas, notably North East England and South Wales, primitive wooden waggonways in collieries and mines were gradually being developed into extensive systems of local horse-drawn tramroads, the precursors of today's railways. It was perhaps inevitable that the enterprising colliery owners and ironmasters of the Forest of Dean would learn of the new technology, and seek to exploit it for their own ends.

The first such venture in the Forest was started without Crown permission in 1795 by James Teague and partners. They then built a second line from Perch Enclosure, close to Edge End, to the Wye near Lydbrook. Used primarily to transport coal, it had a short life, being abandoned in 1815 in the face of mounting concern by the Crown's Deputy Surveyor and other local authorities over the blatant violation of the Forest plus the fact that Teague's colliery was beginning to run out of coal. However, it did serve to show others what was possible, and soon spawned three more successful and longer-lived successors.

The first of these was also commenced without the consent of Parliament. In 1797 Roynon Jones, Margaret Roberts, William Fendall and James Jelf began the construction of a tramroad some 4½ miles in length from Bullo Pill to Cinderford Bridge, on land leased for 100 years. This was almost complete by 1809, when the owners applied to Parliament for permission to extend the tramroad to ' . . . the summit of the Hill above Churchway Engine . . . '.

The Act, dated 10th June, incorporated the entire operation, together with sundry branches, as The Bullo Pill Railway Company, and leased the land to the company at £100 per year plus one guinea per week. It also provided that only Free Miners and HM Surveyor General, who was responsible for the timber in the area, could use the original Cinderford Bridge to Bullo portion, although, according to C. R. Clinker, there is evidence that 'it was pretty generally used as a public railway, with or without permission'.

The extension of just over 2¼ miles was intended to be completed by 25th December 1812, but was first used in March 1814. There is no documentary evidence of gauge, but from measurements of the trackbed taken in the early 1930s, this is estimated to have been 4ft (although this may be the gauge of a later relaying). The permanent way consisted originally of 3ft long cast iron tramplates spiked to stone blocks which acted as sleepers. The space between the tramplates was cobbled and the Act stated the formation was to be not more than seven yards in width except at passing places, embankments, cuttings or where warehouses or wharves were erected. The most notable engineering feature was the 1,100 yard long Haie Hill Tunnel, driven through the hillside at the southern end of Blaise Bailey Wood.

The tramroad was used to transport coal, iron ore, stone, timber and bricks down to the Severn at Bullo for shipment, and to move these and other materials from place to place within the Forest, the many short branches serving coal and iron mines, etc. It continued in use for another 12 years without interruption, but was badly affected by the slump in trade which followed the ending of the Napoleonic Wars in 1815, and eleven years later was almost at a standstill. During this time a connection with the Severn & Wye's tramroad at Churchway was made in 1823, necessitating a change of gauge to 44in, which was effected by adjusting the axle washers of the tram waggons.

The concern was offered for sale and was eventually purchased by Edward Protheroe, a local mining magnate and chairman of the Severn & Wye Co, who, together with three members of his family, and fourteen others, formed a new company, The Forest of Dean Railway Co, with a capital of £125,000 in £50 shares. The company was incorporated by an Act of Parliament dated 5th May 1826 and purchased the line, opening the private section between Cinderford Bridge and Bullo to public traffic. The Act states 'The object of this railway and branches, is to convey, with facility, for shipment on the Severn, the timber, coal, iron-ore, and other minerals, with which the Forest of Dean abounds, thus enabling the owners to transport their superabundant produce to distant markets'.

The tramroad continued in use for more than 25 years, its changing fortunes being illustrated by the £50 shares being offered for sale at £27-£28 in 1835 and 1836, whilst by 1839 and 1840 the Forest of Dean Railway Co distributed a dividend of more than 5%.

By 1836 the limitations of the tramroad were causing complaints, the absence of a double track and stoppages at the tunnel no doubt bringing frequent delays, and by

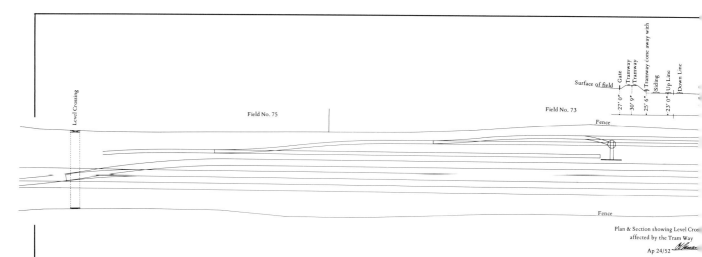

Surface of field

Field No. 75

Level Crossing

Field No. 73

Gate
Tramway
Tramway
Tramway cone away with
Siding
Up Line
Down Line

27' 0"
30' 9"
25' 6"
23' 0"

Fence

Fence

Plan & Section showing Level Cross
affected by the Tram Way
Ap 24/52

October 1837 a railway from Cinderford Bridge to a new harbour at Brimspill or Purton was being considered. This proposal got as far as an application to Parliament, but this was opposed by local landowners and the Severn & Wye Co and was thrown out due to discrepancies in the plans.

At a special general meeting of the company in 1838 consideration had been given to 'the necessity or expedience of applying to Parliament for the powers required to convert part of the said railway into a steam carriage road' but it was not until the South Wales Railway came onto the scene that any steps were taken towards this.

THE BROAD GAUGE LINE
'Minerals and Goods Traffic Only'
The South Wales Railway, really a GWR project, as originally proposed in 1844, was intended to connect Fishguard and Pembroke Dock in West Wales with the Swindon to Gloucester line at Standish on the east bank of the Severn. It would have crossed the river below Bullo Pill by means of a bridge which would have effectively blocked shipping access to the quays serving the Forest of Dean tramroad. Therefore it was agreed that the South Wales Railway would purchase the tramroad.

However, the South Wales Railway Act of 1845 authorised a broad gauge (7ft 0¼in) line only as far as Chepstow. The Severn crossing was dropped in favour of a new proposal for a line along the west bank of the river to a junction with the Gloucester and Dean Forest Railway, which the GWR rapidly gained an interest in. The extension of the SWR to Hagloe Farm in the Parish of Awre was authorised by an Act of 27th July 1846, as was the extension of the G & DF from Grange Court to Hagloe.

Although tramroad access to shipping was no longer threatened, the South Wales Railway still went ahead with the purchase of the FODR with the intention of converting it to a proper locomotive-hauled railway. A price of £90,000 was agreed in November 1849, with the SWR deemed to have taken possession in July.

The South Wales New Works Act of 3rd July 1851 authorised a single line of broad gauge locomotive-worked railway from Churchway Colliery and Whimsey to the

main line at Bullo, using much of the route of the old tramroad. It also allowed the abandonment of the final three-quarters of a mile of tramroad into Bullo Docks, a new railway branch being built from the main line to the riverside in lieu. This arrangement allowed undivided trains to run into sidings where they could be split up for Gloucester, Newport and Bullo Docks.

The South Wales Railway opened between Chepstow and Gloucester on 19th September 1851, but immediately prior to this, at a meeting on 12th September 1851, a letter from Newnham solicitors, Messrs. James & Wintle, was read to the SWR Board 'in reference to the formation of a junction between the Forest of Dean Branch and the main line'. After it had been read, it was resolved that 'Mr. Brunel be instructed to proceed at once with the construction of such junction'. The junction took the form of an interchange siding off the down main line with a new stretch of tramroad extending northwards from the approach to Bullo Dock to run alongside it. Details are hazy but by January 1852 'a booking constable' was employed at Bullo 'in consequence of the completion of the Forest of Dean Branch', and by that November 'additional siding accommodation from the down line' and 'an extra porter' were approved together with the 'occasional use of a horse'.

Conversion of the FoD branch began around 1851. Brunel was responsible for the work which, in order to avoid the sinuous curves of the tramroad, involved the construction of two new tunnels, Bradley Hill (299 yards) and one near Blue Rock (109 yards), and the enlargement of Haie Hill tunnel (1,064 yards). The conversion work was hampered by the need to keep the tramroad open for traffic, a particularly frustrating task during the enlargement of Haie Hill tunnel. Contractors included Tredwell & Co and William Guest, both of whom were involved with work on other portions of the South Wales Railway.

In October 1853 the secretary was instructed to 'make arrangements, with as little inconvenience as possible to the freighters, for giving the contractors more time each day than they are at present allowed for progressing with the works'. This suggests that a period, or periods, of the day were set aside for traffic to pass along the line, but in March 1854 it was reported that the time had finally

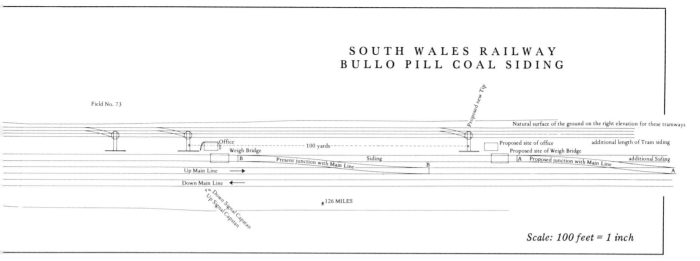

SOUTH WALES RAILWAY
BULLO PILL COAL SIDING

Field No. 73

Proposed new Tip

Natural surface of the ground on the right elevation for these tramways

Office
Weigh Bridge
- - - - - - - 100 yards - - - - - - -

Proposed site of office
Proposed site of Weigh Bridge
additional length of Tram siding

B
Present junction with Main Line
Siding
B
A
Proposed junction with Main Line
additional Siding

Up Main Line →
Down Main Line ←

Down Signal Capstan
Up Signal Capstan

126 MILES

A

Scale: 100 feet = 1 inch

arrived when it was necessary to close portions of the branch to complete the works. Notices were sent to traders to this effect, but stating that the railway would be ready in July. Needless to say, there were complaints. Some colliery owners were also unhappy where various deviations in connection with the easing of curves and building of tunnels had left them isolated from the new railway. One of these, J. F. Corbett, met with the response that 'he could construct a siding but at his own expense'. On the other hand, Aaron Goold, one of the biggest traders, met with a more cooperative attitude and Brunel was instructed to arrange a plan and estimate for a branch to Goold's Crump Meadow Colliery. It was subsequently resolved that 'provided Mr. Goold will construct the road, this company will supply the rails, Mr. Goold undertaking to pay an annual sum of 17% upon the cost of such rails until the whole becomes liquidated'. In the event, Goold offered to guarantee 50,000 tons per annum if the company would construct the branch, which the committee agreed to do.

The minutes of a board meeting on the 26th May 1854 record 'that the general rule by which the whole expense attending the putting in of sidings and junctions required by freighters is defrayed by them so far, varied in the case of the Forest of Dean Railway that the expense of forming the junctions, from time to time approved by the Directors, be defrayed by the Company. That the line when completed be opened in the first instance for the conveyance of Minerals and Goods Traffic only'.

After three years work and expenditure of some £120,000, the 7 mile 20 chain line (including the 53 chain line to the docks) was finally opened as a broad gauge branch of the South Wales Railway on 24th July 1854. From then on, use of the tramroad between 'the junction with the Lightmoor Branch' at Staple Edge and Bullo Pill was discontinued. North of the Lightmoor junction the tramroad to Churchway and Whimsey was retained 'for the accommodation of the coal traffic'.

It would appear that the branch was initially devoted entirely to the handling of coal and mineral traffic with no goods facilities and, whilst in many cases the date of private sidings is unclear, it is likely that those at Scilly Point, Shakemantle, Perseverance, Quidchurch, Staple

Edge, Cinderford Ironworks and either Spero or Regulator were in use at the outset. The SWR provided sidings for tramroad interchange at Whimsey and Churchway and marshalling sidings at Bilson Junction where the Whimsey and Churchway lines diverged.

Several tramroad staff transferred to the railway when it opened, including Thomas Olding and James Dakin who were put in charge at Whimsey and Churchway respectively for 16/- per week. Thomas Holford, who'd been employed as booking constable at Bullo, was put in charge at Bilson Junction 'for present', assisted by Edwin Letcher who attended the weighing machines both on the tramroad and on the broad gauge.

The provision of a passenger station at Churchway was raised at a board meeting in December 1854 but the SWR directors said they 'would give it further consideration when in a position to carry passengers on the branch'. Over fifty years were to pass before the branch would be opened for passenger traffic, but the nomination of Churchway as a suitable location for a station reminds us that, at the time, Cinderford as a settlement was only just beginning to expand from its humble beginnings around Cinderford bridge. A station at Churchway would have served the larger communities at Drybrook and Ruardean.

The growth of Cinderford undoubtedly led to the decision in May 1860 that Cinderford 'be opened as a goods station for invoicing traffic and other purposes'. However, whether the building and platform at Cinderford (later Ruspidge) were provided at this time is not clear as it was not until April 1866 that expenditure of £65 was authorised for a 'lock-up warehouse and crane for the Cinderford station'. A public goods station was also opened at Bilson in 1862 (again no details) and it was not until 1884 that such provision was made at Whimsey.

The early years of so many railways passed largely unrecorded, but we are lucky in being left with a small insight into operation from the reminiscences of a Mr. Dowding, yard foreman at Bullo. These were published in the *Dean Forest Mercury* for Friday, 19th November 1897:

'He says that he arrived at Bullo Pill on Monday, the 26th of January, 1857, at which time the late Mr. Richard Williams was the station master. At that time there were no signal boxes.

The signals and points were worked by hand. There was 'stabling' in the yard for but one locomotive, which then was able to cope with the shunting at Bullo and Bilson, and it alone brought down the whole of the traffic day by day from the Forest of Dean to Bullo Pill. This engine among other things ran daily to the Nelson Pit, taking three empty coal waggons and bringing away three loaded ones. It also fetched wire from Churchway, which was brought in trams to that place from the Lydbrook Mills. The engine also journeyed to Whimsey siding for Edge Hills iron ore, which had to be taken to the mining company's works at Dowlais, South Wales. In a special note Mr. Dowding states this traffic increased very much, and for many years the carriage reached, and sometimes exceeded, £80 a day. The coal traffic (40 years ago) averaged 40 trucks per day. They were generally brought down the line sometime during the afternoon (representing the previous day's work at the pits), and stood in Bullo sidings till the following morning, when these trucks, nearly all of them, were sent up the line by two Swindon trains running down from that centre with empty waggons for the Forest collieries. Besides the coal traffic, about 30 trucks of pig iron from the Soudley Furnaces and the Cinderford Iron Works were brought down in the mornings. There were no brake vans, and the three guards in charge of the trains had to ride on the top of the loaded waggons. A few years later Trafalgar, Foxes Bridge and East Slade Collieries were opened, also Stapledge Coal and Brick Works, and the total amount of traffic per day then reached 80 or 90 waggons, all of which our readers will be astonished to learn were brought down in one train. Mr. Dowding relates an incident (it is well worth repeating), occurring in this connection, when on one occasion a train having been made up, it was found to contain 99 trucks. Bilson yard was searched throughout in vain for another truck, but the guard to his great disappointment was bound to leave with only 99 trucks! Of course this increased traffic meant the need of increased power, and as they did not grow at that time half engines, there was nothing left but to provide a whole one. About this time — it was the autumn of 1863 — something occurred which demonstrated in an awful manner the unwisdom of bringing down such an enormous number of trucks at a time. Describing the circumstances, Mr. Dowding says that a train of 70 trucks was coming down the line, and somewhere in the neighbourhood of Shakmantle the train parted, the driver having 40 waggons attached to his engine, discovering that something was amiss, he pulled up just below Shakmantle siding, with the result that the remaining 30 trucks dashed into the stationary 40, piling them up, then (borrowing the language of a newspaper report of the occurrence) "15 waggons high". We suppose this was a hyperbolical description, which was common in those days. The wreckage took five days to clear away. The lesson taught had the immediate effect of reducing a train to 45 trucks, though they were 12 tonners. This meant the employment of engine No. 3, through which four trains a day were regularly brought down the line to Bullo. About this time, however, the Forest of Dean coal trade increased by leaps and bounds. Its heyday was approaching, and the common experience then was that four or five days out of each week Mr. Dowding was forced to wire to Gloucester for two special engines to be sent to take away the congested traffic. Occasionally when trucks began to accumulate in the yard, a train would be sent to Grange Court, the guard riding on the last truck carrying a red flag and having a supply of detonators. This meant that between the evening and noon of the following day 150 waggons of coal were regularly dealt with. Turning for a moment to what was done at the docks, Mr. Dowding said that during the spring tides as many as 200 coal waggons were dealt with in one day, of which 80 waggons represented close on 1,000 tons of fuel, were shipped at Bullo Docks, chiefly for Bridgewater and Dunball. For our own part we question if that much is dealt with there in a month in the present day. There was also a considerable trade from the docks to Newport in Forest pig iron, it being carried there in barges. As time began to be of value, trains were made up in the evening, and the coal instead of standing all night at Bullo was started on its way, via Swindon to Salisbury in which district at that time Forest coal was chiefly used.'

T. E. R. Morris, a former station master at Cinderford, recorded that the broad gauge line was opened with the locomotive *Virgo* (a 'Leo' class 2—4—0 built in 1841) but this engine could only have been used at the outset, perhaps as a trial or temporary measure, for it does not appear in subsequent listings. Alternatively, he may have meant *Virgil*. The late Eric Mountford was kind enough to provide details of locomotives allocated to Bullo Pill shed from 1854-61:

BULLO PILL

2 wks ending	16.9.1854	Homer
2 wks "	30.9.1854	Homer, Virgil
2 wks "	14.10.1854	Virgil
2 wks "	28.4.1855	Ovid
2 wks "	12.5.1855	Ovid, Bacchus
2 wks "	26.5.1855	Ovid, Bacchus, Virgil
2 wks "	9.6.1855	Sappho, Bacchus, Virgil
3 wks "	30.6.1855	Sappho, Virgil
2 wks "	13.10.1855	Sappho, Virgil, Ovid
2 wks "	27.10.1855	Sappho, Ovid
2 wks "	24.11.1855	Sappho, Ovid, Virgil
2 wks "	8.12.1855	Ovid, Virgil
2 wks "	1.3.1856	Ovid, Virgil, Sappho
2 wks "	15.3.1856	Ovid, Virgil
23 days "	30.6.1856	Ovid, Sappho
19 days "	19.7.1856	Sappho
2 wks "	30.8.1856	Virgil
2 wks "	8.11.1856	Euripides
2 wks "	11.11.1856	Euripides, Virgil
2 wks "	6.12.1856	Virgil
17 days "	17.1.1857	Virgil, Euripides
2 wks "	31.1.1857	Euripides
2 wks "	14.2.1857	Euripides, Sappho
2 wks "	28.2.1857	Sappho
2 wks "	9.5.1857	Sappho, Horace
2 wks "	23.5.1857	Horace
24 days "	30.6.1857	Horace, Sappho, Euripides
18 days "	18.7.1857	Sappho
2 wks "	1.8.1857	Sappho, Euripides
2 wks "	12.9.1857	Sappho, Lucretius
2 wks "	26.9.1857	Lucretius
2 wks "	10.10.1857	Lucretius, Euripides
2 wks "	21.11.1857	Lucretius, Sappho, Hesiod
2 wks "	5.12.1857	Lucretius, Hesiod
4 wks "	13.3.1858	Theocritus, Hesiod
4 wks "	8.5.1858	Theocritus, Hesiod, Virgil
4 wks "	5.6.1858	Theocritus, Virgil
17 days "	17.7.1858	Theocritus
4 wks "	14.8.1858	Theocritus, Virgil
4 wks "	18.11.1858	Theocritus, Virgil, Status
4 wks "	11.6.1859	Theocritus, Virgil, Status, Homer
19 days "	30.6.1859	Virgil, Homer
4 wks "	20.8.1859	Virgil, Homer, Theocritus
4 wks "	17.9.1859	Virgil, Homer, Theocritus, Briarius
4 wks "	12.11.1859	Virgil, Homer, Theocritus, Briarius, Brigand
4 wks "	10.12.1859	Homer, Theocritus
4 wks "	18.2.1860	Virgil, Theocritus
4 wks "	17.3.1860	Virgil, Theocritus, Homer
4 wks "	14.4.1860	Virgil, Homer
4 wks "	12.5.1860	Virgil, Homer, Theocritus
4 wks "	9.6.1860	Homer, Theocritus
4 wks "	18.8.1860	Homer, Theocritus, Virgil
4 wks "	8.12.1860	Homer, Virgil, Euripides
19 days "	19.1.1861	Homer, Euripides
4 wks "	16.2.1861	Homer, Euripides, Hesiod
4 wks "	16.3.1861	Sappho, Euripides, Hesiod

As the line had always been worked by the GWR, the amalgamation of the South Wales Railway with the Great Western on 1st August 1863 probably brought very little change. A supplement to the Great Western working timetable for 1863 shows that there were two engines shedded at Bullo, and most likely a third as spare (as there had been since from before 1854). The No. 1 Bullo Pill engine handled the traffic up and down the branch whilst the No. 2 Forest engine, which assisted the 7.30 a.m. up train from Bullo, worked the line north of Bilson until returning to Bullo with the 2.45 p.m. down train.

The 1863 accident at Shakemantle already referred to resulted in loads being restricted to 45 wagons with a guard to every fifteen. A further effect was that a third engine had to be employed with a fourth as spare at Bullo. The alterations to the working pattern can be seen in the working timetable for 1867. The three engines were known as the Bullo Pill engine, the No. 1 Bullo Pill engine

BRANCH TRAINS. **No. 2.**

Down. **Forest of Dean Branch.—**

Dist.	STATIONS.	1	2	3	4	5	6	7	8	9	10
		a.m.	a.m.	a m.	a.m.	a m.	a.m.	p.m.	p.m.		
	Churchway ....dep	.	.	8 55	.	10 0	11 20	.	.	.	.
½	Whimsey	..	..	—	9 30	—	—	..	..	..	..
1½	**Bilson** ....arr.	...	...	9 0	9 35	10 10	11 30	...	...	R	...
		a.m.	a.m.	a.m.			a.m.	p.m.	p m.	p.m.	
	Bilson ....dep.	7 0	8 0	8 30	.	.	10 45	2 45	4 15	5 20	.
2	Cinderford	—	—	—	..	..	11 0	—	—	—	..
2¾	Meerbrook............	—	—	—	...	...	11 5	—	—	—	...
3	Stapledge	—	—	—	.	.	11 8	—	—	—	.
3¼	Quidchurch .... / Shakemantle	—	—	—	..	..	11 20	—	—	—	..
3¼	Blue Rock............	—	—	—	...	...	11 25	—	—	—	...
3½	Silly Point............	—	—	—	.	.	11 30	—	—	—	.
	Sudely Siding	—	8 10	—	..	..	11 35	—	—	—	..
4½	Cooper's Siding...... / Sudely Furnaces	—	...	—	...	...	11 50	—	—	—	...
7½	**Bullo Pill** ......arr.	7 15	.	8 50	.	.	12 0	3 10	4 35	5 40	.

Bullo Pill Engine will assist up with 7.30 a.m. Train and return Empty.
No. 1 Bullo Pill Engine will go to the Docks for Empty Trucks at 9.5 a.m on arrival of 8.30 a.m. Down Train.
Trains working on this Branch to be made up to a maximum load of 45 Wagons—that is, one Guard to every 15 Wagons. See Notice of Ballast Train. R Runs when required only.
The Forest of Dean Branch is worked by Train Staff, and no Engine or Train will be allowed to leave
be held responsible in case he should start his
Bullo Engine to take the 3.40 Train to Bilson and bring back the 4.15 p.m.

No. 2. **BRANCH TRAINS.** 41

Week Days only. ***Up.***

Dist.	STATIONS.	1	2	3	4	5	6	7	8	9	10
		a.m.	a.m.	a.m.	a.m.		a m.	p.m.	p.m.	p.m.	
	Bullo Pill ......dep.	6 30	7 30	.	.	.	9 45	1 40	3 40	4 50	..
2¾	Sudely Furnaces .... / Cooper's Siding	—	—	..	..	..	—	1 50	—	R	..
	Sudely Siding	—	—	8 15	...	...	—	1 55	—	—	...
3¾	Silly Point	—	—	—	.	.	—	2 0	—	—	.
4	Blue Rock............	—	—	—	..	..	—	2 5	—	—	..
4	Shakemantle........ / Quidchurch	—	—	—	...	...	—	2 10	—	—	...
4¼	Stapledge	—	—	—	.	.	—	2 15	—	—	.
4½	Meerbrook............	—	—	—	..	..	—	2 20	—	—	..
5¼	Cinderford	—	—	—	...	...	10 15	—	—	—	...
6	**Bilson** ....arr.	6 50	7 50	8 25	.	.	10 20	2 25	4 0	5 10	.
				a.m.	a.m.	a.m.	a.m.				
	Bilson ....dep.	.	.	8 40	9 15	9 44	11 0	.	.	.	.
7	Whimsey	..	..	—	9 20	—	—	..	..	..	..
7½	**Churchway** ....arr.	...	...	8 50		9 55	11 10	...	...	...	...

Bullo Engine to assist the 9.45 to Bilston, if required, and return empty.
No. 2 Forest Engine will do the work, as per Time Bill, between Bilson, Whimsey, and Churchway.
Both Engines will return to Bullo for the night with last Down Train.
☞ When required, Special Trips will be run from Bullo Pill to Bilson and *vice versa*.
See Notice of Ballast Train. R Runs when required only.
in either direction without the Staff or a Ticket, which must be carried by the Engineman, and he will
Engine without either a Train Staff or Train Ticket.
Bullo and Forest Engines to assist the 4.50 p.m. Train to Bilson if re uired.

Taken from Working Timetable for July—September 1867.

and the Forest engine. The Bullo Pill engine appears to have worked Bullo Yard and the docks, and assisted certain trains into the Forest. The No. 1 Bullo Pill engine worked the branch, and again the Forest engine worked north of Bilson. During this period ballast was also regularly taken from cinder tips at Cinderford 'between all trains up and down during the night'. It seems unlikely that this was a nightly arrangement, such trains probably running as required.

Trains serving Bullo at this time were as follows:

DOWN TRAINS
5.30 a.m. Swindon to Bullo Pill to take empties for Bullo branch.
8.40 a.m. Gloucester to Bullo Pill to take coal empties, etc.
7.20 p.m. Gloucester to Bullo Pill to take empties to Bullo branch.
11.45 p.m. Swindon to Lydney to take coal empties from stations between Swindon and Gloucester to Bullo Pill. Coal trucks from Cirencester go by this train.

UP TRAINS
8.25 a.m. Bullo Pill to Swindon to take trucks from Bullo Pill for Swindon and stations east of but not for stations between Gloucester and Swindon.
9.35 a.m. Bullo Pill to Swindon. Trucks for all stations Gloucester to Swindon.
11.20 a.m. Bullo Pill to Swindon. Trucks for Swindon and for stations west of Swindon on the Wilts and Somerset lines.

It was probably to work these longer distance trains that, certainly in the early part of the 1900s, Bullo's allocation included several larger saddle tanks and some tender engines. It is unfortunate that the registers do not exist to show the allocations prior to 1901.

The branch was included in the conversion of the South Wales Railway to standard gauge over the weekend of 11th/12th May 1872 so once again traders and colliery owners were faced with the problems and expense of converting their wagons. Presumably they also had to fund the narrowing of their private sidings.

NORTHERN EXTENSIONS
Industrialists had long desired a northern outlet from the Forest, especially for iron ore to South Wales, the first proposals for such a line having been put forward in 1830. After several abortive schemes it looked as though it might come about through the Severn & Wye Railway's proposed Lydbrook branch which, as authorised on 12th May 1870, would link their system with the Ross & Monmouth Railway at Stowfield. However, the impoverished S & W did not start construction until July 1872, and the anticipated delay prompted several notable local industrialists to promote their own line, the ill-fated 'Mitcheldean Road & Whimsey Railway', to link the Forest of Dean branch at Whimsey to the Hereford, Ross & Gloucester Railway close to the latter's Mitcheldean Road station. The idea, resurrected from the abortive Forest of Dean Central, Lydbrook and Hereford Ross & Gloucester Junction Railway scheme of 1856, was for a steeply graded line climbing at 1 in 30 from Mitcheldean Road station and 1 in 34 to the summit near Drybrook and descending at 1 in 40 towards Whimsey.

The Bill was deposited in 1870 and opposed by the GWR and the S & W, both of whom regarded it as a threat. Despite this, the Mitcheldean Road and Forest of Dean Junction Railway Act was passed on 13th July 1871, authorising the company to raise £30,000 capital, with borrowing powers for £10,000, to build 4 miles 5 chains of standard gauge line and lay additional rails for standard gauge on the broad gauge line between Whimsey and Churchway and Cinderford Goods (Ruspidge). The GWR were authorised to subscribe up to half of the capital.

The main promoters of the scheme included Henry and Edwin Crawshay and Alfred Goold, who were undoubtedly seeking an outlet for iron ore, especially Goold, who was seeking to develop deposits around Drybrook and Wigpool. Despite their impatience over the S & W's delay, construction of the MR & FODJ did not commence until 1874, by which time the Severn & Wye's Lydbrook branch was nearing completion! Goold had previously said that if the S & W could have offered any assurance that the Lydbrook line would have been built without delay, the MR & FODJ Bill would not have been promoted, yet curiously, in view of the circumstances, construction work went ahead. The engineer for the line was G. Wells Owen with George Coulthard as his assistant. They furnished revised plans for a ruling gradient of 1 in 35 (but favouring loaded trains) and two tunnels, the 638 yard Hawthorn tunnel and a shorter 97 yard one at Drybrook. The contractors, Messrs. Miller & Roberts, didn't stay long. Relations between them and Coulthard became strained and in November 1875 they abandoned the work, so the company pressed ahead themselves. Eventually, after engaging another contractor, an Act of 6th August 1880 authorised the GWR to absorb and complete the line. In the end, despite a total cost to the GWR of £60,626, the company made no attempt to open the line. The S & W's Lydbrook line provided a more direct outlet for traffic from the northern part of the Forest to South Wales and had been doing so almost since the MR & FODJR was started, so why the line was ever proceeded with remains as big a mystery as why it was never opened after completion. The only reason apparent for not bringing it into operation is the possibility that diverting traffic over the new route might have led to the need for improvements at Mitcheldean Road, etc. and even more expenditure.

A short length of the line from Whimsey to Speedwell siding was opened for mineral traffic in July 1885 and the goods depot at Whimsey was also improved around this time, 'a second junction with the siding' there being added. In January 1884 the GWR accepted a tender from C. W. Whalley for £343 for the construction of a goods shed, offices, and providing and fixing a crane. Following this expenditure, a GWR circular of 26th November 1884 stated 'It has been arranged to open the new goods station for Cinderford, which is situated at the Whimsey sidings on the Forest of Dean branch, on the 1st December and to call it 'Cinderford' instead of Whimsey. On and from the same date the present Cinderford station will be called Ruspidge . . .'

The rest of the MR & FODJR just lay dormant, but was inspected regularly by the local ganger on his trolley. Only a very occasional ballast train ever disturbed the eerie silence of this lonely and forlorn line.

A nicely posed view of No. 1672 and crew near the entrance to Haie Hill Tunnel at Soudley Furnaces. 1672 was one of the '1661' class of outside-framed saddle tanks based on frames ordered for the '2361' class 0–6–0s, which were notable for being somewhat large-wheeled and under-braked for goods tanks. The class were, as a result, generally unpopular across the GWR system, and were certainly unsuitable for the gradients and loads of the Forest of Dean branch.

Parkhouse/Pope Archive

INTRODUCTION

OF

RAIL MOTOR SERVICE

(ONE CLASS ONLY)

FOREST OF DEAN BRANCH.

WEEK DAYS ONLY.

	A.M.	A.M.	P.M.	P.M.	P.M.	P.M.		P.M.
STEAM MILLS CROSSING HALT dep.	7 32	10 21	1 27	4 41	6 55	8 35	....	—
WHIMSEY HALT .. .. .. „	7 34	10 23	1 29	4 43	6 57	8 37	..	—
BILSON (CINDERFORD) HALT .. „	7 38	10 27	1 33	4 47	7 1	8 39	....	8 40
RUSPIDGE HALT .. .. „	7 41	10 30	1 36	4 50	7 4	..	..	8 43
STAPLE EDGE HALT .. .. „	7 44	10 33	1 39	4 53	7 7	....	....	8 46
UPPER SOUDLEY HALT .. .. „	7 48	10 37	1 43	4 57	7 11	..	..	8 50
BULLO CROSS HALT .. .. „	7 53	10 42	1 48	5 2	7 16	....	....	8 55
RUDDLE ROAD HALT .. .. „	7 59	10 48	1 54	5 8	7 22	..	..	9 1
NEWNHAM .. ..arr.	8 1	10 50	1 56	5 10	7 24	....	....	9 3

SATURDAYS ONLY.

	A.M.	A.M.	A.M.	A.M.	P.M.	P.M.	P.M.	P.M.
NEWNHAM .. ..dep.	..	8 30	..	11 30	2 20	5 50	8 0	9 40
RUDDLE ROAD HALT .. .. „	....	8 33	....	11 33	2 23	5 53	8 3	9 43
BULLO CROSS HALT .. .. „	..	8 36	..	11 36	2 26	5 56	8 6	9 46
UPPER SOUDLEY HALT .. .. „	....	8 43	....	11 43	2 33	6 3	8 13	9 53
STAPLE EDGE HALT .. .. „	..	8 48	..	11 48	2 38	6 8	8 18	9 58
RUSPIDGE HALT .. .. .. „	....	8 52	....	11 52	2 42	6 12	8 22	10 2
BILSON (CINDERFORD) HALT .. „	7 20	9 0	..	11 55	2 45	6 15	8 25	10 5
WHIMSEY HALT .. .. .. „	7 23	9 5	10 8	11 58	2 48	6 18	8 28	10 8
STEAM MILLS CROSSING HALT arr.	7 25	..	10 10	12 0	2 50	6 20	8 30	—

SATURDAYS ONLY.

A well-known classic view of the Forest of Dean motor train at Newnham station, showing the strata of the former grassy embankment exposed when the FoD branch bay was built. The loco is '517' class No. 564, and the trailers are two Diagram L 70-footers.

National Railway Museum

PASSENGER SERVICES

By 1904 the threat of motor bus competition in country districts prompted the GWR to exploit the use of steam railmotors, serving a whole new generation of inexpensive and often rail-level halts to serve smaller communities hitherto just passed by. Following trials between Gloucester and Chalford in the Stroud Valley, where competition was successfully staved off, the GWR implemented a comprehensive programme of railmotor-served halts, wrapping the whole defensive scheme into a publicity campaign in which the company proudly proclaimed its intentions of reaching smaller communities throughout their system. Thus, having previously fended off repeated local appeals for a passenger service on the Forest of Dean branch, with expressions of concern over narrow tunnels, congestion at Bilson and lack of siding space at Newnham, the GWR was now only too keen to include the Forest of Dean line in its programme and pushed ahead with indecent haste.

In July 1906 a proposal was put forward to run passenger trains from Cinderford to Newnham and also to 're-open' the Mitcheldean—Cinderford branch! James Inglis, the GWR chairman, recommended that the necessary finance be made available for both the passenger service and for building a branch to the Severn & Wye Joint Committee's station at Cinderford. On 1st November 1906, £14,956 was authorised for the 'adaption of mineral lines in the Forest of Dean for passenger traffic'. Work proceeded quickly with the construction of halts at Bullo Cross, Upper Soudley, Staple Edge, Bilson, Whimsey and Steam Mills. (There was no mention of Ruddle Road Halt at this stage.) The existing building and platform at Ruspidge were adapted for passenger use and at Newnham the down running line was slewed and the platform widened in connection with the provision of a new bay for the railmotor service.

Arrangements were also put in hand for the construction of a 31 chain loop line to provide access to Cinderford station on the recently completed extension of the former Severn & Wye Railway, by now jointly owned by the Midland and Great Western companies. However, in the meantime, the Great Western were anxious to

An official view of the new halt at Upper Soudley, which opened on 3rd August 1907, showing the original 1ft 2in high platform.
National Railway Museum

commence the first stage of passenger services over the existing line and, as soon as the initial work was completed, invited the Board of Trade inspection. The inspecting officer's report was as follows:

Railway Department
Board of Trade
8 Richmond Terrace
Whitehall, London, SW

6th August 1907

Sir,

I have the honour to report for the information of the Board of Trade that in compliance with the instructions contained in your Minute of the 24th July, I have inspected the Forest of Dean Branch of the Great Western Railway, between Bullo Junction and Steam Mills.

This line has been in existence for many years as a mineral railway. The Company are now desirous of bringing it into use for passenger traffic, for which purpose the line has been thoroughly overhauled and, where necessary, relaid and equipped for passenger traffic.

The line extends from Bullo Junction, where it joins the main line from Gloucester to South Wales, as far as Drybrook, a distance of 7m. 24chs., but for the present it is intended to work it for passenger traffic only as far as Steam Mills, a distance of 6m. 2chs., and the present inspection ended at the latter place.

The line is single throughout, and is to be worked as between Bullo Junction and Bilson on the electric train staff system, and as between Bilson and Steam Mills by one engine in steam, or two engines coupled together, carrying an ordinary train staff. Undertakings to this effect have already been furnished by the Company.

The permanent way is laid with second-hand steel rails, weighing 80 or 80½ lbs per yard, cast iron chairs weighing 40 lbs each, and creosoted sleepers of the usual dimensions. The chairs are secured to the sleepers by two 7/8″ bolts, and the sleepers are laid at a maximum distance apart from centre to centre of 2ft. 6ins. The ballast consists of ashes and crushed slag. The fencing is composed of posts and rails, or quick-set hedges.

The gradients on the line are severe, the first 3 miles from Bullo Junction being at inclinations of 1 in 52 and 1 in 58. From here to Ruspidge the inclinations vary from 1 in 49 to 1 in 71, after which they improve as far as Bilson, where the gradient is 1 in 2600. Between Bilson and Steam Mills the steepest gradient is 1 in 56, and this only extends for a short distance.

The curves are numerous, the sharpest at all of which check rails are laid, having radii of 10chs.

The deepest cutting has a depth of 51 feet, and the highest embankment a height of 21 feet.

There are 5 bridges under, and 4 over, the line. Of the underbridges, 1 consists of a segmental arch of masonry, 1 is constructed of wrought iron plate girders with timber flooring, 2 of steel girders with timber flooring, and 1 of steel troughing.

There are 3 tunnels, 1075 yards, 299 yards, and 109 yards long respectively. They are all lined with masonry, the side walls being 2ft. thick, and the arches 1ft. 6ins. thick, and they have a width of 15ft. 10ins. at the springing of the arches. They are provided with platelayers recesses on alternate sides, at intervals of 1 chain.

There are 5 culverts under the line.

All the above works seem to be in good condition and the girders and timber flooring under the line gave moderate deflections under test.

There are 5 public road level-crossings, all of which are provided with gates, signals, and gate-keepers' lodges.

There are 7 stations or stopping places, on the line, namely:- Bullo Cross, Upper Soudley, Staple Edge, Ruspidge, Bilson, Whimsey, and Steam Mills Crossing, in addition to a new station at Ruddle Road, on the main line between Newnham and Bullo Junction.

The line is to be worked by motor-cars, or by what are called auto-cars, namely a small engine with a passenger vehicle at each end, which will run between Newnham Station on the main line and Steam Mills, and the stations have been designed accordingly. Bullo Cross, Upper Soudley, and Staple Edge stations each consist of a single platform, 150 feet long, 7 feet wide, and 14 inches high. Shelters are provided on the platforms at the two latter places. Ruspidge station consists of one platform; 150ft. long, 10 feet wide, and 2ft. 9ins. high. At this station, which seems to be an old one — though it has never previously been brought into use, there is a waiting room. At Bilson, Whimsey, and Steam Mills, the platforms are 150 feet long, 7 feet wide, and 3 feet high. At each of these places a shelter is provided on the platform. All the stations have lamps and name board.

It will be noticed that some of the platforms are only 14 inches high above rail level, while others are 3 feet high. This difference of height is likely to be confusing to passengers. The cars on the line are all fitted with folding steps for use at the low platforms. These steps are opened and closed by the guard, by means of levers inside the car, and should be placed in position by him before the doors are opened. I cannot help thinking that it would have been better if all the platforms had been made of the same height, namely 3 feet. Whatever the saving of expense may be which is due to the adoption of low platforms, it must be fully absorbed by the cost of fitting all the cars with folding steps, which would not have been required had all the platforms been made 3 feet high.

Ruddle station, or stopping place, which is on the main line, between Newnham Station and Bullo Cross, consists of two platforms, each 150 feet long, 7 feet wide and 3 feet high, with shelters, lamps, and name-boards.

The following are the signalling arrangements.

At Bullo Pill West Box, a new junction has been laid in between the up and down main lines & the Forest of Dean Railway. The box is old, and contains 44 levers in use and 5 spare levers. Some boxing in of signal-wires and point rods still remains to be completed at this place.

Soudley Crossing No. 1 ground frame, containing 3 levers, namely 2 distant signal levers for the protection of the level-crossing, & 1 gate lock lever for controlling the gates.

Soudley No. 2 ground frame, containing 4 levers in use and 1 spare lever, namely 2 distant signal levers for the protection of the level-crossing at this place, and 2 levers for working the siding connections, the latter being locked by the key on the staff.

South Shakemantle ground frame, containing 2 levers locked by the key on the electric train staff.

North Shakemantle ground frame, containing 2 levers locked by the key on the train staff.

Ruspidge level-crossing ground frame, containing 3 levers, namely 2 for distant signals protecting the crossing, and one for the gate lock lever.

Ruspidge Goods ground frame, containing 2 levers locked by the key on the train staff.

Bilson signal-box, containing 18 levers in use and 5 spare levers. This is not a passing place for passenger trains, but there is a goods yard, into which a goods train can be placed in order to enable a passenger train to pass.

The working from here to Bullo is by means of the electric train staff, and from here to Drybrook by means of one engine in steam and the ordinary train staff.

Bilson North ground frame, containing 2 levers locked by the key on the train staff.

Duck siding ground frame, containing 2 levers locked by the key on the train staff.

Cinderford Crossing ground frame, containing 6 levers namely 2 distant signal levers for the protection of the level crossing, 1 gate bolt lever, controlling the gates, 2 points levers, and 1 facing point lock lever, the three latter being locked by the key on the train staff.

Cinderford Goods North ground frame, containing 3 levers locked by the key on the train staff.

Steam Mills Crossing ground frame, containing 3 levers namely 2 distant signal levers, and 1 gate lock lever.

The line from Steam Mills to Drybrook, being still worked as a mineral line, catch points have been inserted in the single line at the North end of Steam Mills Station. These are worked from a ground frame containing 1 lever, which is locked by the key on the train staff.

The interlocking being correct and the arrangements satisfactory, I can recommend the Board of Trade to sanction the use of this railway between Bullo and Steam Mills for passenger traffic by means of rail motor-cars or auto-cars.

I have &c.,
(Signed) H. A. Yorke

The passenger service had already commenced on 3rd August 1907, trains starting from Newnham station on the South Wales main line and calling at a new halt at Ruddle Road, only served by branch railmotors, before leaving the main line at Bullo and beginning the long uphill climb 'down' the branch.

The crew of the first train were driver Harry Askew, fireman Jimmy Griffiths and guard Bill Vale. The timetable offered a service of five trains each way with an additional one on Saturday evenings.

During the first six weeks, 20,824 passengers were conveyed, the August Bank Holiday accounting for 3,319. One of the locals recorded his experience of a journey on the reverse of a picture postcard of the first railmotor:

'This is the Car taken just above Newnham Station on the first day. You will see it is all decorated with flags all ready for action. I had a ride in it last Tuesday night for the first time. I went from Newnham to Bullo Cross and it cost me 1½d what a lot wasn't it? It nearly broke me. Mrs. Kerr sent all the girls and the footman to the Forest with it for a picnic one day when I was on my holidays. She told the footman he was to go and take care of the girls and he did too. When he got off it the other end he went up in to Cinderford and left the girls to themselves and the best of it was he missed the 5 o'clock car back and he was left in the lurch so he walked back which is 5 miles across the fields so the next morning she sent for him and asked him about it and she told him she would never send him anywhere else so he has finished I expect.'

The East Dean Parish Council wrote to the GWR expressing their thanks for the service, and, while local people were enjoying the novelty of the long awaited passenger services, the Great Western were busy preparing the abandoned Micheldean Road line north of Steam Mills as far as Drybrook for passenger use. This 1 mile 22 chain extension was opened on 4th November 1907 with halts at Nailbridge and Drybrook. The first train over the line consisted of a '2021' class saddle tank (probably No. 2082) sandwiched between three trailers decorated with flags. Again the new service was evidently eagerly welcomed, the *Dean Forest Guardian* for 15th November

The decorated trailer identifies this 3-car set as the first extended working to Drybrook on 4th November 1907, passing Soudley No. 1 ground frame. The open platform opposite the ground frame was subsequently supplemented by a corrugated goods shed, serviced, like its predecessor, from the running line.

Collection Neil Parkhouse

The photographer has attracted the attention of a youthful audience at the new halt at Drybrook, where an unidentified '2101' class 0–6–0ST and trailer can be seen, perhaps on the first day of passenger services on Monday, 4th November 1907. *Collection A. K. Pope*

reporting that it had been patronised 'far beyond the expectation of the promoters'. According to Harry Paar, some 200 miners used the train each day between Drybrook and Bilson.

Completion of the loop line into Cinderford Joint station concluded the final stage of the railmotor scheme. Climbing a 1 in 51 gradient on a 12 chain radius curve from the north end of Bilson yard to reach the height of the Joint Committee's embankment, the new line joined the Cinderford extension at a point appropriately named Cinderford Junction, just 30 chains short of the terminus. A standard design GWR signal box was provided to control the signalling, single line electric train apparatus and the single point.

The GWR had asked for the junction in 1907, and agreed with the Joint Committee to contribute to the working expenses of the station in the ratio of trains using it, two single-coach auto-trains being equivalent to one S & W train. For the use of the S & W from Cinderford Junction to the terminus, the Joint Committee was credited with a one-mile proportion of gross receipts from traffic carried on GW trains, and station staff were instructed to be strictly impartial in dealing with the two types of traffic.

Work on the line was completed by the end of March 1908 and an inspection took place on 1st April. Again the inspecting officer was Colonel Yorke, who reported as follows:

'This loop, which is 31 chains in length, is single, and connects the Forest of Dean Branch of the GWR with the Cinderford Branch of the GW & Midland Joint Severn & Wye Railway.

'For the greater portion of its length the loop line is on a gradient of 1 in 51, rising towards Cinderford, and the curvature of the loop is 12 chs.

'The permanent way, which is of the usual description used upon the GW Rly, is laid with bull-headed steel rails weighing 86lbs per yard, and cast iron chairs weighing 46lbs each. The sleepers are of the usual dimensions, and are laid at varying distances, in no case exceeding 2ft 6ins from centre to centre. The ballast is of ashes.

'There is only one bridge on the loop, viz. an underbridge of 9ft 6in span, constructed of wrought iron trough girders. The girders gave very small deflections when tested with a heavy engine.

INTERIOR OF FOREST OF DEAN RAIL-MOTOR

A good view of the interior of a Forest of Dean branch auto-trailer. The lady on the left is quite possibly the wife of the photographer,
Will Phillips.   *Collection Neil Parkhouse*

'There are no other works upon the line, except a 9ft arched culvert, and there are no stations or level-crossings.

'Some slight alteration has been made at Bilson signal-box in order to provide for the new junction. The signal-box now contains 23 levers in use and 3 spare levers. A new signal-box has been built at the junction with the Severn & Wye Railway, called Cinderford Junction box. This box contains 8 levers in use and 3 spare levers.

'The only point calling for remark is that the new junction between the loop line and the Cinderford Branch of the Severn & Wye Rly. is a single junction instead of being con-structed, as is usual, as a double junction. But having regard to the nature of the traffic upon the two lines concerned, and the fact that the service over the new loop line will be carried out by means of motor-cars only, there does not seem to me to be any necessity for putting the Company to the expense of constructing a double junction.

'The interlocking in both signal-boxes is correct, and I can recommend the Board of Trade to sanction the use of the new loop line for passenger traffic by means of rail motor cars.

'The new loop is to be worked by means of the tablet system, concerning which the Company have already forwarded to the Board of Trade the usual undertaking.'

When the Cinderford loop was opened on 6th April 1908, trains from Newnham ran to Cinderford Joint and reversed back to Bilson Junction before continuing on to Drybrook. The same arrangement applied in the reverse direction. Bilson Halt, which had temporarily served Cinderford, was closed to the public on the same day but remained in use for workmen, initially on Saturdays only (see timetable). Incidentally, the GWR continued to use Whimsey for all its goods traffic.

Running into Cinderford station, the GWR now offered the shortest journey time to Gloucester with obvious detrimental effects on the S & W.

In November 1908 the GWR authorised expenditure of £423 for raising the height of the platforms at Bullo Cross, Upper Soudley, Staple Edge, Nailbridge and Drybrook from 1ft 2in to 3ft, the work presumably being completed sometime around the introduction of a railmotor service for workmen between Drybrook Halt and Bilson Halt on 4th January 1909. The new train left Drybrook at 5.55 a.m., arriving at Bilson at 6.07. The return service in the afternoon left Bilson at 3.45 p.m. The fares were reduced to about half the normal rate, the weekly fare, Monday to Saturday inclusive, between Drybrook and Bilson being 1s 3d. The workmen's tickets were only valid on the special trains and only for travel between Drybrook and Bilson or the intermediate halts. The service was aimed at colliers from the Drybrook district travelling to Light-moor, Foxes Bridge or Crump Meadow Collieries, all of which were in easy reach of Bilson Halt. Trafalgar and Duck Collieries could be reached from Whimsey Halt. The

GWR SERVICE TIMETABLE FOR 1908

Single Line worked by Electric Train Staff between Bullo Pill West Box and Bilson Jct. and by Train Staff only (one Engine in steam or two or more coupled at a time) between Bilson and Churchway, and Bilson and Drybrook. The only intermediate Crossing Place is Bilson Jct..

For General Instructions, see Mr. Roberts' Notices 6566 and 6680.

DOWN TRAINS.	1	2	3	4	5	6	7	8	9	10	11	12	13	14	15	16	17
WEEK DAYS.	G	B	K	B	B	K	K	B	B	K	B	K	B	B		B	B
STATIONS.	Light Auto Engine.	Passenger Auto Car.	Goods.	Passenger Auto Car.	Passenger Auto Car.	Goods.	RR Gds.	Passenger Auto Car.	Passenger Auto Car.	Goods.	Passenger Auto Car. Q	Goods.	Passenger Auto Car.	Passenger Auto Car.		↑Passenger Auto Car.	Passenger Auto Car. Thurs. & Sats. only.
	dep.	arr. dep.	arr. dep.	arr. dep.	dep.	arr. dep.	dep.	arr. dep.	arr. dep.	arr. dep.	arr. dep.	arr. dep.	arr. dep.	arr. dep.		arr. dep	arr. dep.

m. c.		a.m.	a.m. a.m.	a.m. a.m.	a.m.	a.m. a.m.	a.m.	a.m.	a.m. a.m.	p.m. p.m.	p.m. p.m.	p.m. p.m.	p.m. p.m.	p.m. p.m.	p.m.		p.m. p.m.	p.m. p.m.
—	Newnham	...	... ...	... ...	...	— 8 25	...		— 11 30	— 2 20				— 5 50	...		— 8 0	— 9 35
— 48	Ruddle Road Halt	...	... ...	... ...	— 8 x 0	— 8 28	...		— 11 33	— 2 23				— 5 53	...		— 8 3	— 9 38
— 76	Bullo Pill	6 20	... ...	—	8 29	— 8 31		11 34	— 11 36	— 1 0	2 24		— 3 5	5x54 —		8 4	9,39
1 37	Bullo Cross Halt		... ...	—			Cinderford Goods arr. 10-37.				— 2 26			— 5 56			— 8 6	9 41
2 64	Soudley Furnaces	—	—	—	—					3 15 3 20								
3 12	Soudley Sidings	—	—	—	—					3 25 3 30								
3 22	Upper Soudley Halt	—	—	—	— 8 38				— 11 43		— 2 33			— 6 3			— 8 13	9 48
3 24	Stop Board	—	—	—	—							C R						
4 5	Shakemantle	—	—	—	—													
4 31	Staple Edge Halt	—	—	—	— 8 43				— 11 48	— 2 38		C R		— 6 8			— 8 18	9 53
5 10	Ruspidge Halt	—	—	—	— 8 47				— 11 52	— 2 42		C R		— 6 12			— 8 22	9 57
5 11	Stop Board	—	—	—	—													
5 66	Bilson Halt	...	... ...	... ...	...						Q							
6 1	Bilson Jct.	6 40	— 6†50	—	C 8 49 S				C 11x54 S	C 2 44 S			C 6 14 S	C 8 24 S		C 9 59 S	
*	Cinderford Jct.		C T	C T	C T				C T	C T		C T	C T	C T		C T	
*	Cinderford		6†54 7 1		8 52 9 3	9 50		11 57 11 59	2 47 2 49			4 10	6 17 6 19	8 27 8 29		10 2 10 4	
—	Cinderford Jct.		C T	C T	C T	C T			C T	C T	C T	C T	C T	C T		C T	
—	Bilson Jct.		7 4 7 6		9 6x9 8	9 55		12 2 12 4	1 3 1 5	2 52 x2 54		C T	4 13 x4 15	6 22 6 24		8 32 8 34	10 7 10 9
—	Bilson Goods Yard	...	—	— 8 28 8 38	—		9 20 10x30			1x30 1 45		3 45 x3 55					
7 22	Brick Works Sidings / Churchway	...	—	—	—	9 25 9 30 / 9 35		—	—	—	—	—	—	—		—	—
6 45	Duck Colliery	...	—	—	—			— 12 7	— 1 8		— 2 57		— 4 18	— 6 27		— 8 37	10 12
6 56	Whimsey Halt	...	— 7 9	—	— 9 11 9 58			— 12 9	— 1 10	1 50	— 2 59	4 0	— 4 20	— 6 29		— 8 39	10 14
6 65	Cinderford Goods	...	— 8 43	—		10 42												
7 7	Steam Mills Cross'g Halt	...	— 7 11	—	— 9 13 10 0			— 12 12	— 1 13		— 3 2		— 4 23	— 6 32		— 8 42	10 17
7 59	Nailbridge Halt	...	— 7 14	N	— 9 16 10 3		10 50										
7 68	Speedwell	...	—		—												
8 26	Drybrook Halt	...	7 17	—	9 19 —	10 6		12 15 —	1 15		3 5		4 26	6 35		8 44	10 20

N—When this train is assisted, the Bank Engine must return punctually from Bilson at 9-0 a.m.

* Distance Bilson Jct. to Cinderford Jct. 31 chains, and to Cinderford Station 61 chains.

Q—On Saturdays this trip on returning from Cinderford must run to Bilson Halt to pick up Colliers for direction of Drybrook.

UP TRAINS.	1	2	3	4	5	6	7	8	9	10	11	12	13	14	15	16	17	18
WEEK DAYS.	B	K	B	K	B	K	B	B	K	B	B	K	B	B	G	B	B
STATIONS.	Passenger Auto Car.	Goods.	Pass. Auto Car.	Goods.	Passenger Auto Car.	RR Gds.	Pass. Auto Car.	Passenger Auto Car.	Goods.	Passenger Auto Car.	Passenger Auto Car.	Goods.	Passenger Auto Car.	Pass. Auto Car.	Light Auto Engine.	Passenger Auto Car.	Passenger Auto Car Thurs. & Sats.only. to Bilson.
	arr. dep.	arr. dep.	dep.	arr. dep.	arr. dep.	dep.	dep.	arr. dep.	arr. dep.	arr. dep.	arr. dep.	arr. dep.	arr. dep.	arr. dep.	dep.	arr. dep.	dep. arr.

		a.m. a.m.	a.m. a.m.	a.m.	a.m. a.m.	a.m. a.m.	a.m.	p.m. p.m.	p.m. p.m.		p.m. p.m.	p.m. p.m.		p.m. p.m.	p.m. p.m.	p.m	p.m. p.m.	p.m. p.m.
Drybrook Halt		— 7 20	... ...	9 21		— 10 9	12 26	— 1 17	... ...		— 3 9	— 4 30			— 6 43 8 46			10 23
Speedwell							11 5								Thurs. & Sats. excepted			
Nailbridge Halt		— 7 22		9 23		— 10 11	12 28	— 1 19			— 3 11	— 4 32			— 6 45 8 48		Detach Car at Bilson.	10 25
Steam Mills Crossing Halt		— 7 24	9 0	9 25		— 10 13	12 30	— 1 21			— 3 13	— 4 34			— 6 47 8 50			10 27
Cinderford Goods							11 20		— 2 30						Thurs. & Sats. only.			
Whimsey Halt		— 7 26		9 27		— 10 15	12 32	— 1 23			— 3 15	— 4 36			— 6 49 8 52			10 29
Duck Colliery									2 33 2 40			— 4 8						
Churchway		—		... 9 45		—												
Brick Works Siding		—		9 50 9 55		—												
Bilson Goods Yard		9 5 11x57	— 10 0		11 27		2x45 4x0		4x12 5 10									
Bilson Jct.	7 29 7 T	—		10x18 10 20	12 37	1 26 x1 28	— 3 18 3 20	4 39 4 41		6 52 6 54	8 57		10 32 10 34					
Cinderford Jct.	C T	C T		C T	C T	C T	C T		C T	C T		C T						
Cinderford	7 34 7 36	9 35		10 23 10 25	12 40	1 31 1 33	3 23	4 44 4 46		6 57 6 59	9 0		10 37 10†39					
Cinderford Jct.	C T			C T		C T		C T		C T	C T		C T					
Bilson Jct.	C 7 39 S			C 10 28 S		C 1x36 S		C 4 49 S		C 7 2 S	C 9 5 S		10†42 10∥45					
Bilson Halt																		
Stop Board		12 2 P12 6					4 5 p4 10			5 15 p5 20			9 7					
Ruspidge Halt	— 7 41	C R		— 10 30		— 1 38		— 4 51			— 7 4		9 10					
Staple Edge Halt	— 7 44	C R		— 10 33		— 1 41		— 4 54			— 7 7							
Shakemantle		12 20 p1222					4 25 p4 27			5 35 p5 37			9 14					
Stop Board		C R																
Upper Soudley Halt	— 7 48			— 10 37		— 1 45		— 4 58			— 7 11							
Soudley Sidings		C R																
Soudley Furnaces		C R																
Bullo Cross Halt	— 7 53			— 10 42		— 1 50		— 5 3			— 7 16		9 19					
Bullo Pill	W7x 7 570	12 35	—	W10 10x46 0		W1 540	4 40	W5 70	5x50		W7 200	9 20	W9 230	10∥55				
Ruddle Road Halt	— 7 59			— 10 48		— 1 56		— 5 9			— 7 22							
Newnham	8 1	—	ST. 503		10 50 —	Cinderford Goods arr. 11-13.	1 58	—	... ...		5 11	—		— 7 24		9 27 —	9 25	

Instructions for working Goods Trains between Bullo Pill, Bilson and Drybrook. See Mr. Roberts' Notice 6530, dated July, 1907.

Coal ex Lightmoor Colliery. Immediately on arrival at Bilson Junction, the traffic must be removed from the Lightmoor Siding, so as to release the Colliery Co.'s Engine.

NOTE.—The 4-0 and 5-10 p.m. Trains ex Bilson must run to time whether marshalled or not.

A selection of views of the railmotor accident at Bilson in 1914, showing the telescoping of the two trailers which occurred as a result of the impact with the embankment. The photos also show that a morbid interest in disaster and misfortune by the general public is by no means a modern phenomenon. Signalman Hedley Woodward recalls that one of the priorities after the collision was to retrieve the conductor's takings, which had been scattered inside the trailers, in case the public's curiosity extended to pilfering!

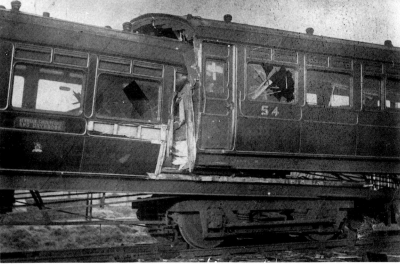

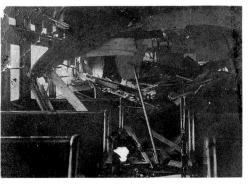

service did not operate on general or Bank Holidays or when the collieries were closed.

Harry Paar mentions that 'on 28th September 1910 the Board of Trade belatedly authorised the use of the branch for passenger traffic by means of 'motor cars', also for excursion trains run between Cinderford and the main line'. As the branch had already been passed for the running of the motor service it is likely that this permission was for the operation of excursion trains, although several trips had been run prior to this date. In June 1910, five hundred men from Lightmoor Colliery travelled to Blackpool (via Grange Court, Hereford, Crewe, Manchester and Wigan) and in August two excursions left on the same Saturday for London. At least one of these was for Foxes Bridge Colliery involving some 450 passengers. It is, of course, possible that the railmotor was used to shuttle the excursionists to Newnham but the number travelling makes this unlikely. If normal passenger rolling stock was used, then application to the Board of Trade may have been due to the success of the trips and the desire to continue them in future years. It may also have been necessary as certain aspects of the branch were approved only on the basis of auto-trains, e.g. the single junction at Cinderford Junction. As excursion trains of regular stock were not allowed to stop at any of the intermediate halts, they ran direct from Cinderford to Newnham and the branch railmotor was run to serve the halts and connect at Newnham with the main train.

In connection with the passenger service, the July—September WTT for 1913 reveals that a truck for meat traffic between Liverpool and Cinderford was attached to the rear of the 8.25 a.m. motor ex-Newnham on average about once a week. The truck was destined for Cinderford Goods but had to be detached from the train at Bilson so the train could be propelled back from Cinderford Joint station. When returning to Bilson, it was re-attached to the train and taken on to Whimsey. Presumably, during its short stay at Bilson, the vehicle was placed in the car siding.

At some point around the First World War, railmotor services off the branch were extended to Gloucester or Grange Court.

The practice of running the motor trains with either one or two trailers according to the traffic needs led to an incident on Saturday, 21st March 1914. The second auto-coach was to be left in the car siding at Bilson but reversing back from Cinderford, with the driver controlling the train from the driving end of the leading auto-coach, the siding was entered rather too quickly and the train ran through the buffer stops, crashing into the embankment beyond. The *Dean Forest Mercury* reported the incident as follows:

RAILWAY ACCIDENT
Mishap with the Motor at Cinderford
ALARMING INCIDENT

The happy circumstance that mishaps on the railways serving Cinderford are of very infrequent occurrence accounted for the unusual excitement which was caused by a mishap on Saturday evening, though it must be conceded that this was of a somewhat alarming character. The disabled coaches concerned in the accident to the GWR motor were inspected on Sunday by very large numbers of people from Cinderford and the surrounding district, and the event was on all hands the principal topic of conversation. Fortunately the mishap was attended by practically no personal injuries, though at least two officials on the motor were in a position of considerable jeopardy. It appears that after the 8 o'clock motor from Newnham to Drybrook, made up of an engine and two carriages, had reached Cinderford Station, and the bulk of the passengers had alighted, one of the coaches being no longer required that evening, it was arranged to leave it in a siding close to the Bilson signal box. By some means not sufficiently accounted for, we understand, the engine which was backing the coaches attained a higher speed than usual. When the position was realised, by the application of brakes everything

Ruspidge, Glos. View near the Half.

Ruspidge level crossing features prominently in this view of Cinderford Bridge. The Forest of Dean branch is seen falling away towards Bullo. The substantial, hip-roofed building along the road on the left is the Bridge Inn, behind which is the course of the Bullo Pill tramroad. The houses around the Bridge Inn, which may have originally been named 'The Railway', formed one of the oldest parts of what became known as Cinderford. The houses on the hillside to the right are in Ruspidge.   *Collection Neil Parkhouse*

was done in the short time and space available to avoid a collision with the stop block under the bank near the bridge on the road leading to Crump Meadow and Foxes Bridge Collieries, but under the circumstances these efforts were not quite effective in entirely stopping the train near the usual appointed place before the stop-block was reached. The coach mounted the bank, which happened, fortunately, to be of a comparatively soft character, and remained in a tilted character as seen in the photograph here given. At the upper end of the coach were Harold Fryers, the assistant conductor, and the driver E. Morris. The former bent down when the coach mounted the bank, and in this way probably escaped injury, but some of the soil fell upon him, and he was in a rather awkward predicament for some time. He was at once seen by a doctor, and, though suffering from shock, was found to have sustained no other injuries. The driver was able, fortunately, to get through the doorway into the coach, though he sustained a few slight scratches. In the position in which it was tilted, some telescoping took place with the other coach and the ends in both cases were considerably splintered, the smoking compartment being greatly damaged. There were no passengers in this coach, but that in front contained about a score. These were naturally alarmed, but, fortunately, no one was injured. The conductor, William Harris, and the fireman, Oram, were also unhurt. The noise caused by the impact was heard throughout the district, and the officials at the station and passengers waiting on the platform hastened to the scene of the collision and for some time a good deal of excitement prevailed. The engine was taken on down to Newnham, and with a carriage taken from a passenger train there, it made the last trip that night at a belated hour. A breakdown gang had by the morning brought

the tilted coach back to the metals, and on Sunday this and the other disabled carriage were an object of great interest to the many hundreds of people who visited the spot.

The passenger services survived during the First World War and it was not until 29th March 1918 that the *Dean Forest Mercury* announced that the 2.40 p.m. and 7.45 p.m. motor trips from Newnham would not run beyond Bilson Halt, which had been re-opened on 2nd April 1917, and that the 8.28 p.m. from Drybrook to Gloucester and the 9.40 p.m. to Bilson on Saturdays would be taken off.

GOODS & MINERAL SERVICES

The branch was always busy with the transport of coal from the collieries around Cinderford, ore from the iron mines loaded at Whimsey, and the produce of the furnaces at Cinderford and Soudley down to Bullo and, of course, the reciprocal movement of empty wagons. However, this traffic was subject to fluctuations in trade and the circumstances of the various works. Within a few years of the conversion of the branch, one or two collieries north of Bilson closed down but these were offset by the development of Trafalgar and Foxes Bridge Collieries and the continued growth of Lightmoor and Crump Meadow. The net result was probably an increase in the traffic as already related in Mr. Dowding's account of the branch.

In 1869 some 1,500 tons a day were carried down the branch, most of which was moved in the morning. During November of that year, 31,556 tons of coal traversed the line. However, the opening of the Severn & Wye's Mineral Loop in 1872 attracted some of this traffic as it gave a more direct outlet for coal from Lightmoor, Foxes Bridge, Crump Meadow and Trafalgar, especially to Lydney Harbour, and the collieries were served by more convenient siding arrangements. The FoD line was further hit when Soudley ironworks closed in 1877 and again in 1894 when Cinderford Ironworks were blown out. The iron ore trade dwindled until by 1900 all traffic of this nature had ended.

couple of times a week or so, delivering perhaps a couple of empties, running round the train in the sidings there, and returning with two or three wagons of roadstone. Although loads weren't very demanding, the rails were often greasy and it was apparently still 'an awkward job' bringing stone out of the quarry, and stopping just short of the catchpoint above Drybrook Halt.

However, of far greater importance was the establishment at the end of the Churchway branch of another large

'1501' class 0—6—0ST No. 1509 at Bilson Junction before departing with the 11.15 a.m. goods to Bullo Pill Junction with coal from Lightmoor, Trafalgar and Crump Meadow collieries sometime in 1917. The wagon next to the loco is a 'Crump' 6-plank open. The cast plate on the bottom plank reads 'Empty to Cinderford'. Staff shown are Reginald May (related to Reginald May, Divisional Inspector at Gloucester), and on the right A. J. J. Williams, who moved to Gloucester in 1943. Both were signalmen/ porters, working at Bilson Junction. *N. Williams*

This just left some of the output of the Lightmoor, Foxes Bridge and Crump Meadow collieries and some smaller concerns at the end of the Churchway branch and Whimsey. It was hardly surprising therefore that by 1907 the GWR felt they had the capacity to run a passenger service!

Things soon took an upturn on the coal front with the opening of a new colliery at Staple Edge. The development of Eastern United began in 1908 but it was not until 1913/14 that a large output was achieved.

The opening of a limestone quarry at Shakemantle, close to the site of the iron mine, and utilising the existing siding, generated some stone traffic, and hopes of a larger traffic of this nature were raised when a quarry was established at Drybrook. The track beyond Drybrook Halt to Mitcheldean Road had been taken up in 1917 but in 1928, just before withdrawal of passenger services to Drybrook, Drybrook Quarries Ltd of Sheffield decided to develop the quarry just north of Drybrook tunnel. So, with the promise of things to come, the line was reinstated through the 97 yard tunnel for some 3 furlongs or so, and private sidings installed to serve the new crushing plant, tarmac plant and a 30-ton weighing machine. Staff remember being told this was 'going to be a big job', but throughout the 1930s traffic expectations were never fulfilled and in practice they only remember serving the quarry a

colliery, Northern United, which by 1935 was dispatching coal, and output soon grew.

By the late 1920s the sheer volume of traffic in the movement of coal, and the corresponding flow of empty wagons, had created serious problems on the branch once again, this time complicated by the passenger service. Eastern United Colliery was in a fairly cramped position and had limited siding space, which required regular clearance, especially during the winter when the colliery was at full output. During the summer there was the problem of loaded wagons of coal awaiting orders. With such limited siding space, the colliery could not hold them and the GWR soon filled any available siding accommodation to capacity.

The output from both Eastern and Northern United Collieries kept the Forest of Dean branch very busy, but the somewhat restricted accommodation at Bullo Junction was critical. About 1932, additional loops were provided at a cost of some £9,000, but at the same time it was proposed to demolish the engine shed, extend the siding through it and extend the adjoining siding to provide accommodation for a further fifty wagons. A decrease in traffic at the time, as well as the cost already spent there, postponed the move and nothing was done. However, in 1935 the Bullo Pill station master revived the idea after it had been necessary to send Eastern United

FOREST OF DEAN BRANCH.

Single Line worked by Electric Train Staff between Bullo Pill West Box, Eastern United Colliery and Bilson Junction and by Train Staff only (one Engine in steam or two or more coupled at a time) between Bilson and Churchway, and Bilson and Drybrook. The only intermediate Crossing Place is Bilson Junction. The Cinderford Loop is worked on the Electric Train Tablet System between Bilson Junction Box and Cinderford Junction Box and Cinderford Joint Station.

Worked by Electric Token between Bullo Pill West and Bilson Junction when Eastern United Box is closed.

Two passenger trains conveying passengers must not cross at Eastern United Colliery unless specially arranged in case of accident.

WEEK DAYS.

DOWN TRAINS.

Distance	STATIONS.	Station No.	Gradient 1 in	Point to point times. Mins.	Allow for stop. Mins.	Allow for start. Mins.	1 Light Auto Engine. dep. a.m.	2 G Goods. arr./dep. a.m.	3 K Auto Car. arr./dep. a.m.	4 B Goods. arr./dep. a.m.	5 K Goods. arr./dep. a.m.	6 K Auto Car. arr./dep. a.m.	7 B Goods arr./dep. a.m.	8 K Auto Car. arr./dep. p.m.	9 B Auto Car SO dep. p.m.	10 Workmen's Car. dep. p.m.	11 dep. p.m.	12 B Auto Car. arr./dep. p.m.	13 B Auto Car. arr./dep. p.m.	14 B Auto Car. Sat. only. arr./dep. p.m.
	Newnham	2569							8 6 / 8 19			11 25 / 11 30			2 46		5 5	5 34 / 5 36	8 26	10 20
76	Bullo Pill	2572				1	5 20		7 37	8 22	8 34	11 34	11 36	1 10	2 46			5 40	8 32	10 24
1 37	Bullo Cross Halt	2575	54 R															5 42		10 26
2 61	Soudley Furnaces	2576	50 R	11		1									2 58					10 33
3 12	Soudley Sidings	2577	48 R	2	1	1				8 31		11 48			2 58			6 49	8 39	
4 6	Shakemantle	2579	49 R							8 36	CR	11 48			2 58			6 54	8 44	10 38
4 31	Staple Edge Halt	2580	49 R	6	1	1						CS	1 30 / 1 35	CS				5 58	8 48	10 42
4 37	Eastern United Colliery	2581	71 R	2	1	1				8 40	9 5	11 52	CR	3 2						
6 1	Ruspidge Halt	2582	58 R																	
6 60	Bilson Halt	2583	99 R				5 47	CS	8 25		Auto. p.m./a.m.	CS	C11 / x 545	CS	CT	8 15 / 8 55	C4	C4	C8 / 6 5	C10 / 6 45
6 79	Bilson Junction	2584					R		CT		11 50 / 11 59	CT	CT	CT	CT	CT	CT	CT	CT
6 62	Cinderford Junction	2586							8 45 / 8 47		11 59		3 7 / 8 10		6 5 / 6 8	N 56	10 47 / 10 49
	Cinderford	2587							8 50 / 8 52				3 13		6 8 / 6 10	8 50	10 52 / 10 54
	Bilson Junction																		
	Bilson Goods Yard	2585			3	1		8 8 / 8 15		9 30			1 45 / 1 55	Q				
	Brick Works Sidings	2588																
7 22	Churchway	2589	41 R						SO									
6 45	Duck Colliery	2590						8 20	8 55		12 7	3 18 / 3 58		6 13		10 57
6 56	Whimsey Halt	2591							8 57		12 9	3 20		6 15		10 59
6 65	Cinderford Goods	2836	82 R	4	1		Engine from shed	9 0			3 23 / 4 4		6 18		11 2
7 3	Steam Mills Cross'g Halt	2592	69 R						9 12 / 9 55		12 12				
7 59	Nailbridge Halt	2593	12 R				5 55	9 0 / 9 3		12 15		3 26 / 4 4		6 21		11 5
7 68	Speedwell	2594	44 R						10 7					
8 30	Drybr'k Halt	2595	48 R											
	Drybrook Quarries													

— When this Train is assisted, the Bank Engine must return punctually from Bilson at 8.5 a.m. * — Distance Bilson Junction to Cinderford Junction 33 chains, and to Cinderford Station 63 chains. R — Attach 2 Trailers at Bilson Junction. The length of the Loop at Eastern United Colliery is 330 yards, capable of holding engine, 50 wagons and van.
Q Runs 5 minutes later Cinderford to Drybrook on Mondays.

FOREST OF DEAN BRANCH—*continued.*

WEEK DAYS.

UP TRAINS.

Distance	STATIONS.	Gradient 1 in	Point to Point Times. Mins.	Allow for Stop. Mins.	Allow for Start. Mins.	1 Workmen's Car. dep. a.m.	2 B Auto Car dep. a.m.	3 K Goods. arr./dep. a.m.	4 B Auto Car to Gloster. dep. a.m.	5 B Goods. arr./dep. a.m.	6 K Goods. arr./dep. a.m.	7 B Auto Car dep. a.m.	8 B Auto Car to Gloster. arr./dep. p.m.	9 K Goods. arr./dep. p.m.	10 K Goods. arr./dep. p.m.	11 B Auto Car to Grange Ct. arr./dep. p.m.	12	13 B Auto Car to Gloster. arr./dep. p.m.	14	15 B Auto Car to Grange Ct. SO arr./dep. p.m.	16 Light Auto Engine. dep. p.m.	17 Auto Car. dep. p.m.
	Drybrook Quarries								10 20								6 29			11 10
41	Drybr'k H lt	48 F					6 0		10 23 / 10 30	12 35				4 10½		6 31		11 12
50	Speedwell	48 F					6 3			12 37				4 12		6 33		11 14
1 22	Nailbridge Halt	48 F		1			6 6	9 8		12 39			2 30			6 35		
1 44	Steam M. Crossing Halt	69 F					6 8	9 10		12 41	Starts from Drybrook 5 min		OR					
1 53	Whimsey Halt							8 30	9 12		12 51							
1 64	Duck Colliery									SO							
	Churchway	41 F															
	Brick W'rks Siding	52 F	2					9 15 / 9 17	19 40 / 11 30	12 36		12 30	2 10 / 3 40	4 16 / 4 18	6 38 / 6 40	
2 80	Bilson Goods Yard	76 F		1	CS	7 5	9 38		CT		CT		N	CT	CT	
	Bilson Junction							9 20 / 9 22	CT	12 39 / 12 59	12 41		1 20 / 4 22	6 43 / 6 45	
	Cinderford Junct.		7½	CT	7 15		CT		CS		C / 4 24 S		CS	C9 / 6 48 S	
	Cinderford			CS		9 25 S		C5	12 44 S				C9 / 6 48 S	
	Cinderford Junct.			CS										
2 30	Bilson Junction	76 F										3 4 / P 349		6 50	
2 43	Bilson Halt													4 26		
3 18	Stop Board	173 F	4				7 20	9 27		12 49			CS	6 53	
3 19	Ruspidge Halt	99 F					CS		11 10 / 11 18	12 49				4 29		
3 72	Eastern United Colliery	55 F					7 23	9 30	9 41 / 11 20 / 11 55		12 53			CS	6 57	9 12
3 78	Staple Edge Halt	71 F	4					CR	9 56	3 5 P2 / 12 4 / 18 P / 4 32				4 33		
4 23	Shakemantle	49 F	3				7 27	9 34	9 56 / 11 3 / 12 P / 12 8						
5	Stop Board	49 F								12 58				4 38		9 17
5 7	Upper Soudley Halt	48 F										3 25	5 X 5	4 41 / 4 42	7 10 / 7 12	9 25 / 9 27
5 17	Soudley Sidings	48 F	1	1												
6 45	Soudley Furnaces	49 F	1				O 9 44	O W 10 10	12 X 28		O W 4 49		O W 8 53	9 15 / 11 35
6 72	Bullo Cross Halt	50 F	1				7 36 / X W					O 7 10 / 7 12	O W 9 25 / 9 27
7 31	Bullo Pill	54 F	12			7 38		9 47					
8 29	Newnham						7 52						

N On Saturdays Bilson Jct. den. 3.35 Stop Board 3P44, Stop Board 4P0, Bullo Pill arr. 4.18 p.m.

STANDARD POINT TO POINT RUNNING ALLOWANCES FOR VACUUM BALLAST TRAINS—FOREST OF DEAN BRANCH

	Point to Point.	Stop.	Start.		Point to Point.	Stop.	Start.
Bilson Junction			1	Bullo Pill	20	1	1
Ruspidge	3	1	1	Ruspidge	8	1	1
Bullo Pill	15	1	1	Bilson Junction			

Colliery 'wait order' wagons to Gloucester, Grange Court and Awre Junction for stabling owing to the lack of accommodation. The cost of the extra accommodation was then estimated at £725 but the outcome is not recorded.

Whether separate from the 1932 scheme or not, official reports also make reference to the consideration of additional storage at Bullo in 1930 due to the problems created by 'wait order' coal, but the provision of extra accommodation was allowed to lapse as the colliery were not prepared to meet the GWR's requirements for their contribution to the scheme. The GWR apparently continued to struggle with the problems, realising that refusal to accept 'wait order' wagons would mean the closure of the colliery for longer periods, and in turn result in loss of traffic.

In July 1935 coal sales were poor and, at the time, 'wait order' coal from Eastern United was stabled as follows: 75 wagons at Bullo, 49 at Gloucester Docks, and 22 at Bilson, a total of 146. Only odd wagons were labelled day by day and many wagons hauled to Gloucester Docks to await orders were eventually labelled for destinations 'down line' and hauled back through Bullo again!

At the end of June 1935, in desperation to keep working, Eastern United appealed to Bilson Junction to hold some of their output. As this was presented as a special case, the wagons were accepted for a 'few' days, but, of the 29 received, only 10 were cleared in a reasonable time, and when, despite pressing, Bilson was left with the remainder, it was resolved not to help out again.

Of course, taking coal to Bilson was extra movement and, although the distance involved was only about two miles, it was 'heavy hauling', twelve Class 1 wagons being a full engine load. There was also difficulty in getting them on the train at the colliery as no traffic was marshalled there, sorting being carried out at Bullo.

The accommodation at the colliery itself was four sidings for loaded wagons holding 23, 16, 13 and 6 wagons each (total 58) whilst the accommodation for empties was 25 on one road and 20 on another. The output of the colliery during the winter months was between 90 and 100 wagons per day, for which continual servicing by the railway was essential.

The number of wagons that could be handled by each train was restricted to 32 empties for 'C' class engines or 24 for 'A' class, and on return to Bullo 40 loaded wagons was the maximum.

In July 1935 empty wagons were worked to Eastern United from Bullo by the 8.50 a.m. to Eastern United, 1 p.m. to Bilson, 1.25 p.m. Eastern United and 6.05 to Eastern United, whilst trains clearing loaded wagons to Bullo were the 10.00 a.m. Eastern United, 10.20 a.m. from Drybrook quarries, 3.08 p.m. ex-Eastern United and 2.45 p.m. ex-Cinderford. The limited accommodation at Eastern frequently meant heavy shunting and, with wagons being labelled as the colliery received orders, it was not unusual for 20 wagons to be labelled out from ten or more positions. Also six wagons of coal for 'country trade' would often be stabled in front of them and had to be moved before they could start to shunt the others, and

returned afterwards. Occasional wagons of coal were also shunted out on to the running loop by the loco for the colliery company's horse to draw into the van siding for country delivery.

All of this shunting was restricted by the lack of head-room for the loco at the screens, and it was not unusual for a loco to take an hour to get out a train of coal.

This shunting was far in excess of the 15 minutes allowed for in the private siding agreement, beyond which the GWR were entitled to charge at least 7s 6d per hour and, according to one report, 10 shillings. This was naturally of some concern to the company and an internal letter of 14th August recorded the excess time, beyond the 15 minutes allowed, spent at Eastern United without charge for 12 months ending 28th July 1935.

4 weeks ending	1934	Hrs	Mins
	26 August	24	35
	23 September	25	55
	21 October	34	45
	18 November	38	20
	16 December	40	15
	1935		
	13 January	32	15
	20 February	35	05
	10 March	37	45
	7 April	39	25
	5 May	33	15
	2 June	32	50
	30 June	38	35
	28 July	35	35

Calculated at 10 shillings per hour, this meant that the GWR were performing shunting for the firm to the value of £224 5s 10d per annum without charge.

At the end of 1935 it was reported that there were anything up to 150 wagons of 'wait order' coal from both Eastern and Northern United Collieries standing at Bilson, Bullo and Gloucester docks from spring to autumn, and equally during the winter months there was difficulty in dealing with empties working in, with the result that frequent stops were imposed and in consequence wagons were held back at Gloucester, Stoke Gifford, etc. to the detriment of general work. Furthermore, the GWR realised the situation was likely to worsen when Northern United was in full operation, as an increase at Bullo was anticipated.

No siding at Bullo would take a train of sixty wagons and it was a nightly occurrence that the 7.35 p.m. Bullo to Gloucester had to be formed up on two roads, resulting in lost time in joining the train, which in consequence frequently missed its path.

The winter brought the usual problems with empties, and examples of vehicles on hand for both Eastern and Northern United in January, February and March were as follows:

	January		
	2nd	3rd	4th
Bullo Pill	155	146	132
Gloucester DBS	199	36	26
Gloucester New Yard	7	19	20
Bilson	81	100	82
Gloucester Docks	50	71	58
Grange Court	–	41	41
	412	443	359

SOUDLEY.

An enlargement from the panoramic view included in the preliminary pages, showing an open-cab '2021' class pannier tank restarting a heavy train of loaded wagons of Forest coal after pinning down brakes at the stop board prior to running down the 1 in 57 gradient through Upper Soudley. On the original postcard, Parkend and Norchard wagons can be seen next to the brake van. Other private owners in this 36-wagon train include Dean Forest Coal Co. and large numbers of Baldwin and Renwick Wilton wagons, but no Eastern United vehicles can be identified. The loco and first few wagons are passing through Upper Soudley Halt, whilst the long low structure behind the centre of the train is the skittle alley built behind the White Horse pub as a memorial to local men killed in the Great War. The large square house beyond the railway at the left of the view is the Post Office, at one time run by Winnie Morgan, the youngest postmistress in the country.   *Collection R. How, cty. Elsie Ibbotson*

	February		
	3rd	4th	5th
Bullo Pill	120	144	108
Gloucester DBS	40	33	36
Gloucester New Yard	—	22	28
Bilson	24	—	—
Gloucester Docks	109	109	109
Grange Court	—	—	—
	213	218	291

	March		
	2nd	3rd	4th
Bullo Pill	82	117	157
Gloucester DBS	51	39	19
Gloucester New Yard	55	83	61
Bilson	35	25	25
Gloucester Docks	48	20	—
Grange Court	—	—	—
	271	284	262

There was a stop on all Eastern and Northern United empties, except Baldwins (Bristol based coal-factors) for several weeks prior to 20th February and considerable numbers were held back in other divisions, principally at Stoke Gifford.

On 29th May 1936 there were 42 trucks of 'wait order' coal from Eastern United at Bullo and 36 from Northern United at Bilson.

On 28th June the following year there were 116 wagons of 'wait order' coal on hand at Bilson and for a few days by the beginning of July, the total had risen to 132 although 80 were sent to Lydney Docks on 2nd July.

In 1937 new sidings, almost ready on 2nd June, were brought into use at Northern United accommodating 80 [another report states 60] empties. This did at least help the situation, but the time spent servicing the colliery still presented problems because of the variation.

Empties for Northern United Colliery (maximum 15 wagons) were always propelled from Bilson with the open end of the guard's van leading, and one of the two guards carrying a horn to warn any persons of the train's approach. If necessary, he had to be prepared to stop the enginemen by exhibition of a red flag or red light at night. On arrival, the brake van was pushed onto the remains of the Nelson branch, clear of the colliery extension. The train was then propelled up the gradient into the empties sidings with one of the two guards walking in front. If more than 15 wagons had been brought up to Bilson, the engine would often make more than one trip between Bilson and the colliery, where the clerk would bring out the paperwork and check wagon numbers, etc. After the empties had been stabled, the engine returned to pick up the brake van and, providing there was time, the crew would leave the engine and van coupled up on the running line and slip into the canteen for tea and a bun. The engine then drew up to the loaded sidings where once again the van was left on the running line while the engine ran into the colliery. The train of loaded vehicles was drawn outside the colliery and the brake van gravitated onto the back of them. Unlike Eastern, which was hard work, Northern had an easy layout and there was never

any waiting. Loaded wagons would always be ready in 'the run', a train load of up to 40 wagons having been formed up there from wagons gravitated from the screens one or two at a time under the control of a skilled colliery employee with a brake stick. The line to Bilson fell at 1 in 41, so, when leaving the colliery, two or three brakes were pinned down before setting out on the run to Bilson.

On separate occasions in May 1937 the time taken from the Bilson Junction ground frame to the colliery, both empties and return, was 20 minutes and 27 minutes, whilst from the ground frame to the colliery, to pick up coal from the south end and return, had taken 30 minutes and 37 minutes. These timings were noted as providing a fair margin without rushing. The result on the second occasion was that the 3.40 p.m. goods got behind the 4.20 p.m. autocar from Cinderford and also did not leave Eastern United until after the departure of the 5.45 p.m. autocar ex Newnham from Staple Edge Halt. The branch was consequently open for an hour longer than otherwise. The situation was expected to worsen as Northern United were steadily increasing output and a new brickworks was being built along the Churchway branch.

One improvement was that the Churchway branch was uprated to a dotted blue route, thus allowing the larger and heavier '57xx' class pannier tanks to work the line. This was a considerable aid in working the Northern United traffic. Previously the maximum load for '20xx' or '21xx' locos had been 35 loaded wagons (originally quoted as 40, but changed by November 1935) at 15 mph, but the more powerful '57xx' could work a maximum of 40 loaded wagons at 25 mph and propel 24 empties from Bilson to Northern United. The new regulation was brought into use on 6th July 1938 but, in practice, three goods guards pointed out in a letter of 20th September, that in propelling 22 wagons along the branch, it was not possible to see the engine and there were two accommodation crossings on the route. After a test on 27th October, the total allowed was restricted to 20.

In 1942 additional accommodation was achieved by the provision of three new loop sidings, with a total capacity of 133 wagons, at Staple Edge. Known as the Cast House Sidings, they were owned by Henry Crawshay & Co and situated at the north end of the running loop on the opposite side of the running line. This work involved the lengthening of a footbridge and resiting of a permanent way hut. However, after much effort and expenditure, the Cast House Sidings were never actually used!

OPERATION
The branch was served from Bullo engine shed, which opened at the same time as the branch and where on average four locomotives were stabled. This was probably the case from the 1860s.

One of the first standard gauge locos known to have been used on the line in 1872 was an unidentified member of the '1076' class double-framed 0—6—0STs. The scarcity of GWR allocation details for the 1870s-1900 leaves an unfortunate gap in our knowledge, but double-frame 0—6—0STs were still very much in evidence in 1902 and on into the 1920s (see Appendix 1), so it is not unreasonable to assume that they were always the mainstay of services.

The 1902 allocation included members of the '1076', '1661', '1813', and '1854' classes of saddle tanks plus two 0—6—0 tender engines, 2364 and 2401. It is unlikely that the tender engines were used on the branch (although in his *Great Western in Dean* Harry Paar records that Dean Goods were used on the branches in times of drought). They were probably employed on the longer distance main line coal trains.

When passenger services commenced in 1907, the rail-motors tried on the line were based at Gloucester where the 1908 allocation included Nos. 40, 48, 50 and 53 — all 70ft types. It has been suggested that steam railmotors were only used experimentally in the first months of the passenger service, but, as Gloucester retained at least one unit until 1st January 1929 (presumably for the Stroud Valley), they may have seen further use in the Forest, but there is no other evidence to confirm this.

Nevertheless, autotrains were always more common and the loco allocations reflect this. Auto-fitted '517' class 0—4—2Ts and '850' class 0—6—0STs were used in the early days of the auto services but they were soon displaced by auto-fitted '2021' class 0—6—0STs.

By 1920 the allocation still included 0—6—0 tanks, by now of both saddle and pannier varieties. Classes recorded were '1016', '1076', '1501', '1661', '2021' and '517' class 0—4—2Ts. Four locos were based there at any one time and there were seven sets of men at Bullo shed, a shedman, Bert Turley, two cleaners on permanent nights, a day chargeman, Fred Jones, and another two cleaners to prepare the engines for the crews, the first of whom booked on at 4.35 a.m. They came off shed at 5.20 (with full tanks) to run light engine to Bilson, where they picked up two trailers from the car siding where they were stabled. They worked empty stock to Drybrook for the 6.00 a.m. or 5.55 a.m. miners train to Bilson to serve Lightmoor, Foxes Bridge and Crump Meadow collieries. One driver, Harry Askew, would hold both whistles open all the way up ('down' in railway terms) the valley to make sure the miners were up and about! He was so well thought of by the men that once when he was ill, a miner called at his house with five sovereigns as a result of a collection for him.

After dropping all the colliers at Bilson, the spare trailer was put back in the car siding and the crew went up in the signal box for breakfast. Afterwards they ran into Cinderford with the single car to work the 7.00 a.m. to Grange Court, calling at all stations, then back to Cinderford with schoolchildren for East Dean Grammar School which was conveniently sited in Station Street.

At 9.00 a.m. they set off to Gloucester, leaving there at 11.08 to run back to Cinderford. For the last leg of their duty, they worked the 12.30 p.m. or thereabouts from Cinderford to Gloucester, as far as Bullo where they handed over to the late crew alongside the water tower, while the cleaners emptied pre-loaded baskets of coal into the bunker and replenished the tanks. (In later years it would appear that this changeover took place earlier when the train arrived from Gloucester.)

The fresh crew worked through to Gloucester, back to Cinderford, then Bilson, where at approximately 3.40

up to 200 miners could be waiting for the journey to Drybrook. Presumably on the way to Bilson Halt, the second trailer was collected from the car siding. For a while, a carriage cleaner was employed at Bilson, yet the second coach was known by some as the 'dirty' trailer as it was kept for the workmen's service. It probably suffered on the afternoon workmen's train, as before the days of the pit-head bath, the men returned home in their pit dirt to soak in a tin bath in front of the fire. At peak periods, such as Gloucester market days, the second trailer was often pressed into service on the normal train. On arrival at Drybrook, the crew had a lay-over of about an hour during which time they cleaned the fire and emptied the ashpan and smokebox. A pit was provided between the rails here for the purpose, and of course the driver could check the engine and oil up. If time allowed, the crew could enjoy a breather at this quiet spot before returning to Cinderford to collect returning school-children. From Cinderford the crew worked to Grange Court and back, connecting with the main line trains at Newnham. The final return trip from Cinderford at 6.00 was booked to leave Gloucester at 7.40 p.m. Afterwards the auto-coaches were left at Bilson and the engine worked light back to the shed.

The second turn involved booking on at 5.20 a.m. (when the first loco was leaving) and, coming off shed at 6.05 a.m., forming a train of goods for Cinderford and empties for the collieries and other industries in Bullo yard. The train set off from Bullo at 7.20 a.m. and ran through to Bilson. After sorting the yard, they ran out to Whimsey with goods, sorted the yard there and brought back empties, etc. Whimsey was quite busy during the 1920s with general goods, timber traffic and occasional coal.

At 10.30 empties were taken down to Eastern where the colliery was shunted ready for a clearance of loaded wagons which departed at 12.00 for Bullo Yard, where the crew handed over to the late men. The fresh crew left at 1.05 with more empties for Bilson. On arrival they sorted the yard and at 3.40 p.m. left Bilson with empties for Eastern, working loaded away from there and down to Bullo to finish.

The crew for the third morning turn worked two round trips to Eastern Colliery, leaving Bullo at 8.40 a.m. and 1.25 p.m. They came off shed about 7.00 to work the 8.40 a.m. colliery empties off Bullo. At one time in the late 1920s, up to 60 empties were taken on the first trip, assisted with a banking engine at the rear. However, progress up the steep banks was a hard steady slog during which it could take up to five minutes to get through Haie Hill tunnel. This was not a pleasant experience struggling through the long narrow bore without the benefit of any intermediate ventilation shaft and, by the time the banking engine entered the tunnel, the whole bore was already absolutely choked with thick sulphurous exhaust left by the straining effort of the train engine which the second engine added to. In such appalling circumstances the crew would struggle for air but, after one fireman was carried away from the footplate on a stretcher, all the Bullo crews signed a letter refusing to bank through the

The postcard view (top) shows the White Horse Public House at Upper Soudley in the lower centre of the photo. The long low building to the right is the skittle alley shown in the previous view, behind which the railway can be glimpsed. A large area of land to the west of the pub was owned by a Mr. Joiner. He was happy for local people to let their horses onto it but would not allow it to be built on. The only exception was the corner plot opposite the White Horse on which he allowed Roy and Fred Bevan to build two houses and a garage for a coach (seen here) which they ran between Blakeney and Cinderford. This was generally reckoned to be more convenient than the train. The Bevans were so successful that after a while Red & White moved in to compete with cheaper prices. Joiner advised the Bevans that if they could keep going for three years, Red & White would give up and the Bevans vowed that even if they had nothing to eat but bread and cheese, they would keep their buses running. They did and Red & White gave up, leaving the Bevans to become very successful, and, at the time of writing, a son of one of the brothers runs the business, which is still based in Soudley. The small building on the hillside, centre left, is Zion Chapel, built by local Methodists in 1879 using rock they quarried from the hillside. The other two photographs show two of Bevans' later 'Soudley Valley' coaches.   *Collection R. How, cty. Elsie Ibbotson*
and Collection A. K. Pope

tunnel. Afterwards the loading was limited to 32 empties and brake van, and later still, the maximum load was further reduced to 28.

On arrival at Eastern the difficulties were not over for the crew. Shunting the cramped colliery is detailed on page 21, but even when this task was over and a train of loaded coal wagons was formed up in Eastern United loop, it was quite usual for it to be held there for half an hour or so before being signalled away for the descent to Bullo. At one time some 50 or 60 wagons were handled on the descent, but one of the main problems was that when pulling away from the loop, it was impossible to see that the guard's van was following, let alone get the tip from the guard. The number of loadeds were later cut to 40 or so, but even handling this number could prove tricky in bad weather.

The brakes were all pinned down before leaving, and the train brought to a stand at Soudley for further adjustment. Controlling a heavily loaded train down the branch called for great skill and years of experience. Once all the heavily laden wagons were on the move, even with brakes rubbing on all wheels, the driver and the guard had to work very hard to check the progress of the train in order to bring it to a stand where required. It was certainly not possible to stop just anywhere without prior warning. They had to know the line intimately and use their knowledge to advantage; even the final check-railed curve into Bullo had a retarding effect which was brought into play when bringing the train to a stand at the home signal. Speeds on the descent were minimal but it was nonetheless unnerving for a crew to find themselves being pushed faster than they wanted at any point. Knowing what was at stake, incidents were rare, but there were times when some drivers didn't quite time it to perfection and found themselves running into the sand drag at Bullo. Such incidents were doubly frustrating, for, apart from the obvious disruption to services, explanations and paperwork for officialdom, there was the embarrassment among colleagues — a severe blow to the pride of any self-respecting engineman and not quickly forgotten.

DECLINE AND ECONOMIES

Despite the problems in coping with the output of the two new collieries at Eastern and Northern United, other traffic was in decline. Passengers were increasingly atracted to the more convenient motor bus services, and other collieries and industries were dwindling. Ruddle Road Halt had been closed on 29th April 1917 and Bilson Halt was closed again from 1st October 1920 although it reappeared in later timetables. The rest of the decade saw further economies in the face of increasing competition from motor buses in the Forest. On 17th May 1927 Cinderford signal box was closed, the signals taken out of use, and the line from Cinderford Junction to the terminus was worked on the 'one engine in steam' principle using a wooden train staff.

Passenger services over the Severn & Wye line were withdrawn on 6th July 1929, so when the Great Western decided to withdraw its passenger service between Cinderford and Drybrook Halt, local feelings ran high, the *Dean Forest Mercury* for 27th June 1930 reporting:

'It is notified through the medium of the Great Western Railway Company's timetables for the summer service, which takes effect on July 7th, that the Forest of Dean Branch Service between Cinderford and Drybrook Halt will be suspended. So the line from Newnham to Cinderford and from Lydney Jcn. to Lydney Town will, on and after July 7th, be all that remains of the comprehensive if not very convenient passenger service which existed up to a year ago. It would occasion no great surprise if, eventually, the Cinderford Branch from Newnham was also abandoned. An indication of this possibility may be found in the fact that the Company will, after July 6th, cease to run the 7.10 a.m. car to Newnham from Cinderford, and the 8.0 p.m. Gloucester to Newnham and Cinderford (except on Saturdays). The 9.22 a.m. Cinderford to Gloucester is to start (on July 7th) at 9.0 a.m. and make a connection at Newham with the South Wales train, which leaves there at 9.37.

GWR SERVICE TIMETABLE for 9th July to 30th September 1934

FOREST OF DEAN BRANCH.

Single Line worked by Electric Train Staff between Bullo Pill West Box, Eastern United Colliery and Bilson Junction and by Train Staff only (one engine in steam or two or more coupled at a time) between Bilson and Churchway, and Bilson and Drybrook. The only intermediate Crossing Place is Bilson Junction. The Cinderford Loop is worked on the Electric Train Tablet System between Bilson Junction Box and Cinderford Junction Box and Cinderford Joint Station.

Worked by Electric Token between Bullo Pill West and Bilson Junction when Eastern United Box is closed.

Two passenger trains conveying passengers must not cross at Eastern United Colliery unless specially arranged in case of accident.

WEEK DAYS.

Distance.	DOWN TRAINS. STATIONS.	Station No.	Gradient.	Time allowances for Ordinary Freight Trains. See page 2. Point to point times.	Allow for stop.	Allow for start.		K Cinderford S. & W. Goods.		B Auto Car.		K Goods.		K Goods.		B Auto Car.		K Goods. SX	K Goods		B Auto Car.			K Goods. SX	B Auto Car.		B Auto Car. SO			
m. c.			1 in	Mins.	Mins.	Mins.		arr. a.m.	dep. a.m.	arr a.m.	dep. a.m.	arr. a.m.	dep. a.m.	arr. a.m.	dep. a.m.	arr. a.m.	dep. a.m.	dep. p.m.	arr. p.m.	dep. p.m.	arr. p.m.	dep. p.m.		dep. p.m.	arr. p.m.	dep. p.m.	arr. p.m.	dep. p.m.		
—	**Newnham**	2569	—	—	—	—	..	..	7 20	8 7	8 28	..	..	..	..	11 25	11 30	..	..	..	2 20	2 35	..	..	5 †5	5 45	8 20	8 22	..	..
- 76	Bullo Pill	2572	—	—	—	1	..	—	—	8 31		..	..	..	8 50	11 33		1 0	—	1 25	2 38		..	6 5	5 X48		8 25		..	..
1 87	Bullo Cross Halt	2575	54 R	—	—	—	..	—	—	—	8 33	..	..	..	..	—	11 35	—	—	—	—	2 40	..	—	—	5 50	—	8 27	..	..
2 61	Soudley Furnaces	2576	51 R	11	1	1	..	—	—	—	—	..	..	—	—	—	—	—	W	—	—	—	..	—	—	—	—	—	..	..
3 12	Soudley Sidings	2577	48 R	2	1	1	..	—	—	—	—	..	..	—	—	—	—	W	L	—	—	—	..	—	—	—	—	—	..	..
3 22	Upper Soudley Halt	2578	48 R	—	—	—	..	—	—	—	8 39½	..	..	—	—	—	11 41½	—	—	—	—	2 46½	..	—	—	5 56½	—	8 34	..	..
4 6	Shakemantle	2579	49 R	6	1	1	..	—	—	—	—	..	..	C	R	—	—	—	—	—	—	—	..	—	—	—	—	—	..	..
4 31	Staple Edge Halt	2580	49 R	—	—	—	..	—	—	—	8 44	..	..	—	—	—	11 46	—	—	—	—	2 51	..	—	—	6 1	—	8 39	..	..
4 37	Eastern United Colliery	2581	71 R	3	1	1	..	—	—	—	—	..	..	9 x 10	—	C	xS	1 20	1 45	1 55	C	S	..	6 25	—	—	—	—	..	..
5 10	Ruspidge Halt	2582	58 R	2	1	1	..	—	—	M	8 47½	..	..			—	11 49½	..	C	R	—	2 54½	..		—	6 4½	—	8 43	..	..
5 66	Bilson Halt	2583	99 R	—	—	—	..	—	—	—	—	..	..	—	..	—	—	..	—	—	—	—	..	..	—	—	—	—	..	..
5 79	Bilson Junction	2584	—	—	—	—	..	C	S	C 8 51	S	..	..	..	..	11 52	x11 54	..	C	S	2 57	2 58	..	..	C 6 8	S	C 8 45	S	..	..
*0 32	Cinderford Junction	2586	—	—	—	—	..	C	S	C	S	..	..	..	..	C	S	..	—	—	C	S	..	..	C	S	C	S	..	..
*0 62	**Cinderford**	2587	—	—	—	—	..	8 0	—	8 55	—	..	..	..	..	11 56	12†0	..	—	—	3 0	3† 5	..	..	6 10	—	8 48	—	..	..
—	Cinderford Junction	—	—	—	—	—	..	..	..	M CR at Bilson Junct. to detach Paddington to	Cinderford Goods wagon 3 minutes allowed.	..	..			C	S	..	—	—	C	S	..	..	—	—	—	—	..	..
—	Bilson Junction	—	—	—	—	—	..	—	—			..	..			12†2	12 10	..	—	—	3† 7	—	..	..	—	—	—	—	..	..
—	Bilson Goods Yard	2585	—	3	1	1	..	7 48	7 55			8 37	X9 15			—	—	..	2 5	2 15			..	..	—	—	—	—	..	..
—	Brick Works Sidings	2588	—	—	—	—	..	..	..			..	..			..	..	—	..	..	..	..	..	..	..	..	..	..	..	..
7 22	Churchway	2589	41 R	—	—	—	..	..	..			..				R	..	..	..	..	..	..	..	..	..	..	..	..	..	..
6 45	Duck Colliery	2590	—	—	—	—	..	..	..			—	—			—	—	..	—	—	—	—	..	..	—	—	—	—	..	..
6 56	Whimsey Halt	2591	—	—	—	—	..	..	..			—	—			12 12	—	..	—	—	—	—	..	..	—	—	—	—	..	..
6 65	Cinderford Goods	2836	82 R	4	1	—	..	..	..			—	—	Worked by Engine ex	Lydney 7.30 a.m.	—	—	..	2 20	—	—	—	..	..	—	—	—	—	..	..
7 7	Steam Mills Cross'g Halt	2592	69 R	—	—	—	..					9 21	9 34			—	—	..	—	—	—	—	..	..	—	—	—	—	..	..
7 59	Nailbridge Halt	2593	42 R	—	—	—	..					—	—			—	—	..	..	..	—	—	..	..	—	—	—	—	..	..
7 68	Speedwell	2594	44 R	—	—	—	..	Engine arrives from Gloucester 6.25 a.m				9 42	9 55			—	—	..	..	..	—	—	..	..	—	—	—	—	..	..
8 29	**Drybr'k Halt**	2595	43 R	—	—	—	..					—	—			—	—	..	..	..	—	—	..	..	—	—	—	—	..	..
—	Drybrook Quarries	—	—	—	—	—	..					10 2	—	..	..	—	—	..	..	..	—	—	..	..	—	—	—	—	..	..

*—Distance Bilson Junction to Cinderford Junction 33 chains, and to Cinderford Station 63 chains. The length of the Loop at Eastern United Colliery is 380 yards, capable of holding engine, 50 wagons and van. **R** Returns empty Cinderford to Bilson Junction to pick up Trucks Goods and work to Whimsey. **W** When the combined load of 1.0 p.m. Bullo to Eastern United and 1.25 p.m. Bullo Pill to Cinderford does not exceed 40 wagons may be run as coupled train.

FOREST OF DEAN BRANCH—*continued.*

WEEK DAYS.

Distance.	UP TRAINS. STATIONS.	Gradient.	Time Allowances for Ordinary Freight Trains. See page 2. Point to Point Times.	Allow for Stop.	Allow for Start.		K Goods.			B Auto Car to Gloster.		K Goods.		K Goods.			B Auto Car to Gloster.		K Goods. SX		K Goods.		Goods.		B Auto Car to Grange Ct.		C Light Auto and Trailer.	B Auto Car to Gloster. SO		K Engine & Brake			C Light Auto and Trailers to Gloster.
M. C		1 in	Mins.	Mins.	Mins.		arr. a.m.	dep. a.m.		arr. a.m.	dep a.m.	arr. a.m	dep. a.m.	arr. a.m.	dep. a.m.		arr. p.m.	dep. p.m	arr. p.m.	dep. p.m.	arr. p.m.	dep. p.m.	arr. p.m	dep. p.m	arr. p.m.	dep. p.m.	dep. p.m	arr. p.m.	dep. p.m.	dep. p.m.			dep. p.m.
—	Drybrook Quarries	—	—	—	—	..	..	..	..	—	—	..	..	—	10 20	..	..	..	..	..	..	..	..	..	—	—	..	—	—	..	..	..	..
—	**Drybr'k H'lt**	—	—	—	—	..	..	..	..	—	—	..	..	—	—	..	..	..	..	..	..	..	..	..	—	—	..	—	—	..	..	..	..
— 41	Speedwell	43 F	—	—	—	..	..	..	..	—	—	..	..	10 25	10 30	..	—	—	..	..	..	..	..	..	—	—	..	—	—	..	..	..	Q
— 50	Nailbridge Halt	44 F	—	—	—	..	..	..	..	—	—	..	..	—	—	..	—	—	..	..	..	..	..	..	—	—	..	—	—	..	..	..	..
1 22	Steam M. Crossing Halt	42 F	—	—	—	..	..	..	..	—	—	..	..	—	—	..	—	—	..	..	..	..	..	..	—	—	..	—	—	SX	..	..	..
1 44	Cinderford Goods	69 F	—	—	1	..	..	..	..	—	—	..	..	—	—	..	—	—	..	..	—	2 45	..	..	—	—	SX	—	—	..	..	..	..
1 53	Whimsey Halt	—	—	—	—	..	..	..	..	—	—	..	..	—	—	..	—	12†25	..	..	—	—	..	..	—	—	..	—	—	..	..	..	..
1 64	Duck Colliery	—	—	—	—	..	..	..	..	—	—	..	..	—	—	..	—	—	..	..	C	R	..	..	—	—	..	—	—	..	..	..	..
—	Churchway	—	—	—	—	..	..	..	..	..	..	..	..	..	..	..	..	..	..	..	..	—	..	..	..	..	..	..	..	..	..	..	..
—	Brick W'rks Siding	41 F	—	—	—	..	..	..	..	..	..	..	..	..	..	..	..	..	..	..	..	—	..	..	..	..	..	..	..	..	..	..	..
—	Bilson Goods Yard	52 F	3	2	1	..	..	..	..	—	—	..	..	10 40	11 5	..	—	—	..	..	2 51	3 40	..	..	—	—	..	—	—	..	..	..	..
2 30	Bilson Junction	76 F	—	—	—	..	..	..	..	—	—	..	..	—	—	..	12†27	12†28	..	..	—	—	..	..	—	4†15	—	—	—	..	..	..	..
—	Cinderford Junct.	—	—	—	—	..	..	..	..	—	—	..	..	—	—	..	—	—	..	..	M		..	..	C	S	..	—	—	..	..	..	..
—	**Cinderford**	—	—	—	—	..	—	8 15	..	—	9 8	..	..	—	—	..	12†30	12 35	..	..	—	—	—	3 20	4†17	4 20	6†20	—	6 40	..	..	..	8†55
—	Cinderford Junct.	—	—	—	—	..	C	S	..	C	S	..	..	—	—	..	C	S	..	..	—	—	C	S	C	S	CS	C	S	..	..	..	CS
—	Stop Board	51 F	—	—	—	..	P	—	..	—	—	..	..	—	—	..	—	—	..	..	—	—	—	—	—	—	—	—	—	..	..	..	—
2 30	Bilson Junction	76 F	—	—	—	..	8‡22	—	..	9 10	9 11	..	..	C	S	..	C 12 37	S	..	..	C	S	3‡25	—	C 4 22	S	CS	C 6 42	S	..	..	..	CS
2 43	Bilson Halt	—	—	—	—	..	‡ Bilson Goods	Yard.	..	—	—	..	..	—	—	..	—	—	..	..	—	—	‡ Bilson Goods	Yard.	—	—	6†23	—	—	..	..	..	—
3 18	Stop Board	178 F	4	1	1	..			..	—	—	..	..	—	—	..	—	—	..	..	3 44	P3 49			—	—	—	—	—	..	..	..	—
3 19	Ruspidge Halt	99 F	—	—	—	..			..	—	9 13	..	..	11 10P	11 15	..	—	12 39	—	—	—	—			—	4 24	—	—	6 44	..	..	..	—
3 72	Eastern United Colliery	58 F	4	1	1	..			..	C	S	..	10 0	11 20	11X55	..	C	S	—	3 0	3 53	4 40			C	S	—	—	—	6†50	..	..	—
3 78	Staple Edge Halt	71 F	—	—	—	..			..	—	9 15½	—	—	—	—	..	—	12 41½	—	—	—	—			—	4 26½	—	—	6 47	—	..	..	—
4 23	Shakemantle	49 F	—	—	—	..			..	—	—	C	R	—	—	..	—	—	—	—	—	—			—	—	—	—	—	—	..	..	—
5 5	Stop Board	49 F	6	1	1	..			..	—	—	10 8P	10 12	12 3P	12 7	..	—	—	3 8P	3 12	4 43P	4 52			—	—	To Lydney.	—	—	6P56	..	..	—
5 7	Upper Soudley Halt	49 F	—	—	—	..			..	—	9 19	—	—	—	—	..	—	12 45	—	—	—	—			—	4 30		—	6 51	—	..	..	—
5 7	Soudley Sidings	48 F	—	—	—	..			..	—	—	—	—	—	—	..	—	—	—	—	—	—			—	—		—	—	—	..	..	—
5 45	Soudley Furnaces	43 F	—	—	—	..			..	—	—	—	—	—	—	..	—	—	—	—	—	—			—	—		—	—	—	..	..	—
6 72	Bullo Cross Halt	50 F	—	—	—	..	..	..	..	—	9 23½	—	—	—	—	..	—	12 49½	—	—	—	—	..	..	—	4 34½	—	—	6 56	—	..	..	—
7 33	Bullo Pill	54 F	‡16	1	1	..	..	..	..	O	9 27 W	10 33	—	12X29	—	..	O	12 54 W	3 34	—	5X14	—	..	..	O	4 39 W	6†40	O	7 0 W	7† 5	..	..	—
8 29	**Newnham**	—	—	—	—	..	..	..	..	9 30	9 31	..	..	..	..	..	12 57	12 58	..	..	..	..	..	..	4 42	4 43	..	7 3	7 4	..	..	..	9†15

Goods worked by Auto Engine and Trailer. Light Auto and Trailers to Gloster: Sats. only.

M On Saturdays Bilson Jct. dep. 3.35 Stop Board 3P44, Stop Board 4P0, Bullo Pill arr. 4.21 p.m.

Q To Gloucester to work 9.50 p.m. Gloster to Lydney **SO**

‡ To Bullo Pill Home Signal—3 mins. allowed thence to Bullo Pill Yard, including one minute to stop. Trains conveying less than equal 25 "Ten Ton" loaded wagons allowed one minute less Eastern United Colliery to Bullo Pill Home Signal.

'It will no longer be possible to leave Gloucester at 8.20 for Awre and Woolaston, as that train will cease to call at those stations.

'So far as the stoppage of the 7.10 motor from Cinderford to Gloucester, which gave a connection to London, is concerned, we understand that the Company will shortly be announcing (no doubt through our columns), a 'bus service, which will replace this train and take passengers direct to Gloucester Great Western Station. It will be remembered that the Great Western Railway Company are now interested in the 'Blue Bus Company' who, therefore, now use the Cinderford Joint Station premises as a garage.'

The closure was also highlighted in the railway press of the time, C. R. Clinker remarking in the *Railway Magazine* for August 1930, 'Perhaps no rural area has suffered so much from the closing of its railway communication as the Forest of Dean'.

The passenger service between Newnham and Cinderford continued well into BR days but, in the search for further economies, the engine shed at Bullo was closed from 23rd March 1931, and thereafter locomotives for the Forest of Dean branch were shedded, along with their S & W counterparts, at Lydney. The loco for the first trip in the morning to Eastern United was sent from Gloucester and tended to be a larger engine, often a '57xx' 0—6—0PT in the '77xx' series. Lydney provided one of the new Collett '58xx' 0—4—2Ts for the auto service and two '2021' class 0—6—0PTs which worked the branch and traffic in the Lydney direction.

The Gloucester crew booked on at 3.20 a.m. and, after preparing the engine and making up the fire, were allowed

20 minutes extra to put another box of coal from the tip on the bunker, until partly overspilling onto the cab roof. They needed to carry every scrap they could for the day's duty ahead. When they came off shed, they ran to Gloucester New Yard to collect the goods vans for Bullo Pill and the Forest branch. They then proceeded to the Gloucester Docks branch to pick up 70 empties. On arrival at Bullo they were relieved by driver Harry Askew and fireman Bob Trigg, the one set of men retained at Bullo. Harry was Bob's father-in-law. The Bullo men carried out any shunting required, and delivered any wagons for the small goods shed at Bullo Docks before forming the train for the branch. They then worked the 7.30 a.m. mixed goods to Cinderford, Whimsey and Drybrook Quarry, then back to Eastern United Colliery to work the 12.00 noon coal train to Bullo. At 1.00 p.m. they worked a train of empties to Eastern, returning at 3.00 p.m. from there with a coal train. At Bullo they were relieved by Gloucester men who worked the train forward, leaving Harry and Bob to book off duty.

At that time Lydney men worked 8.30 a.m. empties to Eastern with a '2021' class pannier tank from Lydney shed. They shunted the colliery and left Eastern at 11.00 a.m. with a coal train for Bullo. Sometimes, when excursions were run from Cinderford on a Saturday night, for Barton Fair for instance, with three trailers, Harry Askew and Bob Trigg would take over from the Gloucester men at Bullo.

The piecemeal utilization of the former Mitcheldean Road line took an unusual turn during June 1939 when,

The GWR 'Docks Branch Siding' at Gloucester, looking south-west towards the docks. To the left of the centre line, kept clear for through running, stand a couple of loaded coal trains awaiting forward shipment. To the right are the outwards wagons including a rake of coal empties. The tall chimney stack in the middle distance marks the location of the electricity power station, latterly an important user of coal brought in by the GWR route. This picture was taken on 20th October 1946. *L. E. Copeland*

Left: Loaded wagons from the screens at Northern United colliery on 27th June 1948.
L. E. Copeland

Below: A solitary tank wagon inhabits the weed-strewn sidings at Drybrook Quarry on 1st August 1949. Although little used by this date, the quarry experienced considerable disruption during the Second World War, with trains of ammunition to and from the Admiralty's storage depot in Hawthorns tunnel.   *L. E. Copeland*

in anticipation of hostilities, the Admiralty requisitioned Hawthorns Tunnel for use as an explosives store. On 1st July it was reported that the branch had been extended to the mouth of the tunnel and Decauville track was being laid to transport the shells inside. The bed of the tunnel was to be concreted. A transfer shed, two 1-ton hand cranes and a guard room were to be erected, and three coaches provided for accommodation.

It seems that the decision to use the tunnel had been made the previous year as correspondence reveals that on 26th September 1938 thirty-three wagons of Admiralty traffic had been despatched from Fareham for Hawthorns Tunnel. It seems the train had reached Bilson and another was also on its way from Fareham before it was pointed out that the tunnel was inaccessible! 'The tunnel is devoid of track — about ¼ mile short. It is in need of examination as water had percolated through for years and there is also a defective culvert'.

It appears that the second train was diverted to Tonmawr near Port Talbot. To accommodate the Admiralty train, coal traffic was moved from Bilson Junction to outlying points but in internal GWR correspondence it is recorded: 'I do not suppose the Admiralty will be content to allow these opens covered with sheets to stand in the open indefinitely'.

In connection with Admiralty traffic, the track layout at Drybrook Quarry was altered and blasting was prohibited while explosives were passing or standing alongside the quarry sidings.

Ammunition traffic was sorted at Bilson Junction and hauled up to Drybrook Quarry sidings where the locomotive ran round its train and propelled it for the final few yards. Crews remember taking box vans of ammunition to the tunnel 'several times a week'.

Other wartime measures included the storage of French wagons and Canadian sleepers at Cinderford Old, the junction between the Churchway branch and the neighbouring Severn & Wye. The S & W also did its bit for the war effort with ammunition storage along the Mineral Loop, in Moseley Green Tunnel and at a new depot created for the purpose at Acorn Patch.

Details of wartime working are inevitably patchy, such movements being irregular and often classified. However, the signalman at Bilson Junction remembers the yard being full of coaches from troop trains and evacuation specials. These used coaching stock from many areas, including the Chalford 'car', and the crews were evidently a mixed bag as well; the loco of one special, pulling out from the yard for Cinderford, dropped a plug and stopped, thus fouling the running line. A loco had to be brought from Eastern United to push it clear.

No enemy action is recorded in the area; however, a notable wartime casualty was Lightmoor Colliery, which closed on 8th June 1940, the connection with Bilson yard being removed the following year.

No doubt the area returned to a semblance of normality in the immediate postwar years, and there were no immediate changes either to the pattern of traffic or the infrastructure of the line. Nationalisation from 1948 brought a change of ownership (the line coming under the control of British Railways Western Region) and a gradual change of livery, but little else. Passenger services continued to be handled by auto-fitted '14XX' 0–4–2Ts and '54XX' 0–6–0PTs, whilst goods services were invariably in the charge of '57XX' pannier tanks, although the '16XX' class, modern successors to the '2021s', were also used occasionally following their introduction in 1949.

Bob Trigg had been made up to driver in 1937 and transferred to South Wales to take up the position. He returned to the Forest in 1939 when a vacancy arose at Lydney shed. By this time his son Harry was a fireman at Lydney and, through exchanging turns for convenience, they were able to cover the Bullo job together, booking on over the telephone at 10.30 a.m. and relieving the Gloucester men at 11.30, shunting until 12.30 and forming the 1.05 p.m. Bullo to Bilson and Northern United Colliery. Empties for Northern were conveyed in two trips with 20 wagons being propelled from Bilson with a brake van leading. A 40-wagon coal train was formed at the colliery and left for Bilson at 3.40 p.m. On return to Bilson, it was sometimes necessary to run to Drybrook, engine and brake van, to collect ammunition from Hawthorn Tunnel. On these occasions it was difficult to get back to Bilson in time for the 4.20 departure so the train ran late on these days. On arrival at Bullo, they shunted the train to form the 7.30 p.m. Bullo to Stoke Gifford, booking off duty at 6.20 p.m.

Sometimes the Triggs exchanged with crews on the Gloucester to Cinderford auto-car which they took over at Newnham, again booking on at 10.30 a.m. Otherwise, if they were unable to exchange, they worked jobs with their own mates in the links, largely on the Severn & Wye, including the Coleford and Lydbrook branches, and the Berkeley Road passenger and, on the main line, the night Lydney to Stoke Gifford coal train.

The branch enjoyed a period of relative prosperity through the late 'forties; however, the steady decline in industrial output in the Forest, plus the widespread increase in private car ownership, meant that this was only an interlude before the now familiar pattern of closure and cutbacks set in.

A tranquil post-WWII interlude at Cinderford with '14XX' class 0–4–2T No. 1456 on a FoD branch auto-train. This is clearly a posed view, the trains normally standing next to the station building between arrival and departure. *W. A. Camwell*

NEWNHAM-ON-SEVERN, THE TOWN CLOCK & LOWER HIGH ST.

A sunny view of Lower High Street, Newnham, looking towards Gloucester. The road leading to Newnham station led off to the left of this picture, past the George Hotel which was also known as the Lower George. The ornate clock tower was built by public subscription in 1875 and is a symbol of the town's importance in the area. With the industrial growth within the Forest of Dean, Cinderford assumed greater importance although Newnham still enjoyed a degree of influence with several firms of solicitors handling mining matters from offices in the town.

Collection R. How

ALONG THE LINE

NEWNHAM

An early Edwardian view of Newnham, with a '3521' class 4—4—0 on a down stopping train. The station is shown here in its original condition, the wide spacing between the tracks serving as a reminder of the former broad gauge.   *Lens of Sutton*

The Forest of Dean branch connected with the South Wales main line at Bullo, about two miles further west, so Newnham station is not strictly part of the line. However, when passenger services were introduced on the branch on 3rd August 1907 it became the junction station and therefore makes the obvious starting point for our description of the branch. Newnham had either opened on, or perhaps soon after, the opening of the South Wales Railway on 19th September 1851 as it was not until 20th August 1852 that a contract was concluded with William Blinkhorn for the construction of Newnham station. Whether there was a temporary arrangement beforehand is not clear. The main station building and goods shed were Brunel designs but 'platform coverings' and a 'platform shed' were not provided until 1857.

For the next fifty years or so those who travelled by rail to the eastern side of the Forest of Dean faced a long and bumpy road journey up the hills to Littledean and beyond. Certainly for over twenty years Newnham would have held a virtual monopoly for both passenger and goods traffic, with Awre Junction and Lydney the only alternatives. It was not until 1875 that the Severn & Wye & Canal Co opened its line from Lydney to Cinderford for passenger traffic and even then travellers from the Gloucester direction would probably still have found it easier (and quicker!) to alight at Newnham and take to the roads. Mail

for the Forest was also offloaded at Newnham and in 1890 Travelling Post Office apparatus was erected there in the 'down' direction.

The station remained little altered until the introduction of the Forest of Dean branch passenger service, when a new bay platform was provided. The broad gauge legacy of the South Wales Railway left surplus spacing between the platforms so the down platform was extended outwards towards its opposite number to allow the building of the new bay with minimal excavation of the steep bank behind. One less predictable feature of the station layout after modification was the absence of a crossover to provide up trains from the Forest with direct access to the bay. However, as many of the passengers from the Forest were probably travelling to Gloucester, they alighted on the correct platform and only had to wait there for the connecting train, thus avoiding the need to use the footbridge. The empty motor train ran forward and reversed onto the down line via the trailing crossover beyond the signal box. It then ran right through the station and reversed into the bay. Of course, passengers returning from Gloucester alighted on the down side and only had to cross the platform to the waiting motor train.

By 1913 several of the Forest services were being extended through to Grange Court and Gloucester and the bay saw less and less use after this time.

'Bulldog' class 4–4–0 No. 3459 *Toronto* with an up passenger train at Newnham not long after the loco was built in February 1904. This view presents a typical lineside scene at any main line station with coal being unloaded in the yard.

Collection J. E. Kite

An unidentified '3521' class 4—4—0 at Newnham alongside the down platform prior to the 1907 building of the FoD bay. In contrast with the loco featured on page 33, this is one of the batch fitted with non-taper standard No. 3 boilers. Both types were rebuilds from standard gauge or broad gauge convertible 0—4—2Ts between 1899 and 1902, and were common on the South Wales main line up to 1927.

Collection Roger Carpenter

G.W.R. STATION, NEWNHAM-ON-SEVERN. "GLOSS" SERIES 4007.

A post 1907 view showing the new bay platform provided for the inauguration of the Forest railmotor service. Taking advantage of the broad gauge legacy, space for the bay was created by slewing the down main running line closer to the up line, extending the platform to meet it and excavating some of the steep bank behind. This view shows one of the new Forest motor trains waiting in the bay for main line connections.

Collection Neil Parkhouse

Another Edwardian scene with passengers about to board a Forest railmotor.

Collection Neil Parkhouse

'388' class 0—6—0 Standard Goods No. 43 with a down goods at Newnham c.1905.

L & GRP, courtesy David & Charles

NEWNHAM
CTION FOR MOTOR SERVICES TO CINDERFORD
AND DRYBROOK DISTRICTS

NEWNHAM-ON-SEVERN. THE STATIO

A wonderfully evocative pre-1911 view of Newnham, looking south-west towards Bullo, with a Forest of Dean motor train waiting in the bay beyond the footbridge. It is probably awaiting both up and down main line connections judging by the number of potential travellers on the platforms.   *Parkhouse/Pope Archive*

NEWNHAM-ON-SEVERN. THE STATION (WEST) & FOREST RAIL MOTOR. W.P. 172.

An unidentified auto-fitted '2021' class 0–6–0ST with a Forest of Dean branch motor train in the bay at Newnham shortly after the introduction of the service. The Forest railmotor, normally only run with one coach, was strengthened with a second vehicle for Saturdays and special events, the extra coach being kept at Bilson. Three coaches were used for trains to Barton Fair in Gloucester with the railmotor running right through to Gloucester.

Parkhouse/Pope Archive

Looking south-west towards Bullo through the rebuilt station, showing the new running-in board proclaiming Newnham as the 'junction for motor services to Cinderford and Drybrook Districts'. The up waiting room on the right of the picture was authorised in January 1911 for £545. The corrugated shed alongside the main building on the down platform served as a parcels office. *Collection A. K. Pope*

4—6—0 No. 2921 *Saint Dunstan* leaving Newnham with a down train c.1934. *A. K. Pope*

Looking east towards Gloucester from Newnham signal box on 5th June 1941, showing the goods yard and cattle pen. Travelling Post Office apparatus erected alongside the down line, 214 yards east of the station, was brought into use in January 1890 when the Cinderford post was routed via RSO Gloucester and put off at Newnham. There was no apparatus on the Gloucester-based (up) side.   *L. E. Copeland*

Signalman Arthur Roberts at Newnham signal box on 5th June 1946. The previous signalman was Frank Tilley who transferred to Bullo East Box.   *L. E. Copeland*

The view from the station footbridge, looking over the combined roof/canopy of the 1911 waiting room, towards Gloucester on 5th June 1946. After arrival from Cinderford, FoD branch motor trains ran out of the station past the trailing crossover visible in the distance. They were then reversed through the crossover to run right through the station on the down line to reverse again into the bay platform

L. E. Copeland

The brick store alongside the main building on the down platform in this 1950s view replaced the corrugated iron parcels shed featured on page 41. *Collection A. K. Pope*

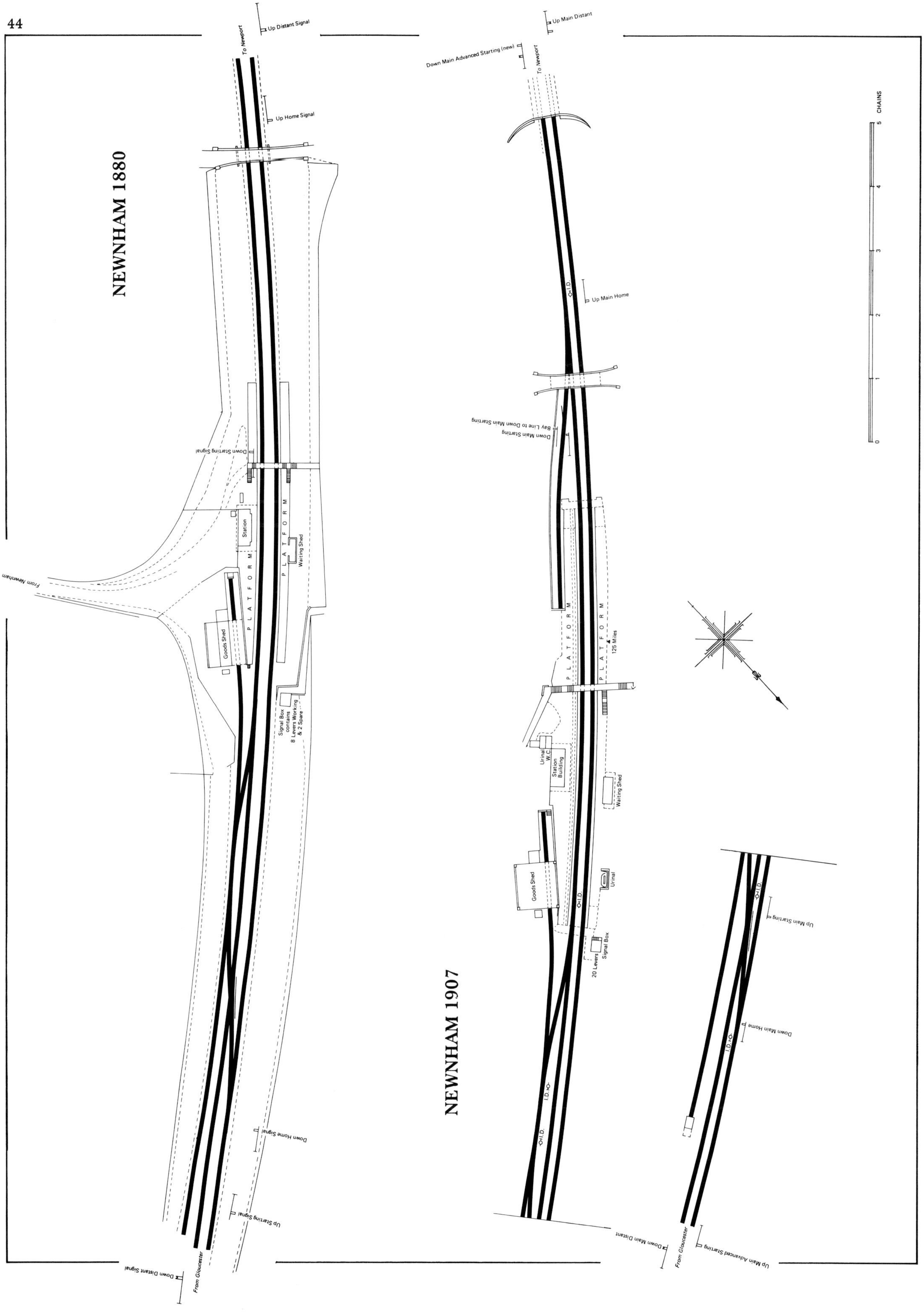

NEWNHAM 1880

Up Distant Signal

Up Home Signal

To Newport

Down Starting Signal

From Newnham

Station

P L A T F O R M

P L A T F O R M

Waiting Shed

Goods Shed

Signal Box
contains
8 Levers Working
& 2 Spare

Down Home Signal

Up Starting Signal

From Gloucester

Down Distant Signal

NEWNHAM 1907

Up Main Distant

Down Main Advanced Starting (new)

To Newport

Up Main Home

I.D.

Down Main Starting

Bay Line to Down Main Starting

P L A T F O R M

P L A T F O R M

125 Miles

Urinal
W.C.

Station
Building

Waiting Shed

Goods Shed

I.D.

Urinal

20 Levers
Signal Box

Up Main Starting

I.D.

Down Main Home

I.D.

I.D.

Up Main Advanced Starting

Down Main Distant

From Gloucester

0 1 2 3 4 5 CHAINS

Having crossed over from the up running line as described on page 43, the Forest motor train is backing into the bay on 5th June 1946. Newnham tunnel can be seen in the background beyond the occupation bridge. *L. E. Copeland*

Collett 0—4—2T No. 1409 starting away from the bay with a train for Cinderford on 11th September 1948. *L. E. Copeland*

An unidentified auto-fitted '2021' class 0—6—0ST propelling an auto trailer from Cinderford towards Newnham tunnel, probably just before the First World War.

Collection Neil Parkhouse

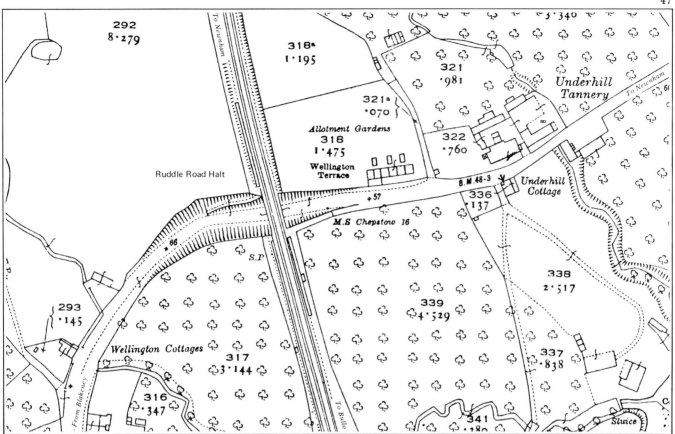

Looking towards Blakeney through Ruddle railway bridge c.1908-10 just after the opening of Ruddle Halt which was built on either side of the bridge. Opening with the Forest of Dean service in 1907, this halt was short-lived, being closed in April 1917 and removed in June 1920. One of the shelters was moved to Bullo Cross halt in 1918. The approach to the halt was to the left just behind the photographer. Unfortunately, no views of the halt itself have been discovered but the third edition 25-in Ordnance Survey shows the platforms staggered either side of the road underbridge.
A. J. Pope

Looking towards Newnham and Gloucester from the north-east end of the yard at Bullo on 11th September 1948, with Bullo Pill East box on the right and the up sidings headshunt (poetically known to staff as 'Rookery Siding') extending into the distance on the left of the up running line.

L. E. Copeland

BULLO YARD

From shortly after the opening of the South Wales Railway in 1851 Bullo had been important for the interchange of traffic with the Forest of Dean branch tramroad, the output from which had formerly all gone for shipment from Bullo Pill dock. When the tramroad was converted to a railway, 'Bullo Pill station' became a proper junction and, as already mentioned on page 2, facilities were rapidly expanded.

The small wooden 'station' was destroyed by fire on 16th September 1855, the *Gloucester Journal* reporting:

'It appeared that a policeman named Richard Fryer was at the station about five o'clock in the evening and lighted his lamps as usual with a Lucifer match. After lighting the lamps he proceeded down the line for half a mile and on his return he saw the station on fire. He endeavoured to remove the company's goods etc., and succeeded in removing some of the account books. The cash box containing eight £5 notes, some gold and silver amounting to about £10 were destroyed.'

Fryer was later cautioned by the South Wales Traffic Committee to be very careful when lighting his lamps in future.

Instigation of a replacement 'station' prompted the replacement of the engine shed with a larger structure (see page 54) but little else is known of the site at this time. Subsequent expansion, if vague in detail, included additional sidings authorised in April 1865 at £507 4s 0d; a 'reservoir for the supply of water at Bullo Pill', July 1865, £120; 'Extra shunter at Bullo', February 1868; 'locking gear at Bullo Pill' £12 10s 0d, and an 'additional lad clerk to attend telegraph Bullo Branch', August 1867; 'erecting grease house Bullo Pill Station', June 1868, £12 0s 0d; and a 'Switchman Bullo' in December 1872, all of the work presumably taking us towards the situation shown on the first edition OS map surveyed in 1879 and reproduced on pages 60/61.

On 27th October 1897, £1,234 was authorised for 'the improvement of signalling arrangements', the work involving the replacement of the old Middle and West Boxes by a new 34-lever West Box situated opposite the divergence of the FoD branch, not far from the old Middle Box (see plan on page 58). The work also involved the provision of a new crossover road between up and down main lines to replace

Bullo yard, seen in the opposite direction (from the north-east) on the same date, providing a particularly clear view of the down goods running loop. This clearly later addition, running to the left behind the East box, was provided in 1930. The outermost of the up sidings on the right of this view, running round the back of the offices, was known as 'new road'. It is believed to have been provided in 1941. The adjacent siding terminating just short of the offices, was known as 'Muckhole'.   *L. E. Copeland*

the existing down main to up main and refuge sidings connection which, further west, had been controlled from the previous West Box, but would now be beyond the limits of mechanical working from the new one. At the same time, the East Box was fitted with a new 22-lever frame and the layout was extensively resignalled. The work was completed and ready for inspection on 20th December 1898.

The introduction of passenger services on the Forest of Dean branch in 1907 must have brought about the direct connections between the branch and the up and down main running lines. The provision of a new down goods running loop, conversion of the old refuge or 'long siding' on the up side of the line into an up goods running loop, and the provision of a sand drag for the FoD branch was authorised on 23rd January 1930, the cost of £9,610, made up of £6,050 Engineering Department, £2,790 Signalling Department and £770 Chief Mechanical Engineer's Department, plus £250 for land.

In November 1930 the Gloucester District Goods Manager, Mr. E. A. Chapman, wrote to Messrs. Henry Crawshay & Co Ltd, the owners of Eastern United Colliery (see page 151), suggesting the provision of three extra sidings at Bullo Pill to relieve the congestion of traffic at their colliery. The estimated cost was £3,500 and it was suggested that Crawshays might contribute half of the amount or alternatively pay 10% of £1,750 per year for ten years. That the GWR would have first call on the use of the sidings did not impress Crawshays who declined the offer, supposing that it was Chapman's duty to try and induce them to do so. The debate was revived in January 1931 when in Crawshays' daily quota of wagons there was some fuss over the required selection of empty wagons. The GWR felt that if the coal factors required a special selection then they should contribute to the proposed sidings! Crawshays offered to contribute £1,000 towards this but their minute books record that the GWR were not 'nearly so well pleased with our offer to contribute £1,000 towards the cost of the proposed additional sidings at Bullo as he [Crawshays' managing director] had anticipated they would be'. When the matter surfaced again in February 1932, Crawshays expressed the opinion that with the volume of traffic from Eastern United, the proposed sidings should be provided free of charge, and the following month the GWR decided that the matter could rest until further difficulties arose!

The final development took place during the war when in desperation for more accommodation, a new siding (the 'new road') was added behind the offices. The 'short road' and middle roads were also extended as described on page 52. Much of this work is evident in the pictures, especially when compared with the track plan.

The layout at Bullo Pill was primarily concerned with the interchange of traffic between the Forest of Dean branch and the main line and, of course, the docks branch,

Bullo Pill East box on 18th June 1933. This was an early style GWR box dating from the period 1869-1875.   *L. E. Copeland*

The signalman's view from the East box towards Newnham and Gloucester, with a down train held at the down home and down main to down goods loop signals on 11th September 1948. *L. E. Copeland*

but it also provided vital refuge accommodation for up and down goods trains which could be held in the goods running loops and watered if necessary while higher priority trains sped through.

An example of operational procedure here might be a train of 70 Forest-bound empties from Gloucester. This might enter Bullo on the down goods running loop where it was divided. A portion would then be drawn forward onto the down main in front of the West Box and reversed hard back into the 'straight road' where the wagons were secured while the loco ran round to the other end of them. They would then be taken over the down sidings to up goods running loop trailing crossover and placed in the yard via the headshunt as required. Trains of empties for the Forest were marshalled on either the 'middle' or branch roads and always left for the Forest with two guards.

Another view of the box on 2nd April 1968.
A. K. Pope

The interior of East Box on 5th April 1968, showing the 20-lever frame. Frank Tilley was a regular signalman here from the mid-30s after leaving Newnham box.
A. K. Pope

This picture of an up passenger passing a down goods train on the main running lines on 11th September 1948, provides a glimpse of the offices which accommodated the Bullo station master, three or four shunters and six guards. The two structures nearer the camera presumably date from the 1855 replacement of the wooden building destroyed by fire, the adjacent one obviously being a later design. The siding behind the offices was known as 'new road' and, as shown here, extended right up to the engine shed. The next one diverging in front of the offices was 'short road' and the adjacent one 'middle road'. The next line, occupied by a single wagon, was the 'branch' along which, just beyond the end of 'middle' and 'short' roads, were the points leading into the engine shed. However, by this time the connection had been taken out, and the shed line reconnected to the 'middle road' to form a much longer siding. At the same time the 'short road' was extended to run alongside the shed as shown on page 55. It is believed this work was carried out as part of the 1941 improvements. Still working across the picture, the line alongside the branch was the up goods running loop with its adjacent water-crane, then the up main and down main running lines, the 'straight road' (officially marshalling siding), 'dock road' leading to the docks, and the down goods running loop.

L. E. Copeland

One of the 20-ton goods brake vans or 'Toads' photographed at Gloucester in June 1933.

L. E. Copeland

Looking south towards Lydney, this picture, taken on 11th September 1948, shows the long crossover alongside the engine shed, providing a facing connection from the down main to Forest of Dean branch, and, in the opposite direction, up branch to up sidings, up goods loop and up main. The simple crossover beyond provided exit from the first portion of the up goods running loop to up main line. The two water cranes on the left of this view stood between the down goods running line and the 'dock road' and the 'straight road' and the down main line.

L. E. Copeland

According to official shed records, Bullo Pill shed was built for the broad gauge in 1851, but this date may apply to a previous structure, for in September 1855, following a fire which destroyed the station, the South Wales Railway Secretary was instructed to get estimates for 'providing additional engine house accommodation for a second locomotive at Bullo' in addition to a new 'station'. The resulting structure was built to a standard GWR design of the mid-1850s with brick side walls enclosed with wooden ends and a slate roof. The internal dimensions were 104ft by 20ft, and the heights to the wall plate and ridge of 15ft 10in and 21ft. In 1897 it had a full length smoke trough and a 95ft 3in inspection pit. There was also a 29ft 3in pit outside the north entrance to the shed. Lean-to appendages on the east wall provided a stone-built enginemen's cabin 12ft x 9ft and WCs, both featured in this picture. The enginemen's cabin was later used as a stores, crews being displaced to an old 24ft x 7ft coach body situated on the east side of the track between the sand house and the water tower, and mounted on a brick base. Official records indicate that it was probably provided in October 1919, the accommodation being divided equally between enginemen in the southern end and cleaners in the other. The corrugated iron building beyond the shed measured 15ft 6in by 14ft 9in and housed a sand furnace, sand drying being one of the cleaners' duties. The shed was closed on 21st March 1931, at which time there were four sets of men based there. Locos and men were transferred to the former S & W shed at Lydney. Afterwards the shed road was reconnected to the middle road and relegated to wagon storage, as shown in this picture taken in June 1936.

W. A. Camwell

The south-eastern end of the shed shortly before demolition. The wrought iron coal bunker on the left, measuring 15ft 10in by 14ft 9in, had been there since at least 1897 when it featured on an official survey of the shed. (Broad gauge tender?) *Lens of Sutton*

The north-western end of the derelict shed building in 1949. The stores and WC appendages, shown in the picture opposite, were taken down to make room for the siding shown here, which was the short road extended in 1941 to increase desperately needed accommodation, perhaps as an indirect result of the more ambitious suggestions mentioned on page 50. *L & GRP, courtesy David & Charles*

The steep 1 in 54 gradient by which the branch climbed away from the main line is very obvious in this view towards Gloucester from Bullo West Signal Box on 5th October 1946. The more ornate water tower alongside the running line incorporated a coal stage measuring 29ft 6in by 10ft 9in. In earlier years this was also equipped with a small crane to assist with coaling. As there was no supply at Newnham, branch auto trains would usually stop here for water on their way from the Forest, two cleaners standing by to take the opportunity of loading at least one tub of coal into the small bunker of the engine while it was stood alongside the coal platform. However, the working timetable appendix for 1914 specified 'when a car is running late in the direction of Newnham, and is likely to cause delay to a main line train through stopping for water at Bullo Pill, this work to be done on return trip from Newnham.' A second water tank, to the left in the picture, was authorised in December 1922 for £3,935 including the renewal of the water main. The supply 'spring water obtained by gravity through Bullo Tunnel' proved inadequate for the increased traffic during the Second World War so 'provision of emergency water supply from dock feeder' was authorised on 30th October 1942 for £1,373. The work, completed the following July at the expense of the Ministry of War Transport, involved the installation of a second-hand 6hp oil engine removed from Didcot and a new Pulsometer centrifugal pump to obtain water from an adjacent dock feeder. The equipment was housed in a small hut constructed from 'Taunton concrete building blocks with a reinforced concrete roof (see page 75). The 'Toad' at the end of the shed siding may have been condemned goods brake No. 35854 which was repaired and weatherproofed for the temporary accommodation of examining staff at Bullo. The official authorisation for the work was granted the same month this picture was taken. The train featured on the right was a down goods being held on the down goods running loop which extended from the East box, and, at 500 yards long, could accommodate a tender engine with 70 wagons and a brake van.

L. E. Copeland

Still looking out of the West Box but this time in the opposite direction towards Lydney and South Wales, on 11th September 1948. The lines on the far side of the main running lines were the up goods running loop and beyond that, to the right, a cripple siding, which, accessed by a padlocked ground lever (key kept in the custody of the signalman in the West Box), would hold 30 wagons. The up goods running loop extending to the East Box was divided by the FoD branch junction. It could accommodate two trains, the first section ending at the ringed arms on the bracket signal controlling the exit crossover from the loop line to the up main featured on the opposite page. Trains occupying this portion of the loop had to stand clear of the foot crossing from the West Box to the FoD branch line (see page 78), the length of loop available then being 433 yards, which would accommodate a tender engine with 60 wagons and a brake van. The second or easternmost portion of the goods loop extended from a catchpoint, 15 yards on the east side of the branch junction, to the exit at the East Box. The length of line available was 373 yards which would accommodate a tender engine with 50 wagons and a brake van. The line descending steeply on the left was the Bullo Pill Dock branch which was worked using a train staff kept in the West Box. The 'dock, wharves and switches' were under the supervision of the station master, all the points at the dock being worked by local hand levers locked with switch locks, the key to which was kept by the porter in charge. Trains to the dock had to be accompanied by the Bullo Pill yard shunter who, according to the WTT Appendix, had to ensure that sufficient brakes were pinned down before starting the descent. At one time the docks were served every day with perhaps a couple of wagons for the general siding. Incoming traffic included materials for the rubber works, whilst outgoings included wool. Coal for the tip was apparently propelled down the gradient, rakes of six wagons (60 tons) being taken at a time, with the shunter pinning down the brakes on the lead wagon. In the 1920s coal for loading at the tip was only taken down every 2-3 weeks. Inevitably there were run-aways, one lively incident involving a '31XX' 2-6-2T on the Severn Tunnel pick-up goods which was collecting wagons from the

docks road. It seems that the signalman had somehow turned it out down the overgrown docks line, some 8 or 10 loaded coal wagons proving too much for the engine's steam brake on the steep incline, the whole ensemble running out of control into the rubber works siding, smashing a couple of vans. The vehicles concerned had already been unloaded but, far more fortunate was the absence of local children who apparently spent much of their time playing in and around such empty vehicles.

L. E. Copeland

The overgrown throat of the sidings serving the dock, the line to the extreme right leading to the old wagon works which closed c.1916, the siding latterly serving a rubber works. The next siding was known as 'town trade', serving a timber-built goods shed which was later moved to Upper Soudley Halt. The building was replaced with a corrugated iron structure. The next two sidings served the loading tip, empty wagons being returned along an empties road, the last siding on the left. Reference to the track plan on page 65 should make this all clear. A short siding at right-angles to the tip had apparently been used for occasional wagons held for mixing when loading.

L. E. Copeland

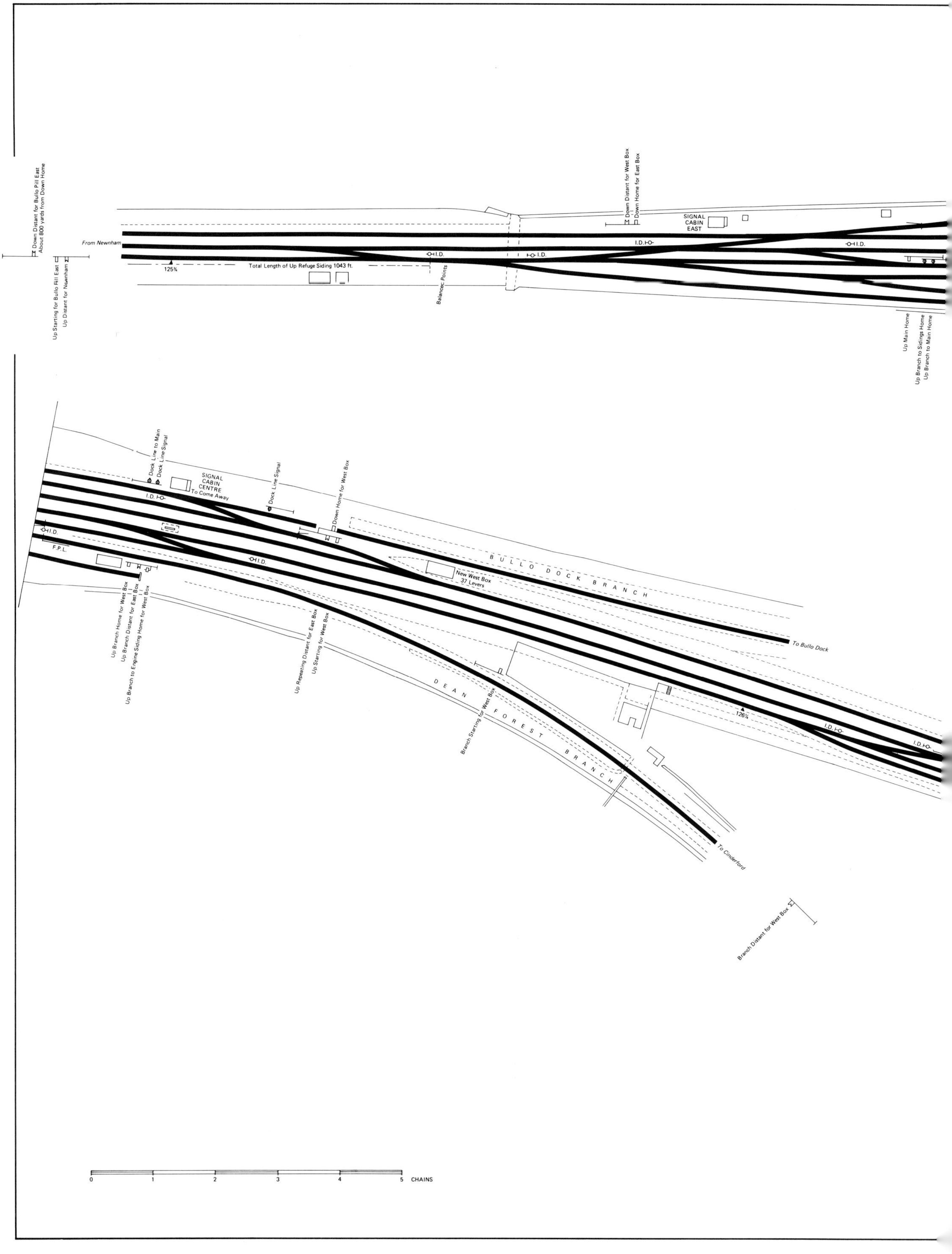

Down Distant for Bullo Pill East
About 800 yards from Down Home

Up Starting for Bullo Pill East

Up Distant for Newnham

From Newnham

125%

Total Length of Up Refuge Siding 1043 ft.

Balance Points

I.D.

I.D.

Down Distant for West Box

Down Home for East Box

I.D.

SIGNAL
CABIN
EAST

I.D.

Up Main Home

Up Branch to Sidings Home

Up Branch to Main Home

Dock Line to Main Line Signal

Dock Line Signal

I.D.

SIGNAL
CABIN
CENTRE
To Come Away

Dock Line Signal

Down Home for West Box

BULLO DOCK BRANCH

I.D.

F.P.L.

Up Branch Home for West Box

Up Branch Distant for East Box

Up Branch to Engine Siding Home for West Box

I.D.

New West Box
37 Levers

To Bullo Dock

Up Repeating Distant for East Box

Up Starting for West Box

DEAN FOREST BRANCH

Branch Starting for West Box

126%

I.D.

I.D.

To Cinderford

Branch Distant for West Box

0   1   2   3   4   5 CHAINS

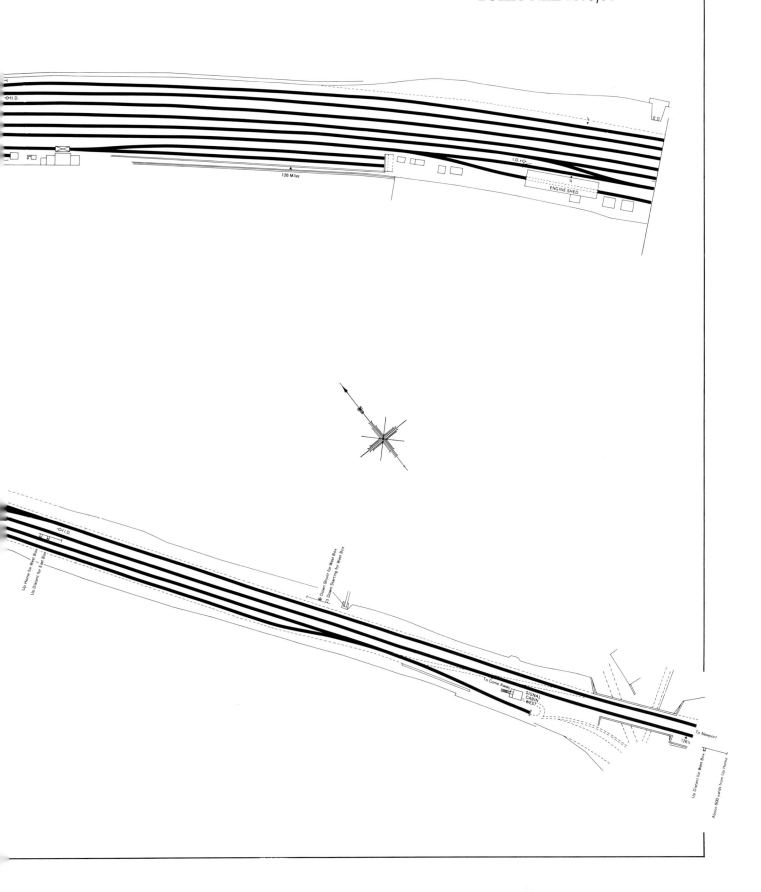

BULLO PILL 1898/99

H.I.D.

126 Miles

I.D.

ENGINE SHED

Up Home for West Box
Up Distant for East Box

I.D.

Down Shunt for West Box
Down Starting for West Box

To Come Away

SIGNAL
CABIN
WEST

To Newport

126½

Up Distant for West Box

About 800 yards from Up Home

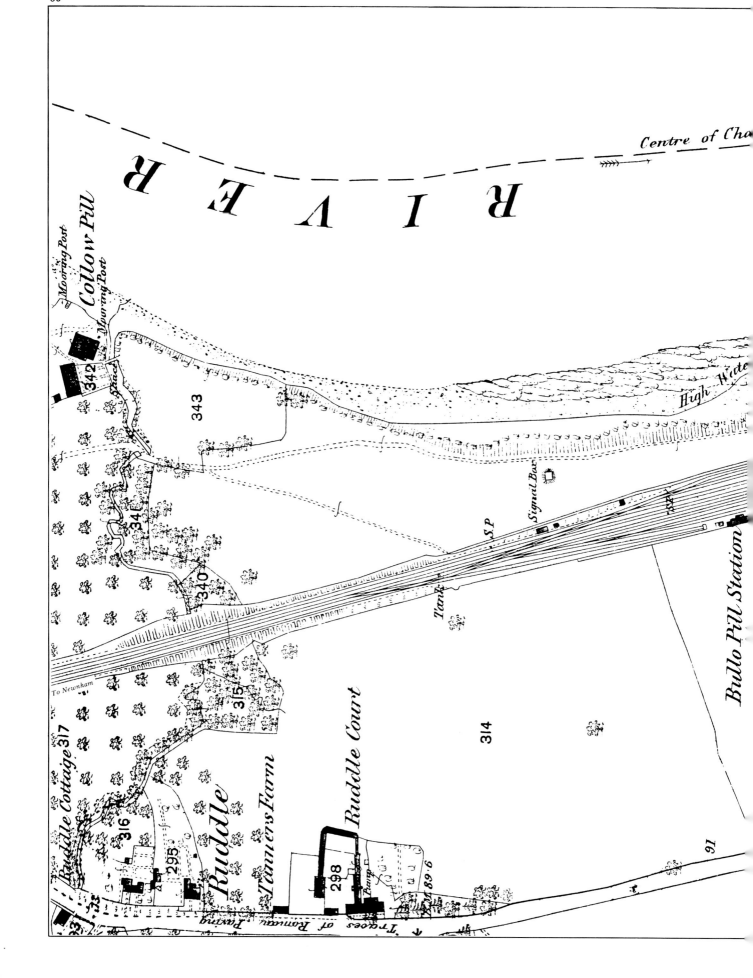

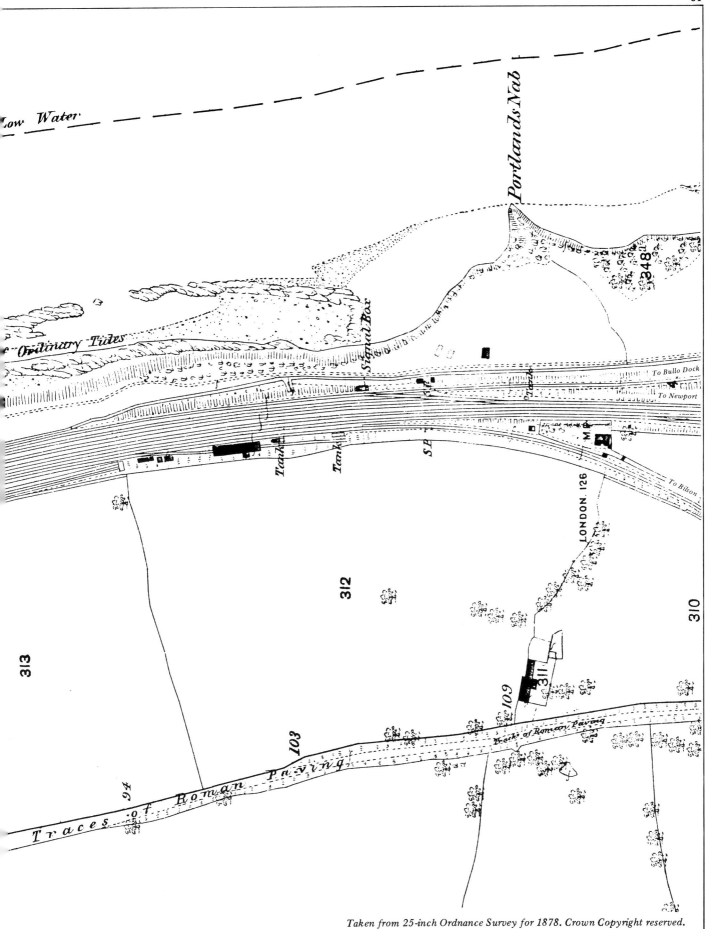

Low Water

Ordinary Tides

Portlands Nab

348

Signal Box

To Bullo Dock

To Newport

Tank

Tank

S.P.

M

To Bilson

LONDON. 126

312

313

310

311

109

94

103

Traces of Roman Paving

Track of Roman Paving

Taken from 25-inch Ordnance Survey for 1878. Crown Copyright reserved.

62

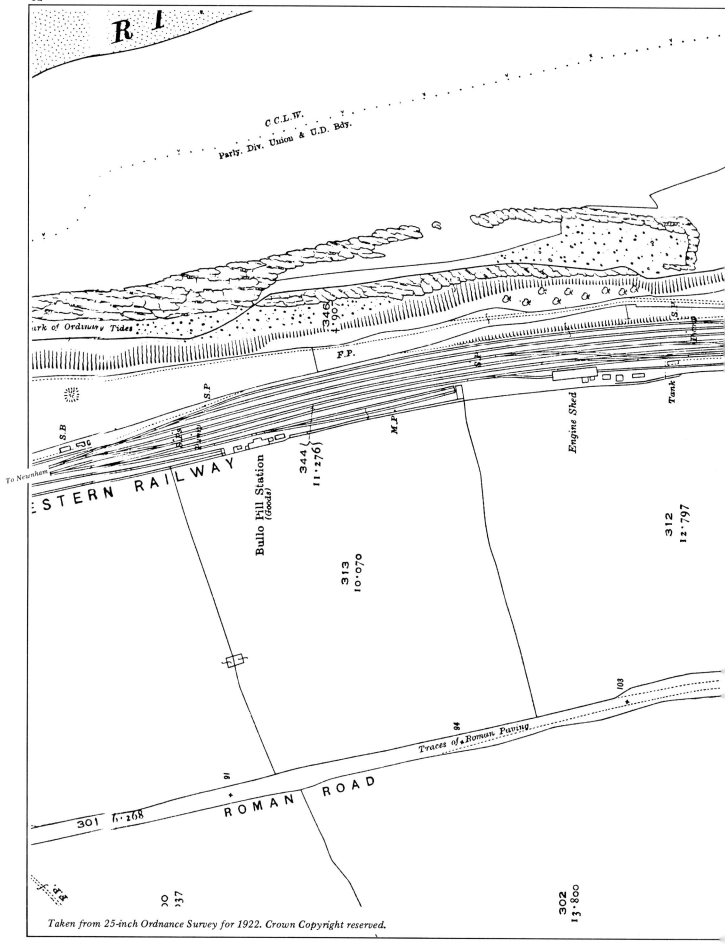

R I

C.C.L.W.
Parly. Div. Union & U.D. Bdy.

ark of Ordinary Tides

346
4·90

F.P.

S.P

S.P

S.B

S.Box

To Newnham

ESTERN RAILWAY

Bullo Pill Station
(Goods)

344
11·276

M.P.

Engine Shed

Tank

313
10·070

312
12·797

103

94

Traces of Roman Paving

91

301 6·268

ROMAN ROAD

302
13·800

037

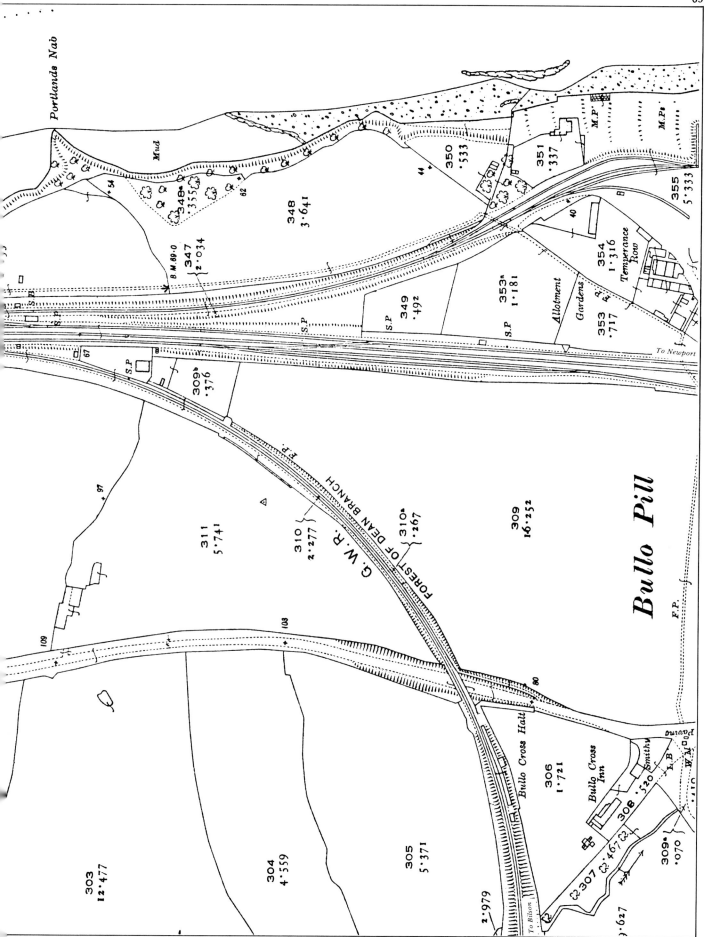

Portlands Nab

Mud

Bullo Pill

FOREST OF DEAN BRANCH

G.W.R.

Temperance Row

To Newport

Bullo Cross Halt

Bullo Cross Inn

To Bilson

Smithy

Gardens

Allotment

The trow *Finis* owned by the Triggs and crewed part time by members of the family, being loaded at Bullo. Occasional cargoes included coal to the tar works at Gloucester and stone to Stonebench, and Elmore Back for river bank repairs. The stone used was often brought down the Forest of Dean branch from the quarry at Shakemantle. Another regular trip after 1912 was to take Eastern United Colliery steam coal to Messrs. Cadbury's works at Frampton on the Sharpness–Gloucester canal. In earlier times Bullo was much busier, with trows, at times four abreast, waiting to load. By 1815 some 1,000 tons of stone and coal were shipped each day, along with bark, pig iron, slate and hides from nearby tanneries, and activity increased until the 1850s even Lydney harbour was losing trade to Bullo. In 1872 sixty-four craft were trading regularly from Bullo, traffic increasing in the decade before the opening of the Severn Bridge in 1879. Coal was shipped both from collieries on the Forest of Dean branch and on the Forest of Dean Central Railway which ran from Awre Junction, through Blakeney, to Howbeech. In January 1883 the *Dean Forest Mercury* reported that coals from Messrs. Gollop & Co.'s Howbeech Colliery which were hewn from the ground in the morning were shipped at Bullo in the afternoon and sailed on the evening tide. Surviving records for the late 1880s show that coal was shipped to Berkeley, Bristol, Barry, Minehead and up the Bridgwater river to Bridgwater, Dunball and Highbridge, total tonnage varying between some 1,300 and 2,500 tons per month at that time.

Harry Trigg

BULLO DOCK

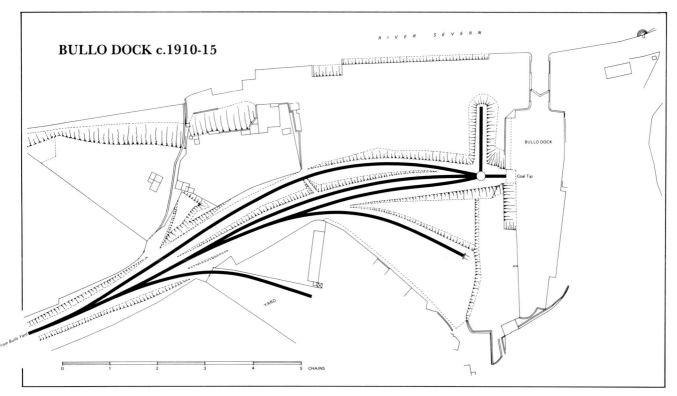

BULLO DOCK c.1910-15

Coal was shipped from Bullo Pill virtually as soon as the tramroad was completed to Cinderford Bridge as in June 1810 coal was on sale at Bullo Pill wharf. The wharf was undoubtedly a river wharf as it seems unlikely that work had started on the dock. Indeed, at this time one of the main destinations for coal shipped from Bullo was the Thames & Severn Canal which entered the Severn at Framilode, some 5¾ miles upstream from Bullo. The Thames & Severn Company, however, soon realised that coal from Bullo had lain on the wharf for too long a period and thus suffered from exposure to the weather, so when the Severn & Wye opened their dock at Lydney in 1813 they switched to getting supplies from there. Bullo was unable to regain the trade until improvements were made at the wharves and by the construction of a wet dock. By January 1815, Bullo could dispatch 1,000 tons of coal and stone daily. From an inscription carved on the dock entrance it would seem that the dock itself was started in 1818, the same year in which one William Greening was appointed to the position of shipping agent at Bullo — a post he was to hold until August 1872.

The dock was reported as complete in October 1827, but little is known of the facilities provided at this time. The tramroad approached the dock from the west and divided to serve either side of the dock where some form of tips may have been provided. Tips may also have been provided on the river wharves which lay on both sides of the dock entrance although cranes and muscle power may have been the sole method of loading vessels here. With the completion of the dock, trade at Bullo boomed, especially with traffic to the Thames & Severn Canal, and there was soon a need for increased facilities. In January 1832 a proposal was put forward for a new deep water wharf

at Box Meadow, south of Bullo, as the other wharves were only available at certain states of the tide. Construction of the new wharf, capable of taking three vessels, started in October 1833.

Things then changed little at Bullo until the arrival of the South Wales Railway in 1851. Immediately to the west of the dock, the tramroad was crossed by a stone viaduct and to the north-west an interchange with the tramroad was constructed. This undoubtedly siphoned off some of the traffic from the dock. Further traffic would have been lost once the tramroad was converted to a broad gauge line in 1854.

In the meantime, a branch had been constructed off the South Wales line down to the dock. This crossed the dock entrance by a lifting bridge, marked on the Ordnance Survey as a drawbridge, for which the sum of £144 12s 10d was paid to Messrs. Tredwell & Co in November 1854. A further sum of £12 12s 6d for work to the drawbridge went to Geo. Hennett in February 1855. The line then ran to Box Meadow where two coal tips and a crane were provided at the deep water wharf. At the dock itself two coal tips were constructed, one on either side of the basin. In April 1855 it was reported that Charles Hewlett was putting up coal drops at Bullo Wharf and in August consideration was being given to a 'proposed tipping place' to be provided at an estimated cost of £526 10s 0d. This may have been for one of the tips at the dock. All the activity in constructing new tips seems to have upset at least one resident at Bullo. In September Mr. John Heyworth, who was an agent for the firm of Messrs. A. Goold & Co, applied for permission to plant a piece of railway-owned ground in order to screen the view of the coal wharves from his window. In March 1856 money was voted by the South

Wales Board for Bullo Wharf and 'swings' £188 15s 8d and for a new 'swing', £44 6s 4d. Presumably the swings had some connection with the coal tips and in May Hewlett was paid a further £142 14s 7d in connection with work on the tips.

In 1869 the dock was described by a GWR civil engineer as 'a fair port, with a couple of quays, a dock, cranes, etc.' but this seems to have been biased as a report prepared at the same time for the Severn & Wye stated that Bullo had 'very small dimensions, very shallow water and with dangerous navigation', which, despite being S & W propaganda in favour of Lydney, was all true. From around this time Bullo and Lydney vied for traffic, especially for the Stroud Valley and for the Bridgwater area. There is no doubt that Bullo's fortunes were affected by Lydney but in the early 1880s Bullo gained the upper hand for a while. In April 1881 traders to the Stroud Valley saved 5d per ton by shipping at Bullo rather than Lydney and a period of cost-cutting in terms of the tipping rates charged at both places followed in order to attract business. Despite Bullo having the might of the GWR behind it, Lydney had the great advantage, but in October 1887 it was noted in Severn & Wye minutes that the previous month's shipments at Bullo had increased, with 2,200 tons being dispatched, mainly to the Bridgwater area. During October, shipments continued to increase but dropped again in November. The figures were:

	October	November
Bristol	99	99
Minehead	85	—
Bridgwater River		
Bridgwater	1728	1055
Dunball	605	88
Highbridge	—	95
	2517	1337

1,461 tons were shipped in December, increasing to 1,895 tons (of which 1,725 went to the Bridgwater River and 170 tons to Bristol) in January 1888. February saw a further increase, due mainly to Lydney charging 3d per ton more for shipping. When one of the large traders from Bridgwater, Messrs Bryant & Co, looked like moving their trade to Bullo, the Severn & Wye countered by offering a 1d per ton rebate if they shipped all their coal at Lydney.

From the early 1890s Bullo began to suffer a loss of trade until in 1903 an average of only eight cargoes a month were being loaded. This decline was at least partly attributable to competition from steam vessels which had become available on the Berkeley Canal and all river routes other than the one passing Bullo Dock. The days of the sailing trow were numbered.

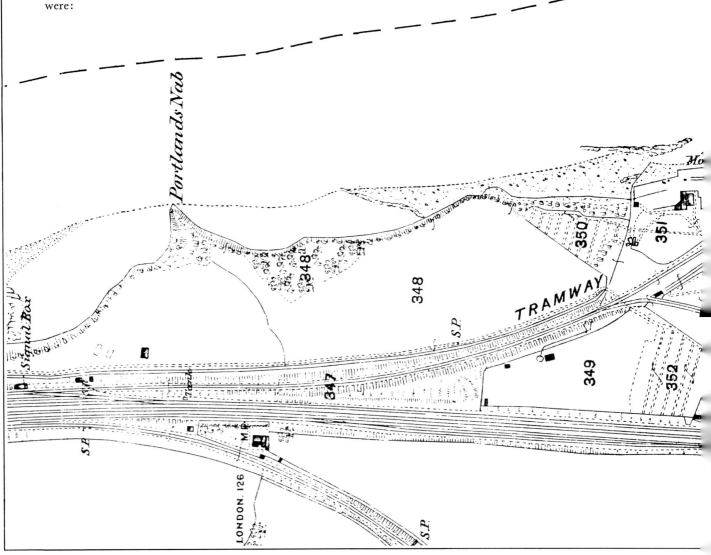

With the decline in traffic, the facilities at Bullo were cut back. The tips at Box Meadow and the one on the south side of the basin were removed in April 1907, the sidings serving them were lifted and the liftbridge over the dock entrance removed. The dock entrance was originally designed to have two sets of gates but the provision of the bridge had precluded the use of the outer set. At the time of writing, Bullo Dock is undergoing restoration and both sets of gates have been refitted.

After the First World War, the occasional trow took a load of coal to Framilode lock for the mills in the Stroud Valley, and riverside dwellers took their small boats into the once busy dock for just a few hundredweights of coal. The last vessel to use the dock officially was the *Finis* in 1926. It was owned by the Trigg family of Bullo and had

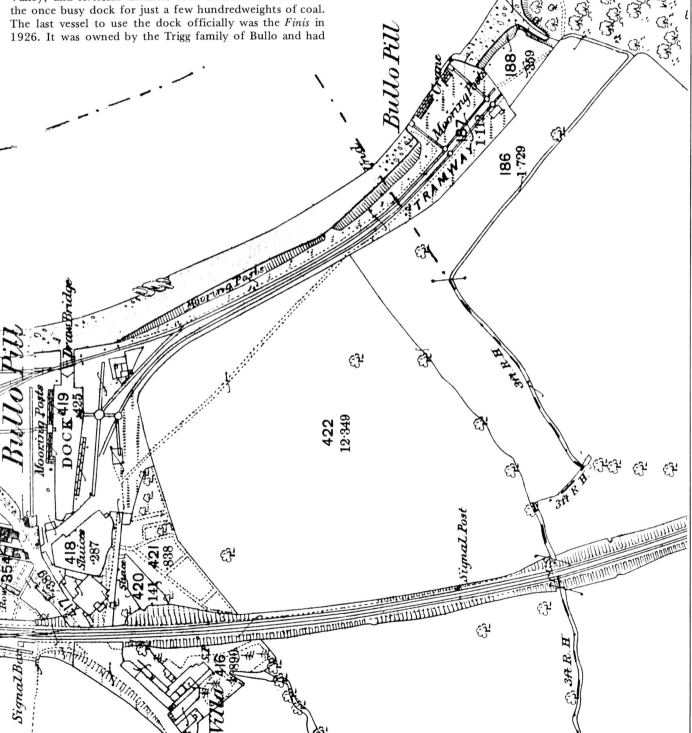

Taken from 25-inch Ordnance Survey for 1878. Crown Copyright reserved.

been used for taking cargoes of stone up river to Framilode and coal up the canal between Sharpness and Gloucester to Messrs Cadbury's works at Frampton. After 1st November 1926, Bullo Dock was only available as a tidal basin, the dock gate being disused, probably due to decay. The wooden loading chute was kept in working order until the early 1930s. However, the dock rapidly silted up after the gate was left open, and it is doubtful that large vessels could berth there. A New Works Order No. 6573, dated 14th September 1940, records the sale to the New Bowson Coal Co, Cinderford, of the old coal chute, dock gates, hand winches and flood gates at Bullo Pill. However, it is not clear whether this was carried through as the derelict tip remained in position until about 1950 and the remains of the original gates can still be seen at Bullo to this day.

RULES FOR WORKING THE BULLO DOCK SIDINGS

In 1895 the following rules were in use on the Bullo Dock branch:

Train staff held at Centre Box.

The Dock Branch, the Lift Bridge, the Wharves and the Switches at the Docks are under the control of the Company's Wharfinger.

The eight Lever Ground Frame, which has been fixed near the Drawbridge, and to which all the Points and Signals between Bullo Yard Centre Box and the Wharfinger's Office have been concentrated and interlocked (except the Points leading to the Wagon Works, which are connected to a Ground Lever close to the Points, and are wire locked with the Down Auxiliary Home Signal) must, when not in use, be kept locked, and the key must be kept in the possession of the Wharfinger. The Bridge is also interlocked with the Signals, and must be kept shut down when not actually in use.

Engines proceeding from Bullo Pill Station Yard to the Docks must not leave the Centre Box in Bullo Pill yard until the Dock Branch Auxiliary Home Signal has been lowered, and they must at all times, on the Down or Up Journey, come to a stand at the Lift Bridge. The Bullo Yard Foreman or Head Shunter will at all times accompany the Trains or Engines down and up the Dock Branch.

Trucks for the Docks must not, at any time, be put on the Docks Branch unless the Wharfinger is present to superintend their removal from the Sidings; and he is responsible for seeing that proper precautions are taken for working them safely down to the Docks. He must accompany the Trucks down the Branch, to apply Brakes etc, having first satisfied himself that the Bridge is shut and the Line clear from any obstruction.

1914 APPENDIX TO WTT:

The Dock Branch, the Wharves, and the Switches at the Docks, are under the control of the Company's Wharfinger.

All the points at Bullo Docks are worked by hand levers, and locked with a Switch lock. The Key of these locks must be kept in the possession of the Wharfinger, and when any Train or Engine requires to go into any of the Sidings the Wharfinger must be present to let them in.

An Engine or Train in possession of the Train Staff proceeding from Bullo Pill Yard may leave the West Box but must be brought to a stand at the first Siding points on the Branch and then proceed as directed by the Wharfinger.

The Bullo Yard Head Shunter must at all times accompany the Train or Engine down and up the Dock Branch, and before proceeding down the Dock Branch must pin sufficient brakes down to ensure the train working safely over the Section.

Train staff: Round, Black.

An enlargement of a postcard view from St. Peter's churchyard, Newnham, looking along the Severn in the direction of Bullo Pill, with the loco shed and water tank clearly visible amidst the lines of wagons to the right. The churchyard occupies a vantage point atop a hill to the south of the town with panoramic views, as shown here. The seat, provided in 1884 in memory of one John Hill, was a popular spot for peaceful contemplation, and we know of at least one Forester, Elsie Ibbotson, who regularly took the 'Motor Car' from Soudley to Newnham in order to escape domestic pressures and relax here. *Collection Ian Pope*

BULLO WAGON WORKS

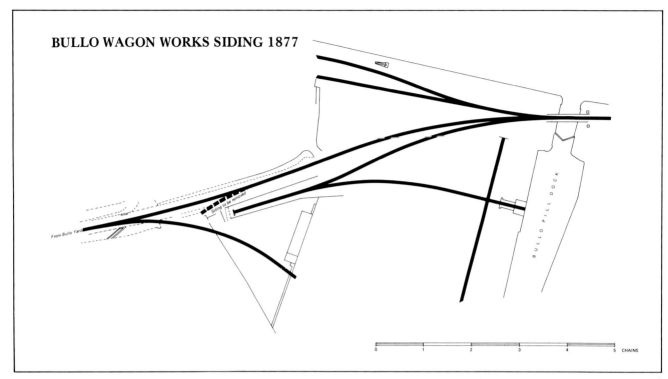

BULLO WAGON WORKS SIDING 1877

Wagon building at Bullo was started by Joseph Boucher who, it is believed, transferred the business from London. Great Western Board minutes for 16th April 1873 record that a connection to Messrs Boucher's works at Bullo was to be provided at a cost of £37 to be paid by Boucher. A siding agreement was signed on 21st July for a siding to give 'convenient access' to and from the Docks Branch.

In 1874 local directories describe Boucher as a railway carriage and wagon builder and also a brass and ironfounder. His advertisements stated that he built wagons for cash or on redemption terms for three, five or seven years; he also made railway wheels and undertook wagon repairs, covering the Great Western main line from Reading to Chepstow. In the early years Boucher obtained some of his ironwork from the Gloucester Wagon Company, ordering various pieces of wagon ironwork such as side-knees, brake gear, etc on a regular basis.

In March 1875 a company, the Bullo Pill and Forest of Dean Wagon Co Ltd, was formed to acquire Boucher's interests. Although nothing came of the plan, the company prospectus does give some idea of the scope of the works at Bullo. There was an iron foundry and forges, a steam engine to provide power, hydraulic clipping and other machinery, tanks, sawmills, shops, offices, building, stock in trade, plant, railway trucks let on hire, nine dwelling houses, land tenements, hereditaments, etc. It would appear that Boucher may have been trading as the Newnham & Bullo Wagon Works Co, which, according to *Engineering* for July 1876, was to work an extra three hours per week. It was Boucher who mutually agreed with the GWR for the siding to be moved in July 1877. The original siding serving the wagon works had kicked back off the docks branch whereas the new siding gave direct access. Joseph Boucher was still listed as a wagon builder at

Bullo in 1879 and in January 1884 it is reported in the *Dean Forest Mercury* that Joseph Boucher had filed a petition for liquidation, having liabilities of £11,500. His creditors had to accept 6s 8d in the pound. Despite this, Boucher seems to have hung on until June 1888 when the works were put up for sale by auction on the 15th under an execution from the Sheriff of Gloucester. A fitters shop at Lydney Junction was included in the sale. The outcome was not recorded but by 1889 the works were being run by 'William Boucher'. It is not clear whether William was a son of Joseph or Joseph trading under his second forename!

By 1889 William Boucher was trading as the Forest of Dean Wagon Co, which took a lease of land at Lydney Junction that year. In February 1890 the Forest of Dean Wagon Co Ltd was formed with a capital of £5,000 in £5 shares to purchase the business 'now carried on by William Boucher' at Bullo Pill and elsewhere. At this time the company had seventy-four wagons let out on hire and ten trucks recently bought from Sir Hussey Vivian. It was bought for the sum of £900 plus 130 fully paid up shares. The new company also took on the liabilities of the old one which amounted to some £1,895, but this must have proved too great a burden as in October the Gloucester Carriage & Wagon Co were approached to see if they would purchase the works and ninety-three wagons let on hire together with the repairing contracts on 921 wagons at an average of £2 16s 6d each per year. The Gloucester board declined. A siding agreement signed on 17th October 1891 describes Boucher as manager and agent, then in March 1892 the Forest of Dean Wagon Co Ltd was wound up with William Boucher and Phipps Williams taking over all liabilities and assets for the paid up capital which amounted to £3,290. The siding agreement was transferred on 11th July 1892 to Boucher and Williams who had formed a partnership and were trading as Messrs Boucher, Williams & Co.

In April 1893 the Standard Wagon Co Ltd was incorporated to take over the Bullo works. With a capital of £10,000 in £1 shares, the subscribers to the new company included William Boucher, who was again manager and agent, together with Thomas King, a carpenter; William Ingram, sawyer; Oliver Lloyd, moulder; and George Drew, engineer; all of Newnham. Each took one share and from their occupations it seems likely that they were employed at the works. In January 1894 an agreement was signed with Stephen Haddingham, a bank manager from Newnham, for the purchase of 125 railway wagons held on 7-year leases dated 1st April 1893 from the British Wagon Co, for the sum of £1,500. Another siding agreement was signed with the Great Western on 12th February 1894.

In May 1895 it was announced that because of its liabilities, the Standard Wagon Co Ltd was unable to continue trading. William Boucher, described as works manager and appointed liquidator, informed the Board of Trade that a new company was to take over the works as a going concern. In October 1895 another Standard Wagon Company Ltd was formed after gaining permission to use the old company name. Not only was it the same name but the subscribers were virtually those of the 1893 concern. The capital was now £5,000 in £1 shares.

The new company was tied up with the Railway Wagon & Engineering Co Ltd of Swansea whose engineer was also William Boucher. Several directors were also common to the two companies. The Railway Wagon & Engineering Co was incorporated in December 1894 with a capital of £10,000. At some point they amalgamated with the Standard Wagon Co but it is not clear which Standard Wagon Co it was! It may have been the earlier company as a note in the 1895 company's files gives the Railway Wagon & Engineering Co as the vendors to the new company.

Whatever the size of the new Standard Wagon Co, it was as unsuccessful in attracting shareholders as its predecessor had been, and in February 1899 an Extraordinary General Meeting was called at which it was stated the company was to be wound up and once again Boucher was appointed liquidator. Three days prior to the EGM, which was held on the 6th, a fire occurred at the works which damaged the offices.

Yet another new company was formed to take over the works and once again consent was sought for the use of the old name. On 23rd February 1899 the Standard Wagon & Carriage Co Ltd was incorporated with a capital of £50,000. This time most of the subscribers were those who had been connected with the Railway Wagon & Engineering Co. The purchase price for the works from the old company was £28,600, but despite another fresh start, things did not improve and at an EGM on the 11th February 1901 it was announced that the foundry side of the business had been sold to the Forest Foundry Co Ltd, which, incorporated in December 1900 with a capital of £6,000, never traded. It was also announced that the railway wagons, out-station depots, stock in trade and goodwill on the wagon repair and

'1016' class 0—6—0ST No. 1019 collecting a newly completed vehicle (still to be weighed and numbered) from the wagon works c.1900. Many of the components came from the Gloucester Wagon Co. The steeply graded line in the foreground led down to Bullo Dock.

Collection Peter Ball

hiring side, had been sold to the Albion Carriage Co Ltd which had been formed in May 1900 with a works at Grange Court, the junction between the South Wales and Hereford lines. This time Boucher was managing director and agent of the Albion Co, and once again wagon building and repair continued at Bullo. A private siding agreement was signed on 31st December 1901 but, like its predecessors at Bullo, the Albion Carriage Co had a short life and was wound up in September 1902 with Boucher as liquidator again.

It would appear that William Boucher and a Charles Boucher continued trading at Bullo under the title of the National Wagon Co as wagon repairers and buffer makers. In 1903 they took out a patent for 'improvements in and concerning buffers for railway vehicles'; details are unknown but the product was known as 'Boucher's buffer'. In November they agreed to sell all rights in the buffer, together with the land and buildings of the Bullo Pill wagon works, to the National Trading Co Ltd which was incorporated on 15th October that year with a capital of £3,000 in £1 shares, most of which were held by Herbert Gopsill Brown, a merchant from Gloucester, and David Northway, described as a wagon builder from Westbury on Severn, both of whom became directors. A further £2,000 was raised almost immediately on mortgage. Prior to incorporation, subscribers to the company included several who had been involved in previous schemes at Bullo and once again William Boucher was manager.

When the National Trading Co Ltd signed an agreement for the wagon works siding on 9th January 1904, the chairman of the company was Thomas Goldsworthy, and it was said that the company had acquired all of the interests of

the Albion Carriage Co Ltd, although when the company was formed it was stated that the Bouchers had acquired the works from the receivers of the Standard Wagon Co.

Rather like its predecessors at Bullo, the National Trading Co had a fairly short trading life, and was in difficulties by 1906. As no returns were made, the company was dissolved in May 1907. During the end of the company's life, the Bullo works were leased to Messrs Gordon, Boucher & Co, but the period of their tenure is unknown. The siding agreement was terminated on 31st May 1916, the works being dismantled at, or soon after, this date. In October 1918 it was reported that the GWR had purchased the buildings from the representatives of the late T. Goldsworthy for the sum of £90.

The workforce of the wagon works c.1900.

Two more products of the Bullo works with the proud workmen posing for the camera.

Collection M. Rees

BULLO RUBBER MILL

Joseph Calvert Healey had been works manager at the Hawkwell brick works (see Volume 2) and had taken over the works there in 1910. After the First World War he set up an India rubber works in part of the brickworks buildings. By 1923 the works were described as now in a 'substantial and well constructed building, having a superficial area of 2,420 sq ft', which suggests that a new building may have been put up alongside the old brickworks. In June, when it was said that Healey Bros. were on the eve of considerable development, they decided to give up the brickworks and the site at Hawkwell and move to new premises in the old wagon works at Bullo. In August the former wagon works were leased to Messrs Healey.

In 1924 the Bullo premises were extended, but otherwise things remained little changed. A steam engine still provided the power to machinery, and lighting was by candle until a diesel engine and generating plant was installed.

The main products of the works were pram tyres, tubing, catapult rubber, rubber bands and car hoses. All raw materials were delivered by rail, the rubber in hundredweight bales direct from London Docks. It is not known when the siding into the works was removed; it may well have been prior to the commencement of operations by the rubber company for in later years materials were unloaded at the small goods shed on the dock line. The last wagon of Cornish china clay was unloaded at the works in May/June 1963. Thereafter it arrived by road.

The rubber mill continues in use at the time of writing.

This charming portrait provides a record of the Bullo Dock approach road which ran along the course of the old tramroad. This was a private road belonging to the GWR and a notice to this effect was provided at the junction with the main road. To maintain rights, it was roped off every Good Friday. The bridge carried the South Wales main line. Each arch had a set of gates which were locked every night, at 6.00 p.m. in summer and 5.00 p.m. in winter. The wicket gate under the first arch allowed pedestrians access to the cottages beyond.

Collection Frances Webb

A similar view along the approach road to the dock on 2nd June 1946. The signal on the embankment was the up main home bracket signal for the Bullo West signal box. The lower (bracketed) arm applied from the up main to up goods running loop.   *L. E. Copeland*

This 1950s view over the abandoned dock is the only photograph so far discovered showing the corrugated iron goods shed which features on the left in the distance. In such an eerie quietness it is difficult to appreciate the frustrations of one lady who in busier times insisted on a gap being left between the wagons so that she could get to her fowl run. So much in life is of a temporary nature — now only dwindling memories can revive the social structures and fellowship of this lost age.   *R. Dagley Morris*

The reservoir to top up the basin is illustrated in this view of the abandoned dock on 5th October 1946. The derelict coal tip still served by overgrown track marks the edge of the basin, and the fresh masonry of the new wartime pump house described on page 56 is fairly obvious in the foreground. *L. E. Copeland*

On the same day, a closer view of the now silted-up basin and derelict tip. A drawbridge spanning the entrance had carried a track leading to the deep water wharf (Box Meadow) where there were another two tips, and to a fourth tip on the other side of the basin, opposite the surviving one shown. The drawbridge had a span of 26ft 6in square, 26ft 10in on the skew, and consisted of stone abutments with wrought iron main and cross girders. It was removed and the sidings rearranged in 1907 at a cost of £500. The lock gates were removed during, or certainly by, 1926. *L. E. Copeland*

Looking back towards the basin from Box Meadow, with the deep water wharf behind the photographer, on 11th April 1948. Just before the war the wharf was used for craning power boats into the river for racing. The ruin standing close to the wharf is the remains of the lock-keeper's cottage and office.

H. G. W. Household

Workmen's cottages on 3rd April 1952, since demolished. The terrace on the left was known as Temperance Row.   *H. G. W. Household*

The basin entrance lock and remains of one of the lock gates on 11th April 1948.   *H. G. W. Household*

Returning to Bullo yard, this view was taken from the original water tower, looking towards Lydney with the Forest of Dean branch in the foreground, on 11th September 1948. As explained on page 51, the boarded crossing from the West Box to the FoD branch single line token apparatus, was the easternmost point at which trains on the first portion of the up goods running loop were allowed to wait so that the signalman's path was unobstructed. The water crane at this point would have been used by crews, sometimes simply taking advantage of the time they were held on the loop and sometimes desperately filling empty tanks! The new building adjacent to the dock line, which can be seen descending behind the signal box, was the examiner's cabin and grease house which, authorised in June 1946, was completed on 29th January 1947, replacing the condemned Toad mentioned on page 56. A new works order for the building lists a table, office desk, six lockers, office stool, fitter's bench with vice, shelves for stores, and water connection. At this end of Bullo Yard no shunting movements were permitted beyond the illuminated limit of the shunt board featured in front of the examiner's cabin in this view. *L. E. Copeland*

Bullo Pill West signal box was provided as part of the extensive 1897 improvement of signalling arrangements, replacing two previous signal boxes, Bullo Pill West, situated adjacent to the bridge over the road/tramroad approach to the dock, and Bullo Pill Middle, which was almost opposite the water tower. Unfortunately, there are no pictures of these earlier structures. This picture was taken on 5th October 1946. *L. E. Copeland*

During the final years of the passenger service, the Cinderford train was often a B set and siphon as shown in this view of a down train stopped to take water. The steep climb out of the yard was no problem for the short passenger trains but if rushed with goods or empty minerals, problems could ensue. Engines of goods trains would normally have watered in the yard beforehand to get a steady run at the bank. In 1915 goods guard Aust struck his head against the hopper or 'tundish' of the water crane shown on the left of this view between the down main and what had been the goods loop. When it transpired there was just 8ft 10½in between the rails at this point, the old loop line or 'straight road' was slewed to give 11ft. For safety, the hopper was taken away immediately but it is not clear whether it was ever replaced, this view showing the alternative generous catchment area around the drain.
A. E. Bennett

The single line token apparatus was always used at Bullo to exchange the electric train token which gave a driver authority to occupy the line from Bullo to Bilson Junction. The electric token equipment had replaced the former electric train staff as from 22nd March 1937. No system operates without occasional problems but the failure of the electric train staff at 6 a.m. one Sunday morning in August 1909 marred the return of passengers from an excursion to Blackpool. The motor train with two trailers containing approximately 100 excursionists, was held at Bullo while workmen were despatched from Bilson to Bullo on a permanent way trolley. The *Dean Forest Mercury* reported, 'this was a work of time but arrival of the human staff (in the place of the machinery appliance) as he was able to assure the officials that the line was clear and as this procedure met with the company's working requirements, the motor, and its tired out passengers, after 1½ hours weary waiting were soon at their journey's end'. This picture was taken on 11th September 1948.

L. E. Copeland

This view from the steeply graded Forest of Dean branch curve towards Bullo in March 1968 also features the Bullo Pill station master's house.

Bob Marrows

The descent of the steep gradient from the Forest of Dean branch into Bullo has already been discussed on page 27. The 240 yard sand drag, authorised in January 1930, protected the junction from any train unable to be brought to a stand before the up branch home signal. The trailing points at the lower end of the drag were locked by clip and padlock. The working timetable appendix stated 'In the event of a train entering the Sand Drag, arrangements must be made for the Engineering Department gang to attend and clear sand from the drag.' A senior Bullo driver simply said 'Some trains have been in the sand drag'. This picture, which also features the down branch advanced starting signal, was taken on 5th October 1946.

L. E. Copeland

BULLO CROSS HALT

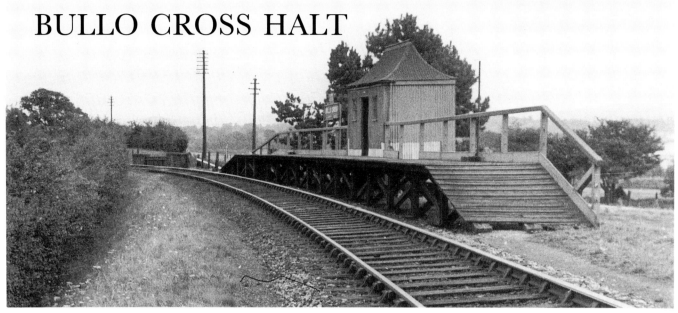

Bullo Cross was the first halt up the line, 1 mile 37 chains from Newnham. Originally provided with a 153ft x 7ft rail level platform, the halt was opened for the introduction of passenger services in August 1907. Although served by railmotor trains with folding steps, the platforms at Bullo Cross, Upper Soudley, Staple Edge, Nailbridge and Drybrook were nevertheless soon raised from 1ft 2in to the standard height of 3ft, the work being authorised on 5th November 1908 for £423. For some inexplicable reason, Bullo Cross was the only halt not originally equipped with a shelter, but this deficiency was remedied in 1918 when one of the redundant shelters from the recently closed Ruddle Road halt was moved to Bullo Cross. In April 1927 £355 was authorised for platform renewals on the Forest of Dean branch 'to a length of 126ft', but later official records show Bullo Cross platform as 153ft (others were anything but 126ft). In August 1933 part of the platform was 'completely burnt' and the waiting room damaged beyond repair. A railway employee raised the alarm and a locomotive was summoned for water. According to the local press, when the engine arrived, the middle part of the platform was a 'roaring mass of flames', which was got under control after about one hour. Damage was confined to the middle third of the platform and both ends were saved. The shelter was evidently replaced, presumably with a structure from one of the halts closed in 1930. This picture was taken looking down the 1 in 54 gradient towards Bullo Pill on 5th October 1946.

L. E. Copeland

The bridge adjacent to Bullo Cross Halt originally crossed the A48 by means of a wrought iron girder span with timber decking. It was reconstructed in 1918 with second-hand steel girders, but in the motor vehicle age it suffered several times being struck by high vehicles. On one such occasion in 1962 one of the main girders was seriously weakened and the bridge had to be propped up while steel plates were affixed to the girder. The span of the bridge was brought down in the early hours of Friday, 2nd October 1964 when it was hit by an excavator on a low loader lorry. The line was closed until the 7th while a temporary span was put in place. This picture shows the structure on 6th January that year, with 0-6-0PT No. 4614 passing over it on the descent to Bullo Pill.

A. K. Pope

Loco crews recall 'there were always a few passengers, mostly on Saturdays for shopping in Gloucester'. This picture shows the Newnham auto approaching the halt on 5th October 1946.

L. E. Copeland

Approaching on a 1 in 54 gradient, steepening to 1 in 50 beyond Bullo Cross halt, the line continued to climb through the long narrow bore of Haie Hill tunnel at 1 in 56. As mentioned earlier, a train of empty mineral wagons could take up to five minutes to climb through the 1,064 yards which was quite unventilated. The boarded area adjacent to the permanent way hut was a 'run off' point for the gangers' petrol motor trolley. Gang No. 117, based at Bilson Junction, were responsible for this section of the line. *L. E. Copeland*

Looking back towards Bullo Pill from the bank behind the PW hut with the Bullo fixed distant on the right. The noticeboard in the foreground (184 yds from the tunnel) and the 5 mph speed restriction on the signal post reminded crews of the severe speed restriction for 'up' goods and mineral trains on the long steep descent. The wire crossing the picture diagonally led to telephone box No. 2 at the PW hut. This provided communication for the single line occupation key system between the ganger and signalmen at either end of the section. Both pictures were taken on 5th October 1946. *L. E. Copeland*

Soudley No. 1 crossing down distant mounted above one of the deep stone retaining walls just outside the tunnel entrance. *L. E. Copeland*

The rail level view of the stone-lined approach to Haie Hill tunnel. The line was back on the old tramroad course here, the original bore dating from 1809 and being enlarged while the tramroad was still in use. The milepost on the right was cast by Hewlett at Soudley and followed the pattern of the original tramroad mileposts. Between Bullo and the tunnel the tramroad had followed a much more sinuous course, its route being crossed and recrossed several times by the railway on its more direct alignment. *John Norris*

'2021' class No. 2114 emerging into the daylight at the top end of Haie Hill tunnel with a train of empties on 16th September 1946.   *L. E. Copeland*

The western portal of Haie Hill tunnel on 16th September 1946. The hinges on the tunnel face suggest that at one time it may have been gated. The 'gain stroke wheel' in the right foreground was in the wire to the down distant signal for Soudley No. 1 crossing. *L. E. Copeland*

Soudley No. 1 crossing was uncomfortably close to the tunnel. The signal in the foreground of this picture, taken on 18th July 1948, was the down distant for Soudley No. 2 crossing. This stretch of line was referred to as 'between the tunnels'. The pulley wheel in the finial of the distant for Soudley No. 2 crossing was part of an arrangement which allowed the lamp to be lowered for refilling. Soudley Ironworks had formerly stood to the right of this view.

L. E. Copeland

COOPER'S SIDING

This short siding, capable of taking at the most two wagons, was provided by the South Wales Railway for Mr. John Cooper who, in June 1854, applied for a siding in connection with his 'Forest Stone Trade'. The exact quarry, or quarries, worked by Cooper have not been established, the first edition of the OS 25-inch showing several small quarries in the vicinity. In September 1877 a John Cooper was applying for the lease of quarry No. 555 at Soudley adjoining quarry No. 389, both of which were immediately north of the entrance to Bradley Hill tunnel. A John Cooper, quarryman of Soudley, is mentioned in local trade directories until at least 1885 but not in 1889. This may provide a clue as to when the siding was used. By 1892 it had been removed.

Looking back towards the western portal of Haie Hill tunnel (just visible on the left), this early view, taken from above Bradley Hill tunnel c.1876-7, shows the area when it was dominated by Soudley ironworks. At this time it was owned by the Great Western Iron Co. Ltd. which, having rebuilt the furnaces, had recently commenced operations. The works had its own locomotive (a Fox Walker) which was housed in the engine shed adjacent to the left-hand chimney. The incline alongside the approach to Haie Hill was used to convey the charge for the furnaces (i.e. coke from the wagons in the middle foreground) to the higher level where it could be discharged ready for conveyance to the top of the furnaces. Coopers siding in the right foreground, and much of the running line, retained baulk road which survived from the broad gauge conversion. The signal box, behind the locomotive, is presumed to have controlled entry to the sidings but details of the signalling of this early period on the FoD branch are virtually unknown. The Civil Engineer's papers note the existence of a signal box here, at 2 miles 6 chains from Newnham, but the entry related to a box recorded as being opened on 22nd July 1907, presumably Soudley No. 1 crossing.   *Collection A. K. Pope*

A general view of the iron works with Bradley Hill tunnel in the centre of the picture, again featuring the signal box. The structure on the right, behind the engine, was the charging house — effectively a covered way — adjacent to which are the two furnaces. The building in the foreground contained a blowing engine used to create the draught for the furnaces.

Collection A. K. Pope

SOUDLEY IRONWORKS

The front of the furnaces features behind the low twin hip-roofed building which housed the 'pig beds', and was known as the casting house. After the closure of the works in 1877 the buildings remained unused. In May 1898 the inhabitants living close to the furnace were disturbed by a loud crash when the roof of the casting house fell in. *Collection A. K. Pope*

Iron had been worked in the Soudley area since 1565 but it was not until 1836/7 that Edward Protheroe erected a pair of blast furnaces. These, together with a pair of steam engines, probably blowing engines, were completed by October 1837 at a cost of over £10,000. The works were managed for Protheroe by a Mr. Broad with Protheroe's agent Aaron Goold keeping an overall check, but the furnaces were only in production for four years, until 1842, and had even been idle for a period in March 1841. It seems likely that the furnaces then remained blown out until purchased by Mr. Benjamin Gibbon of Staffordshire. In March 1857 Mr. Wintle, a local solicitor, approached the South Wales Railway on behalf of a client who was in treaty for the purchase of the works. It would appear that in constructing the Forest of Dean branch, the SWR had taken land formerly used as the coke yard for the works, and the client, Gibbon, wanted to know if he could purchase the land. By June 1857 the purchase was evidently complete as Gibbon was asking for a siding at Soudley. The SWR bore the cost of the connection and Gibbon provided the siding.

He only worked the furnaces for a year or two and sold them to Messrs Goold Brothers in 1863. Using Forest of Dean ore, they worked one of the furnaces in 1864, producing about twenty tons of iron at each casting. About eighty workmen were employed under the management

of Mr. John Y. Jarrett, and the coke used in the process was brought from South Wales.

In November 1866 it was reported that the works had for some time been on the market, and on the 15th of that month they were offered for sale at Gloucester, but bids did not reach the reserve price of £5,000 and in December all the workforce, about fifty men, were given a fortnight's notice to suspend work. It was said that the stoppage was due to defects in the furnaces rather than a shortage of orders as plenty of work was on hand, and it was estimated that repairs would take about three months. At this time the average make had been around 580 tons of various grades, the greater portion of which was mainly disposed of to South Wales and Staffordshire, with some iron also being supplied to tinplate works in the Forest itself. The closure led to great hardship for the idle workforce during a very severe winter when the rest of the Forest's industries were doing well. The works were re-opened in May 1867 but certainly between 1871 and 1875 only one of the furnaces was in blast at any one time, so perhaps only one had been repaired. It was during this period that the Goolds finally managed to sell off the works, the *Gloucester Journal* in February 1873 reporting that the furnaces, together with Scilly Point and Tingle's Iron Level mines, had been sold to a 'wealthy London company' who, it was hoped, would bring a new energy to the works and increase the number of furnaces in blast. The agent for the sale was a Mr. J. Shields who informed the newspaper that the purchase price was more than £20,000 and that the new owner was a Mr. Maximilian Low of Threadneedle Street in the City of London.

There then followed a period where the ownership changed hands several times. The actual purchase from the Goolds appears to have been concluded by January 1873, in which month Low entered into an agreement with one Thomas Key. Then came an indenture between Key and a Thomas Leopold Fox. Later in the year, on 22nd August, an agreement was entered into between Fox, Alfred William Maberly and Maximilian Low. One or more of these arrangements, probably the indenture, may have concerned a mortgage on the property as a note refers to the agreements being subject to the payment of £9,000 less any profits on the property which might be received and retained by the mortgagees.

A further agreement, dated 29th August 1873, was between Fox and the Soudley Ironworks, Forest of Dean, Limited. This company was incorporated on 5th September 1873 with a capital of £70,000 divided into 7,000 £10 shares, of which 2,500 were 'A', or non-preference, and the rest 'B', preference shares. The company return for 1874 shows that there were only seven shareholders, but it seems that the company soon floundered as there are no returns after that and in 1877 the company was dissolved. It is possible that none of the above listed arrangements were carried through and that the furnaces remained in the Goolds' hands, but at the beginning of 1874 it seems certain that the works were acquired by a Mr. C. W. Spark who installed a new blast engine made by the Haigh Foundry Co. of Wigan. During the brief nine month period of his ownership, which was not a good time to attempt to revive moribund furnaces, Spark had to contend with a high price for coal, iron ore and labour, whilst the demand for iron was at a low point. By January 1875 Spark was apparently making a last attempt to avoid closure and offered his creditors five shillings in the pound, which they declined, the Severn & Wye Railway offsetting his debts by the 50 tons of ore which were on their system at the time the failure was announced.

By May 1875 the furnaces and the Scilly Point, Kings Moor, Noxon Park and Tingles Level iron mines, were again under new ownership. They had been purchased by Messrs. Morrison and Beauclerk who set about modernising the works. They also formed a limited liability company, the Great Western Iron Co. Ltd., which was incorporated on 21st October 1875. The authorised capital was £150,000 in £10 shares. Of this £60,000 worth of fully paid-up shares were to be issued to Arthur Duff Morrison and William Arthur De Vere Beauclerk, plus a cash payment of £12,500. The debts of the vendors, Morrison and Beauclerk, were to be discharged, presumably the costs incurred in buying the property, and a first mortgage of £15,000 plus other mortgages totalling £8,000 were also to be settled.

The services of a Mr. Jarrett were retained as manager, and work on the improvements began. The management of the extension and alterations was placed in the hands of Mr. Coulthard, a civil engineer of Westminster, whilst the contractors for the work were Messrs. Fielding & Platt of Gloucester. The alterations were completed by October 1875 and on the 20th a celebratory luncheon was held to mark the re-opening of the works.

The *Dean Forest Mercury* report of the event gives a valuable description of the new works including the main feature of the utilisation of the waste gases from the furnaces. This process had been attempted a few years earlier at the Parkend furnaces with a certain amount of success, but greater results were achieved at Soudley, where gas produced was taken off at the furnace throat by means of apertures leading to a circular flue around the throat. From the flue the gas was conveyed to the stoves and boilers through a wrought iron pipe, 4ft 9in diameter and lined with firebricks. On the principle patented by Messrs. Jones, there were two stoves with each furnace, which could be heated by either coal or gas. Each stove contained a set of ten tun-pipes 12in diameter surrounded by firebricks, with a central flue along which the gases were drawn to the chimney via an underground flue 4ft 3in by 3ft 9in. There was also a gas tube from the stoves to the boilers which was carried on wrought iron trellis standards. The boilers themselves were of the double flue principle and in front of each was a combustion chamber which the gases entered by downpipes with shut-off valves. After passing through the tubes, the gas was conveyed along the sides of the boilers and underneath to the chimney. Each boiler worked at 60 lbs, a pressure apparently hitherto unknown in the Forest. The steam from the boilers was taken to a direct acting high pressure engine which was capable of blowing 10-15,000 cubic feet of air per minute. The exhaust steam was then passed into a 40ft high water heater at the top of which water entered by a self-acting valve in the form of a spray. As the water droplets fell, they met an upward current of steam and so were heated to boiling point before being conveyed to a donkey pump which pumped the water into the boilers. The donkey pump also served to pump cold water into the tank. The air blast generated by the blowing engine was conveyed in a 4ft 6in diameter wrought iron pipe direct to the stoves, where it was heated to about 800 degrees and then to the fire tuyeres of the furnace.

The system worked well and after a month's trial it was clearly demonstrated that pig iron could be produced without the use of coal. Initially, only one furnace worked on this principle, effecting a saving of about £10 per day. The company were so satisfied that in December they were contemplating putting the second furnace back into blast. In February 1876 the first shareholders meeting was held at the Victoria Hotel, Newnham. Here the company again repeated their satisfaction with the new works and also reported that they had purchased a 'costly locomotive engine of novel construction', apparently especially designed for the iron trade.

The *Gloucester Journal* for 3rd June 1876 reported a fatal accident at the works during preparations for the provision of a second furnace. The contractor was a Mr. Gideon Bourne of Dudley. The accident occurred when an old locomotive belonging to the Great Western Iron Co. was being tested after repair work carried out by Messrs. Fielding & Platt. It is interesting to speculate whether this engine was that of 'novel construction'. A train of wagons had been hauled up the cinder tip on a sharp gradient adjacent to the casting shed, but having reached the summit, the driver ran back along the wrong line. Instead of taking the main line, he took a siding to the slag beds, the gradient of which was very steep all the way. He lost control of the engine and a collision occurred at the base

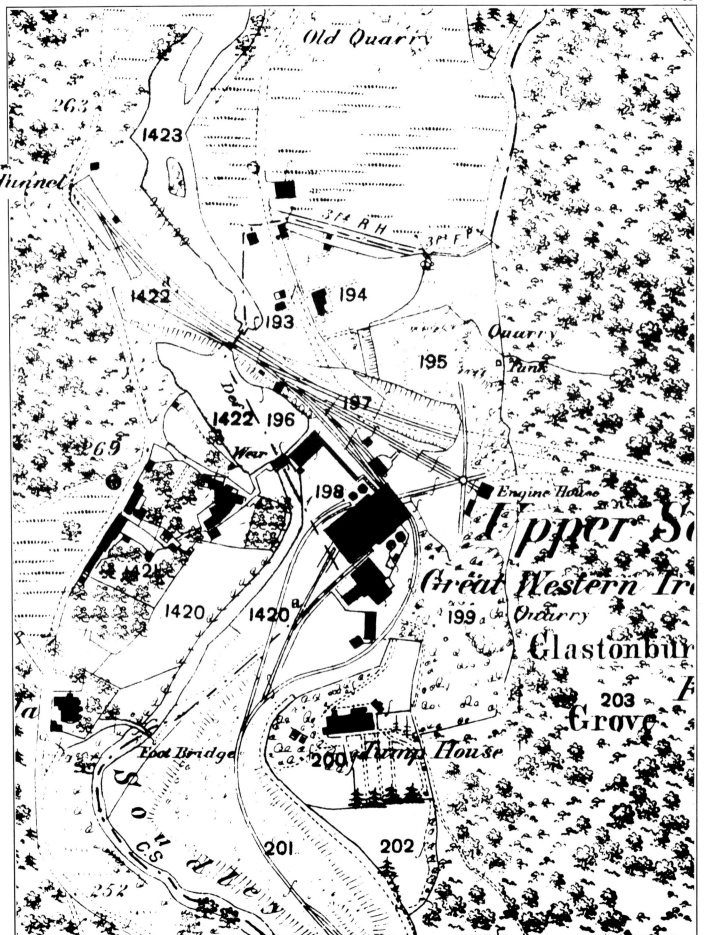

93

Old Quarry

263

1423

Tunnel

1422

3ft RH   3ft FP

194

193

Quarry

195   Quarry   Tank

197

1422   196

Weir

269

198

Engine House

Upper S

Great Western Tr

1420   1420ᵃ   199   Quarry

Glastonbur

203

Grove

Foot Bridge

200   Pump House

201   202

Taken from 25-inch Ordnance Survey for 1879. Crown Copyright reserved.

of the furnace, smashing one of the company's new trucks and damaging others. It was fortunate that the wagons absorbed the full force of the collision instead of the masonry work and piping which took the hot-blast to the furnace, otherwise there would have been far greater consequences. One of Bourne's workmen, a Frederick Pugh of Dudley, who was riding on the engine, was unfortunately killed.

It is possible that the demise of this 'old engine' in the accident led to the purchase of a new locomotive from Fox, Walker & Co. of Bristol. This was an 0—4—0ST, works number 325.

A further *Gloucester Journal* article in November 1876 stated that it was about twelve months since the company had blown in their first furnace and that 'some months ago' they commenced to build a second furnace which was by this date completed. A duplicate engine was under construction and a second chimney stack which would become the highest in the Forest. It was hoped that the furnace would be blown in early in 1877. The company was also said to be about to let the contract for a third furnace, which was to be iron cased and fed by a hydraulic lift.

Although it appears that the second furnace was virtually completed, indeed a report in 1899 stated that there were two iron furnaces of 'modern construction', it is unlikely that the second furnace was ever blown, as from 1877 no iron was produced at Soudley.

Any prosperity that the company may have enjoyed was short-lived, as the chairman, Robert McEwen, placed a petition before the Court of Chancery for its winding up in July 1879. It would appear that the works had been using Spanish ore, the cost of which became prohibitive due to increasing railway carriage charges at a time of depression in the iron trade.

The furnaces were never re-started but the works remained intact for a considerable period, and by April 1892 were in the hands of the Benton family of Clyne House, Stetford, Lancashire, several of whom were described as 'contractors'. It is likely that they had purchased them for demolition and the recovery of materials and scrap. On 5th April an agreement was signed with the Bentons for the siding into the works.

In May 1895 the GWR authorised a 'new siding at Soudley' for taking delivery of ballast supplied by the Cinderford Crushing Co, who were to form the trackbed and ballast it. The Crushing Company, which set about clearing the large volume of cinders and slag left on the site of the ironworks, consisted of Arthur Morgan, E. W. Morgan, G. F. Morgan, F. G. Washbourn and William Crawshay, all of whom had connections with the firm of

This view of the iron works being demolished shows the remains of the covered way, probably when the sidings were in use by Cinderford Crushing Co.

Dean Heritage Museum

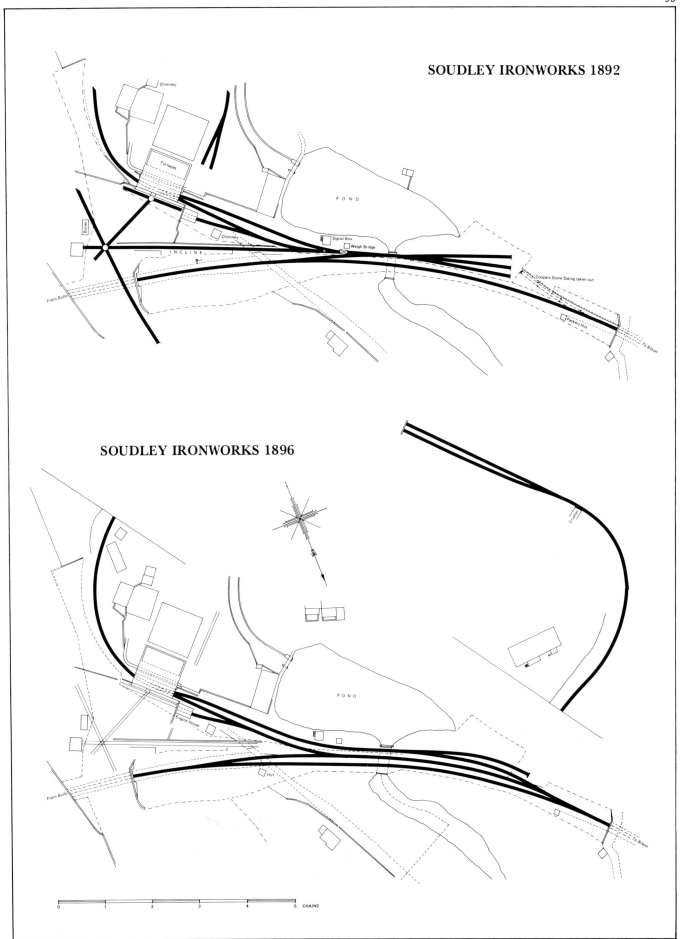

SOUDLEY IRONWORKS 1892

SOUDLEY IRONWORKS 1896

A further view taken during the demolition of the ironworks. The sidings were being used by the Cinderford Crushing Co.
Dean Heritage Museum

Henry Crawshay & Co Ltd. Arthur Morgan began his ballast business at Crawshay's Cinderford ironworks following its closure in 1894. At Soudley the company installed a crusher to the south of Tump House, and the GWR working regulations for 1895 stated:

'The siding from the points under the arch to the crusher must only be worked by the special engine provided for the purpose.'

Unfortunately, the form and ownership of this 'special engine' is unknown.

In January 1896 the Bentons gave the Cinderford Crushing Co permission to remove the old siding and lay down new sidings with the proviso that the old lines had to be restored when the Crushing Co had finished. In May a new agreement was taken out with the GWR for the re-arrangement of the sidings alongside the branch and for the new connections at either end of the site. It was probably permission for these alterations that had been granted in May 1895. In 1899 ballast from Soudley was provided for use on the Cinderford Extension of the Severn & Wye Joint Railway, then in course of construction, and for the new road from Ruspidge to Blakeney which was constructed by the Crown at around this period.

In May 1899 it was reported that the works had been sold off piecemeal at the 'great auction' a few weeks earlier. Much of the property and the two large chimney stacks were bought by Messrs Ponsford of Newport and it would appear that the remains of the works had been sold for £3,000. The boilers were described as 'quite ruined by rust', which is hardly surprising considering that they had been disused for over 20 years.

The first of the large chimneys was felled on Monday, 15th May, and the second (nearest the railway) followed on Sunday, the 21st. The Sunday was apparently chosen to avoid interference with the railway as the chimney listed considerably towards the line! It transpired that the second chimney had never been used so it seems likely that this was the one built in connection with the second furnace in 1877. The Cinderford Crushing Co used the sidings until December 1899 when they terminated the siding agreement.

The site of the ironworks was still not completely cleared and in November 1907 it was reported locally that 'a large steam engine', probably the blowing engine, had been purchased by the Staffordshire Iron & Coal Co which intended to rebuild it at Stoke. Whether this was done is not known, but presumably the site was cleared soon after this date. Photographs of the engine reveal that the sidings were not removed until after this date, although the connection to the branch may have been severed.

The blowing engines made by Haigh Foundry of Wigan in 1874.
Collection A. K. Pope

In contrast to the previous views, the site of the iron works gave way to this charming rural scene. This picture, taken from an old postcard, shows one of the steam railmotor trials of 1907 with what appears to be two railmotors sandwiching two Diagram J trailers, passing Soudley No. 1 ground frame, also known as Soudley Furnace crossing. The corrugated goods lock-up erected alongside the existing timber loading platform is believed to have been solely for the use of Dulcote Leather Board who were at Camp Mill, Soudley, now occupied by the Dean Heritage Museum. Trains simply stopped here for loading, the wagons concerned being marshalled directly behind the engine. General merchandise was also handled on the adjacent platform, and a delivery book was kept to record all traffic and cash taken here and at Soudley siding, details being sent to Bilson Junction. At one time Bob Fear looked after the crossing and goods shed, living in the nearby crossing keeper's cottage, the gable end of which features on the right of this view, the gate at the end of the garden (on the right) providing convenient access.   *Collection Neil Parkhouse*

The mill board manufacturing business established at Soudley by Moses Mason in 1888 was acquired by the Dulcote Leather Board Co. of Wells in Somerset in 1901/2. This was in the buildings to the right which were originally constructed for use as a corn mill, named Camp Mill, in 1876. Prior to this, from c.1821, the site had been in use as an iron foundry owned by Samuel Hewlett, then by his son George. Many castings for the local tramroads and railways were produced here.
Collection A. K. Pope

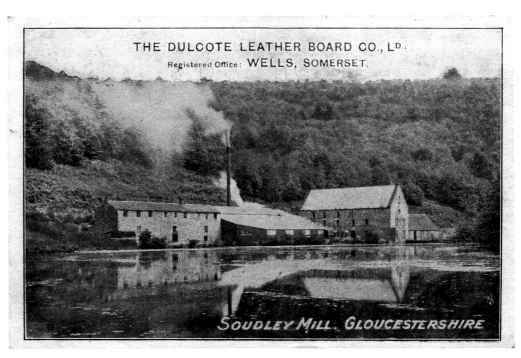

THE DULCOTE LEATHER BOARD CO., Lᴰ.
Registered Office: WELLS, SOMERSET.

SOUDLEY MILL. GLOUCESTERSHIRE

A slightly later view c.1909 of Soudley No. 1 Crossing with a motor train passing by on its way to Cinderford. Unlike the picture on page 97, this saddle tank and auto trailer are truly representative of the regular branch trains which served the local communities up and down the valley for many years.   *Collection A. K. Pope*

Soudley No. 1 crossing ground frame on 18th June 1933. The devices in front of the hut are the apparatus for taking the slack out of the distant signal wires on sunny days. These were normally placed inside the hut rather than the very inconvenient arrangement shown here.

L. E. Copeland

The train featured on page 86 about to plunge into Bradley Hill tunnel after a brief breath of fresh air. The goods shed and platform had been removed by this time.

L. E. Copeland

A light engine drifting bunker first on its way back to Bullo in the early 1960s.

A. K. Pope

Compare this tranquil scene, taken from above Bradley Hill tunnel in the 1960s, with page 89.

A. K. Pope

Again, in sharp contrast to the earlier scene depicted on page 90, the wooded surroundings at the east end of Bradley Hill tunnel now lend a totally different character to its surroundings. With an even steeper gradient of 1 in 48 on a curve, the 299 yard tunnel was regarded by many crews as more difficult to negotiate than Haie Hill tunnel. The picture, taken in the early 1960s, shows the rear of a goods train heading towards Cinderford.

A. K. Pope

UPPER SOUDLEY. TUNNELL. FROM ROMAN CAMP. FOREST OF DEAN.　W.P. 44.

Collection I. A. Pope

The northern end of Bradley Hill tunnel where the line emerged into the rather idyllic surroundings of Upper Soudley. The crossing keeper's house, known locally as 'The Gates', was authorised in February 1894 for £338. It followed standard GWR design and was occupied at one time by Fred James, a former member of the permanent way gang who, after an accident at work on the line, was transferred to look after the gates and siding at the crossing at Upper Soudley. The local children were always pleased if Fred closed the gates across the road on their way to school as it gave them an excuse for being late! The crossing keeper's house was later occupied by Mr. Rowbotham and his wife. It seems he was sent there following the loss of one of his legs on his first day of railway service at Branches Fork in South Wales. This postcard view was taken by Will Phillips, a painter and signwriter from Gloucester who took photographs of the area for an album kept in Mr. and Mrs. Thomas's guest house at Box Cottage, Soudley. Guests could order their own copies from them. Phillips was a friend of the family through the Methodist Church and attended Rechabite and other religious meetings at Box Cottage. Later, his cards appeared in one or two shops in Cinderford; they are identified by the initials 'WP' followed by the negative number. The charming little group sitting above the loading bank consisted of Mrs. Phillips, her sister and (possibly) the young Elsie Thomas (now Elsie Ibbotson) aged about six or seven, which would date the photo around 1911-13.

A closer view of the northern portal of Bradley Hill tunnel on 5th November 1946. Before the First World War, PW men Fred James and Arthur Nelmes used to get up at 5 a.m. each morning and walk down to Bullo with their foreman, Mr. Bullock, to start work at daybreak. During the winter they worked from dawn till dusk looking after the stretch from Bullo Pill to Ruspidge. Their pump trolley was kept at Bullo. Forester Elsie Ibbotson, who grew up at Soudley, remembers that the railway between Bullo and Soudley was regularly used as a footpath by locals and children from the Bullo area who used to go to school at Soudley, the railway route being several miles shorter than the roads. This dangerous tradition was particularly hazardous through the restricted bore of the tunnels but she said they knew the times of the trains and were careful to avoid being caught in the tunnels! The signal is the up distant for Soudley No. 1 crossing ground frame. The telegraph insulators on the signal post carried the wires working the electric repeater in the crossing hut to show that the signal arm had properly responded to the lever. This nicely highlighted telegraph pole provides a good example of alternative spars of different lengths so that one wire was not directly above another, a practice designed to minimise the risk of accidental contact should a wire sag.

L. E. Copeland

VIEW FROM "BEECHCROFT". SOUDLEY. N? NEWNHAM. GLOS: ZP. SY.

A panorama of Upper Soudley, taken from Beechcroft, showing from left to right, Soudley Halt, Soudley No. 2 Crossing, Soudley Siding and the crossing keeper's house before the line disappears behind Bradley Hill towards Bullo. The Anglican church of St. Michael and All Saints, in the centre of this view, was built in 1909 and envied by local Methodists for its bell.

Dean Heritage Museum Trust

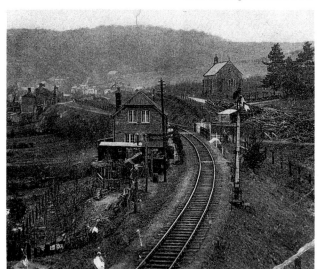

Looking towards Cinderford from above Bradley Hill tunnel some time between the wars. The large pile of timber stacked between the road and the wharf at Soudley siding was probably for one of Henry Workman's contracts and waiting for a Sunday clearance. The adjacent hut on the wharf (to the left of the distant arm) was probably used in connection with the coal traffic to the siding.

Collection Ian Pope

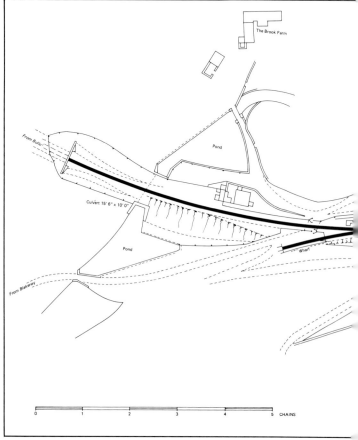

VIEW FROM BEECHCROFT, SOUDLEY, NR. NEWNHAM. GLOS. UP ST.6.B.

SOUDLEY SIDING AND UPPER SOUDLEY HALT

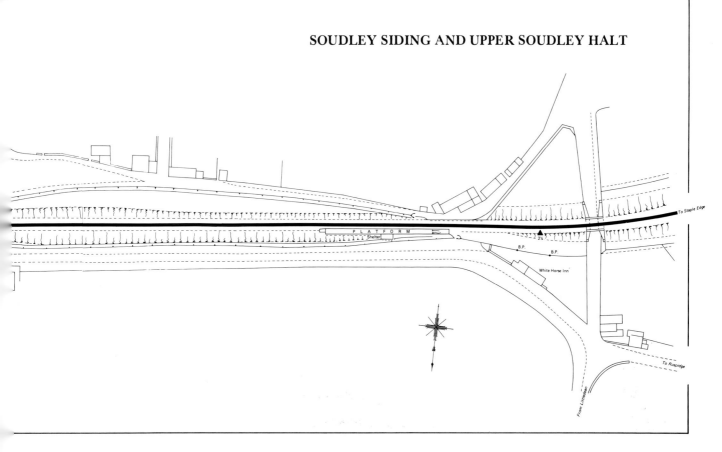

Two more views of Soudley No. 2 Crossing where a simple lane crossed the line to serve the scattered community of Upper Soudley. These pictures were taken on 11th October 1965 and 5th November 1946.

W. Potter and L. E. Copeland

SOUDLEY SIDING

Soudley Siding (3 miles 12 chains) had a capacity of just three wagons. Laid on the course of the former tramroad which skirted Bradley Hill, it was provided at some point prior to 1880. By 1902, the siding was retained by the Commissioners of Woods and Forest, who had owned the land, for Crown traffic, presumably pit props and other timber. That year they granted the GWR use of the siding for general traffic for 'an acknowledgement of 5/- per annum', the GWR agreeing to maintain the siding. Surviving records indicate that in 1904 a Mrs. Moore was using the land for a coal wharf. In 1907 she had sub-let it to Mr. W. Jones who in turn sub-let it to John Woodward, who apparently thought he had sole loading rights. However, it transpired that Mrs. Moore had no right to sub-let, and furthermore the Crown had retained rights to load timber there.

Although without licence, Dulcote Leather Board frequently used the siding. This is borne out by Elsie Ibbotson who remembers sheeted wagons on the siding full of rags destined for Camp Mill. As young children, she and her cousin used to reach under the tarpaulins and pick out ribbon and lace, etc., to clothe their dolls.

At such a restricted site it is hardly surprising that loading problems should have arisen, and in 1913 Woodward was apparently persuaded to 'move his shed to allow for timber loading'. The timber concerned was from the Abbotswood Estate to the north. It had been sold to Mr. Henry Workman of Woodchester Saw Mills, Stroud, but in July he was complaining that the siding was of little use to him. In August he wrote to the Crown asking if he could be given possession of the land occupied by the coal wharf as during 1914 he would have a large quantity of timber to load there from the Drywood and Blaize Bailey.

The quantity of timber being moved from Soudley prompted a debate in February 1915 over the extension of the siding to hold four wagons and a crane. It was proposed that a crane should be placed in the centre of the siding to load wagons on either side of it on any day of the week. The estimated cost of the work was £145. Without the extension, timber could only be loaded on a Sunday, presumably when a crane could be set up on the running line. The railway would only entertain such special arrangements when there was sufficient timber at Soudley to justify it. The difficulty for Workman arose when there was not enough timber at Soudley for a special train, but not enough space on the wharf to stack a further week's supply. The extension of the siding would have required land from the Abbotswood Estate owned by Arthur Morgan. The Crown felt that pressure could be brought to bear on him to give the land because a lot of the coal unloaded at Soudley came from the Lightmoor Colliery of Henry Crawshay & Co. Ltd., of which company Morgan was managing director. There is no evidence that the siding was ever extended but arrangements were later made at Shakemantle (see page 125). In 1915 Woodward was sub-letting to Emmanuel Matthews who continued selling coal there for approximately 12 months.

The GWR's arrangement with the Crown was terminated in 1921 but the siding was retained for Crown timber, mostly pit props, and crews remember calling there about once a week.   *L. E. Copeland*

Soudley No. 2 Crossing ground frame on 18th June 1933 and 4th December 1943.   *L. E. Copeland*

UPPER SOUDLEY. DEAN FOREST. (G.W.R. RAIL MOTOR.)

W.P. 463.

Collection I. A. Pope

Another of the postcard views taken by Will Phillips, looking north-west towards Ruspidge over the railway shortly after the halt had been rebuilt in 1908.

UPPER SOUDLEY HALT

Upper Soudley Halt with the original 1ft 2in high platform which lasted from 1907 to 1908. The village name had formerly been spelt 'Sewdley', and this version of the name was in common use in the area. The first edition Ordnance Survey shows it as Soudley but few locals would have been aware of that. The halt was built for the introduction of the FoD passenger service, and, much to their dismay, the GWR nameboard read 'Upper Soudley Halt'. The older locals refused to change, but the new spelling was taught in schools and gradually came to be accepted as the youngsters grew up.
Dean Heritage Museum Trust

The Forest railmotor at Upper Soudley Halt c.1910. The entrance gate just visible to the right is remembered as a popular gathering place for the young men of the village. In this picture, another by Will Phillips, they appear to have been displaced by the pony trap.
Dean Heritage Museum Trust

A closer view of the small bridge carrying the line over the road into the village. Part of the halt is just visible on the right of the picture. The bridge had a 12ft span with a steel trough floor supported on stone abutments. *Dean Heritage Museum Trust*

Upper Soudley Halt on 5th November 1946 showing the 3ft high platform built with old sleepers and a spoil/ash infill topped with cinders. Crews recall the halt as 'fairly busy with school children to Cinderford'. The little goods shed on the platform 'came from Bullo' and was looked after by the crossing keeper from Soudley No. 2 crossing. There was an additional passenger entrance on the right, behind the parapet railings, but no boarded crossing over the track. *L. E. Copeland*

The remains of the halt after closure. All up goods and mineral trains were required to be brought to a stand at the stop board shown, in order to pin down sufficient brakes to ensure the train could be kept under control 'so that it may pass the Notice Board fixed 184 yds from the Bullo Pill end of the long tunnel at a speed not greater than 5 mph'.

No. 8701 approaching Upper Soudley Halt with coal and vans for Bullo Pill in June 1962. In latter years some crews of trains going in the opposite (uphill) direction often claimed to have run short of steam here and abandoned trains could be found stabled securely on the gradient alongside the fence of the White Horse public house!

R. H. Marrows

Heading on through Soudley, the line was on successive gradients of 1 in 66, 1 in 49 and 1 in 71, so local inhabitants can hardly have been unaware of the heavy trains of empties struggling past on their way to the collieries. This view was taken looking towards Bullo with the Cinderford to Blakeney main road passing under the line and snaking across the picture, little more than a track at the time of this postcard view c.1910. The bridge over the road in the foreground was known as Gullet bridge. It had a 10ft square span with steel rolled joists and a timber floor supported on stone abutments.   *Dean Heritage Museum Trust*

UPPER SOUDLEY. FROM STAPLE EDGE

NEAR NEWNHAM. GLOS:

SCILLY POINT SIDING

Scilly Point, taken on the same occasion as the previous view but looking north-east from further along the hillside. The road bridge over the stream featured in the foreground of the previous view can be seen in the centre. The site of the siding for Findall Iron Mine can just be discerned to the left of the short cutting in the centre of the scene. The freshly cut timber on the hillside in the foreground was stacked neatly in 'cords' (a measure of 128 cubic feet of timber consisting mainly of the branches which were stacked about four feet wide and four feet high, every eight feet along the stack).

Dean Heritage Museum

The siding at Scilly Point, also known in early documents as 'Silly Point', was probably provided from the opening of the broad gauge branch to replace a tramroad connection. It served the Findall Iron Mine Level to which it was connected by a tramway. The Findall Level formed part of the Perseverance and Findall Iron Mine gale. By 1841 it was in the hands of Edward Protheroe and William Crawshay, Protheroe's holding having a pit (Perseverance) and a level (Findall) in operation as separate mines.

Protheroe undoubtedly used Findall ore for his nearby blast furnaces at Soudley (see page 91), but after the first closure of the furnaces c.1842, the level may have continued in production to supply other Forest or South Wales works. In December 1845 it was reported that Protheroe was to sell Findall level to a Mr. James of Lydney for the sum of £9,999. Whether this figure was just for the iron mine or for Protheroe's entire interest in the furnaces as well is not known. James was evidently still the owner in 1854 as the South Wales Railway gradient diagram shows Scilly Point as 'Siding to James' Iron Ore'.

It is possible that the level passed to Benjamin Gibbon when he purchased the Soudley furnaces from James in 1857, if the level and the furnaces were part of the same estate. What is known is that in February 1873 the level was sold, along with the furnaces, to Maximilian Low. The various agreements that were arrived at over the furnaces around this time and the complications therewith may have led to the temporary closure of the iron mine in June 1873. This was reported in the *Gloucester Journal* on the 21st of the month when it was stated:

'These works were closed a few days since and most of the men paid off, they having had the requisite notice from the props. This step was occasioned mainly we believe, not through the badness of the iron trade, or has been stated in some papers, the firm not being short of orders, but because the manager is in delicate health, and being about to rusticate with a view to its improvement, the partners determined for a few months, or at least until his return, to stop the works rather than introduce new arrangements.'

The level ceased production around the time the furnaces closed in 1877. The date at which the siding was removed is unknown but it had certainly gone by 1902.

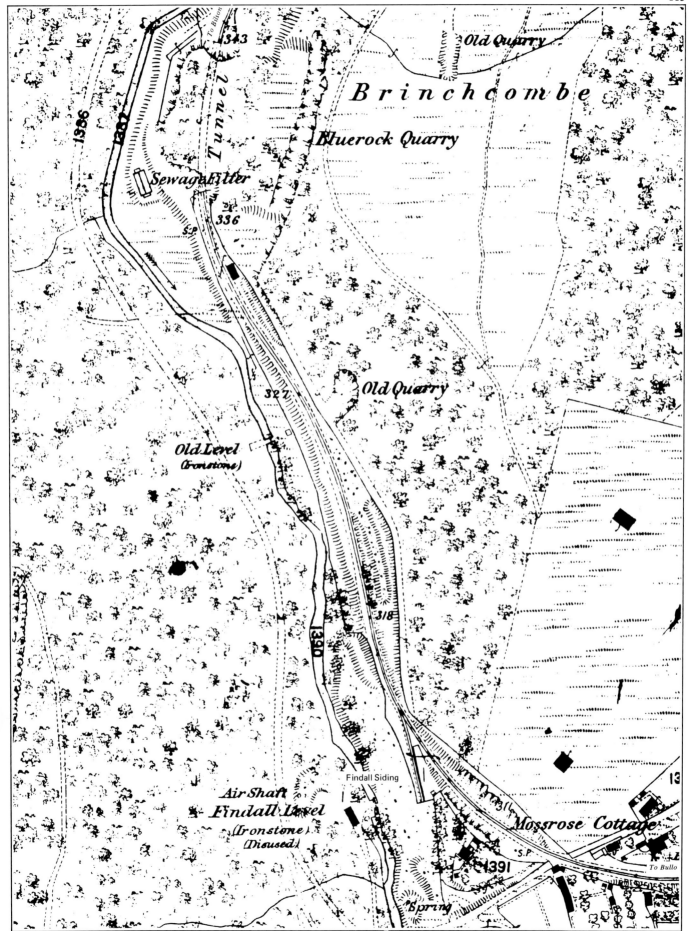

Taken from 25-inch Ordnance Survey for 1878. Crown Copyright reserved.

After leaving Soudley, the line ran north towards Blue Rock tunnel, following the tramroad course and the Cinderford Brook. The tramroad ran around the spur of hillside at Blue Rock whereas the railway tunnelled through. The width of the formation at this point may have resulted from the need to accommodate the tramroad while the railway was being built. In this official view, the entrance of Blue Rock Tunnel can be seen near the centre of the photograph above a platelayers' hut. This was a particularly attractive stretch of line, and was relatively free from signs of industrial activity. *National Railway Museum*

The southern portal of the 109 yd Blue Rock Tunnel. During the First World War, locals were told to make for Blue Rock Tunnel in the event of a Zeppelin flying over, because its bore through solid rock was considered a natural shelter. However, the general opinion was that this was not such a good idea, as since it was so far, they would be hit trying to get there! *R. H. Marrows*

The northern end of Blue Rock Tunnel, looking downhill towards Soudley and Bullo in June 1962 and April 1968.
Keith Allford and R. H. Marrows

The Eastern United down distant signal was usually off as the box was switched out most of the time. After leaving Blue Rock Tunnel, the gradient steepened to 1 in 37 against trains proceeding towards Bilson Junction.

Keith Allford

VIEW FROM BRITISH CAMP. LITTLEDEAN. GLOS: WP. L.103

Taken from another Will Phillips postcard, this view, looking down the Ruspidge Valley from above Shakemantle Quarry, shows how the line weaved its way between tree-clad slopes, plunging into the darkness of Blue Rock Tunnel. The southern connection and gate into Shakemantle Siding can just be discerned.
Collection I. A. Pope

SHAKEMANTLE IRON MINE

Shakemantle formed the southernmost point of an extensive area of iron mine workings which stretched about two and a half miles northwards under the Linegar Woods, Ruspidge Meend and Littledean Woodside. As it was also the lowest point on the property, all pumping was concentrated here. The first pumping station in the area appears to have been erected in 1829 when the Cinderford Iron Co., owner of blast furnaces at Cinderford (see page 187), sunk a shaft here and, in connection with opening the Lime Kiln Iron Mine, erected a steam pumping engine at a cost of about £7,000. From the bottom of the shaft, a level was driven into the iron measures, and by 1831 rich quality ore was being raised. It is possible that the Lime Kiln Iron Mine was part of the Cinderford Iron Mine gale on which the shafts at Shakemantle were situated. Other gales were added to the area, including the Drybrook Mine Level, Trowditch, Brinchcombe Level, a portion of Perseverance, Cooper's Level, Old Orles, As You Like It, and Hattons Level, all of which formed a part of Buckshaft Iron Mine held under a lease for 1,000 years from 17th February 1834 granted by Richard Cooper.

The 1841 Awards confirmed the gales as being in the possession of William Crawshay of Cyfartha Castle, Merthyr Tydfil, and Moses Teague of Cinderford, Crawshay having three-quarters of the share. This partnership was also involved in the operation of the Cinderford furnaces and at Lightmoor Colliery.

A shaft had been sunk on Buckshaft in 1835, and further north another was started in 1849 at the St. Annal's Iron Mine gale which was added to the area. These were connected underground with Shakemantle by levels driven in the Crease limestone.

In the 1850s a second shaft was sunk at Shakemantle, about ninety yards from the original. This became the Deep Pit. The original shaft, which became known as the Land Pit, was oval in shape, 22ft 6in by 11ft 6in and was 72 yards deep. It was equipped with a pumping engine with a 36in cylinder and an 8ft stroke. Working at 50lbs pressure and connected to two 27in diameter pumps, it operated at between 6 and 10 strokes per minute. The new shaft, also oval, 19ft 6in by 11ft 6in, was equipped with a new and larger pumping engine with a 60in diameter cylinder, 10ft stroke. The piston came out of the bottom of the cylinder and attached direct to the pump rods. This increase in pumping power was necessary to cope with the extensions to the worked area and the greater depths from which the ore was being won.

Insole & Bunning, writing in 1880, listed the pumping plant as:

High Pressure Bull Engine	60 in cylinder	10 ft stroke
Auxiliary Bull Engine	30 in cylinder	5 ft stroke
Rotary Condensing Beam Engine (not working)	70 in cylinder	12 ft stroke

Another source in 1882 states that at Shakemantle there was 'a ponderous double-acting pumping engine' designed by P. Teague and made and erected by the Neath Abbey Ironworks. This was probably the engine described by Insole and Bunning as 'not working'. With its 70 in cylinder and 12 ft stroke, the piston rod was 8 in diameter. The beam was 36 ft long, 6 ft 6 in deep and weighed over 30 tons. The engine was placed on a wall 6 ft thick and 43 ft above the basement of the engine house. The flywheel of the engine was 20 ft in diameter and weighed 32 tons. This massive engine may have been the subject of an accident at Shakemantle reported in the *Dean Forest Mercury* in March 1887. On Sunday the 13th, the engineman, one Elijah Wintle, heard a scraping sound and a thud, whereupon he promptly stopped the engine. On investigation, he found that the crankshaft had broken off, luckily at half stroke, thus minimising the damage to the engine and pumps. Interestingly, the report stated that although the pump had been 'completed some months', it had only been used regularly for the last three, pumping some 1,300 gallons per minute.

As already mentioned, Shakemantle, Buckshaft and St. Annal's were connected underground and eventually there were four main levels at various depths. The two shafts at Shakemantle were Land, about 230 ft deep, and Deep, about 470 ft deep. Buckshaft Pit, begun in 1835, reached a depth of about 620 feet and St. Annal's Shaft, begun in 1849, reached 657 feet.

The four main levels were all driven in the Crease limestone. The No. 1 Level, completed in 1855, ran northwards from Buckshaft for 9,200 feet and was connected to both the Buckshaft and St. Annal's Shafts by means of cross-cuts. The level was at 280 ft above Ordnance Datum and the cross-cuts joined the Buckshaft Shaft at 330 ft from the surface and the St. Annal's Shaft at 525 feet from the top.

The No. 2 Level, completed in 1876, was 140 ft above OD and ran northwards from Shakemantle, connecting with both the Buckshaft and St. Annal's shafts along its length of 12,950 ft. Starting from the Shakemantle Land Shaft, at a depth of 230 feet, it intercepted Buckshaft at 470 feet in the shaft and St. Annal's at 657 feet. No bodies of ore were found to the rise of the level, but to the dip numerous deposits were found as far as 2,250 feet north from Buckshaft, after which point the ground proved virtually barren.

No. 3 Level, at approximately 10 ft below OD, was driven northwards from an incline which joined the Nos. 2, 3 and 4 Levels alongside the shafts at Shakemantle. The level ran 12,600 ft and was completed in 1886. At

The remains of the southern connection to Shakemantle Siding which originally served Shakemantle Iron Mine and latterly the large quarry scarring the hillside. Although at this period the siding took the form of a loop, it appears to have originally been two separate sidings as shown in the first edition Ordnance Survey and on a GWR official plan of 1880. The southern portion of the siding served a limestone quarry and limekilns whilst the northern half served Shakemantle Iron Mine. The connection was removed in June 1953.   *R. Dagley-Morris*

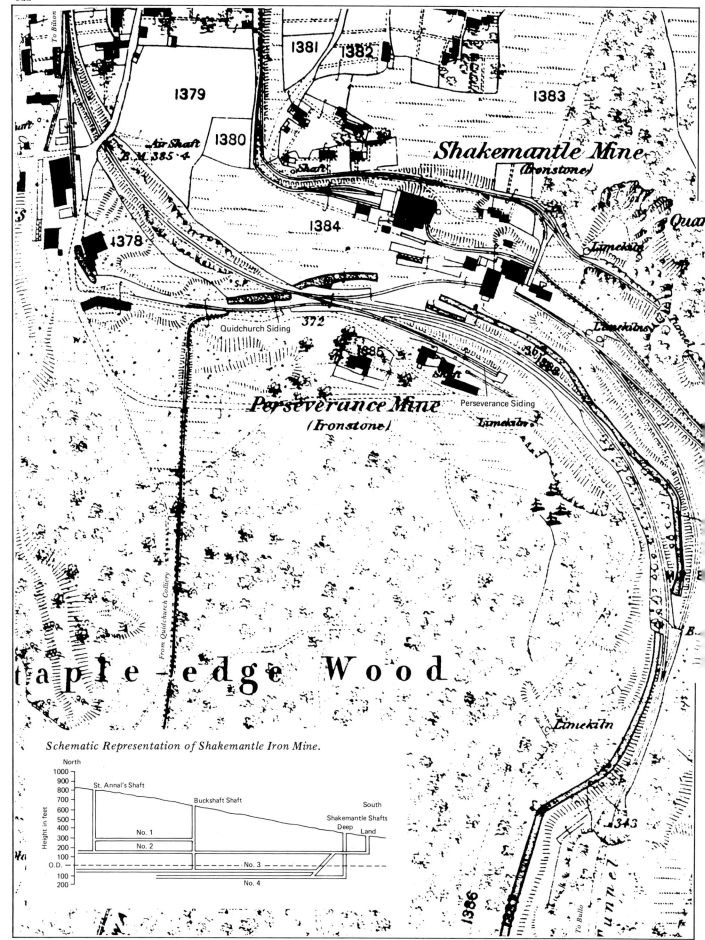

To Bilson

1381 1382

1379

1383

Shakemantle Mine
(Ironstone)

Air Shaft
B.M. 385·4

1380

Shaft

1384

Quar

Limekiln

1378

S.P.

372

Quidchurch Siding

Limekilns

1385

Shaft

Perseverance Siding

Perseverance Mine

(Ironstone)

Limekiln

From Quidchurch Colliery

taple edge Wood

Limekiln

1343

Schematic Representation of Shakemantle Iron Mine.

North

1000
900 St. Annal's Shaft
800
700 Buckshaft Shaft
600
500 South
400 Shakemantle Shafts
300 No. 1 Deep Land
200 No. 2
100
O.D. — — — — No. 3 — — — —
100
200 No. 4

Height in feet

1386

To Bullo

Tunnel

The Shakemantle Iron Mine of Henry Crawshay & Co. c.1900 with the large pumping engine house prominent in the centre. The wagons belonging to Henry Crawshay & Co. were standing on the northern of the two sidings at Shakemantle.
Collection A. K. Pope

Buckshaft a cross-cut driven westwards from the shaft met the level 90ft away. At the southern end of the level the ore bodies proved plentiful but the last 4,000 feet at the northern end proved practically barren.

The deepest level, at 140ft below OD, was the No. 4 which also ran northwards from Shakemantle for 7,100 ft and again the last 2,200 ft showed little or no ore.

The iron measures were thus worked to a vertical depth of nearly 900 ft so the big problem to be overcome was the water which, laying naturally at about 290ft above OD, had to be pumped out. It was allowed to drain to Shakemantle where all the pumping plant was located. As the mine went deeper, the pumping problems became greater and thus the pumping capacity at Shakemantle had to be increased.

It is likely that the greatest use made of the siding, provided from the opening of the broad gauge line, was to bring in coal for the pumping plant boilers, as all ore was brought to the surface at either Buckshaft or St. Annal's. Ore could have been loaded at Shakemantle as Crawshays' private tramroad system, linking their various interests, connected Shakemantle, Buckshaft and St. Annal's on the surface, together with Lightmoor Colliery and Cinderford Ironworks. However, with its own independent link to Cinderford Ironworks, the main consumer of the ore, the mine was largely independent of the Forest of Dean branch and its traffic charges.

Throughout the 1890s the mine suffered a series of setbacks, the greatest of which was the closure of the furnaces at Cinderford in 1894. It was to these works that the greatest portion of the ore had been sent, so now new markets had to be found. As the mine was beginning to run out of easily won ore, output declined from some 3,000-4,000 tons per month to 1,200-1,500 tons. Of course, overheads of pumping water, etc. were constant, so the profit margin was being eaten away. Although large deposits of ore remained at deeper levels, winning this would have entailed sinking new shafts, a large capital outlay which, in the face of cheap ore imported from Spain, was not a viable option.

The accounts for the mine between 1893 and 1896 showed an average loss of £209 11s 4d per year which, it was thought by the Crown, could have been met by a modification in the salaries. The fixed cost of pumping in 1894 was £4,812 15s 2d and in 1895 £3,696 13s 4d. To assist with keeping the mine open, the Crown reduced the dead rents on the gales and the royalty payments on the ore but it was not enough to prevent the inevitable. In July 1896 Crawshay & Co. decided to relinquish the gales and then changed their minds. However, the losses on the mines continued to rise and for the half-year ending December 1896 a loss of £520 was recorded, whilst by August 1897 it was up to £151 per month. In October £300 was allowed

Looking over Shakemantle Quarry towards Cinderford, showing the heavily overgrown siding and a portion of the quarry workings on 4th August 1947.

L. E. Copeland

for new exploration work which evidently proceeded, for in April 1898 Mr. Thomas Smith, the manager, reported that a new heading was in about 767 yards and going well. He also estimated that there was a stock of about 5,000 tons of iron ore on the pit bank. With Crawshays selling their produce on the open market since the closure of the Cinderford furnaces in 1894, it seems likely that ore was thereafter loaded onto the railway at Shakemantle, having been brought along the tramroad from St. Annal's and Buckshaft.

In August 1898 it was decided that although they would continue with the new heading, which was said to be about to cut the ore in the sandstone, if it proved a failure then the whole was to be surrendered to the Crown, if a buyer could not be found in the meantime. Two months later the heading had gone some 31 yards beyond where the ore was expected to be found and losses were reported of £95 for July, £286 for August, £215 for September and the expectation of a larger figure for October. In January 1899 it was decided the position could not continue and a meeting of the shareholders was called for 16th February to sanction the closure. The gales were to be surrendered to the Crown on 29th September. On 15th September 1899 the local press announced that all the men employed in the mine had been paid off, some 160 men and boys being affected; at its peak the mines had employed over 300. The closure was all the more sad as a few years earlier a large deposit of red oxide had been struck which became known in the colour trade as 'Crawshay's Red' and commanded a high price. At one time 300 tons per month were being won with a selling price of between £7 and £10. It is little wonder that when deposits of colour were found it was preferred to the iron ore!

The *Dean Forest Mercury* for 6th October reported that the machinery, buildings and appurtenances 'are not equalled in the Forest, or excelled in the country', after which the intrepid reporter was taken underground.

'Leaving the bottom and proceeding into the workings we observe a small tramway runs one side of the road and a small river the other, the river being the water that has found its way into the pit. It is about 9ft wide and 10in deep and flows quietly and smoothly to the sump. [Another account states that this 'perpetual stream' was of beautifully pure water and ran into a large reservoir from where it was pumped to the surface. This reservoir held about four hours worth of water.] Nearly all of the road and top of the archway is composed of good hard rock, timber only being used when the top is shaley or loose, and as the journey is made into the workings it can be seen from where the ore was obtained, some of the holes from where the mine has been excavated taking the most remarkable shapes, some small, whilst others are large enough to build a chapel in, and the veins of ore run in peculiar and awkward positions.'

The pumping plant was also described, there being a 'large pump assisted by a smaller one' which delivered 11,600 tons of water every 24 hours, some 2 million gallons. Each stroke of the large pump sent 300 gallons out of the pit and it worked at 6 strokes to the minute with a stroke of 12 feet. The smaller pump called 'Little Alice' was let into the pit on the opposite side to the large one, and anchored with four large iron sling rods, and was driven by a Bull engine. When working, it threw 1,400 gallons a minute but it was only used when the large pump was overpowered or being repaired.

In November 1898 the plant was sold off to a Mr. James Clements for the sum of £3,000 and on 9th December the large pump was stopped, thus allowing the workings to fill.

0–6–0PT No. 1627 passing Shakemantle Quarry on 1st May 1962. *R. Dagley-Morris*

By this time the machinery at Buckshaft had already been dismantled and the engine from Perseverance was in the course of being taken down. Crawshays were given six months to clear the site but the removal of the plant was no small problem and in the event this proved impossible.

Ore was still being sold in April 1900, some going to the Lilleshall Company, whilst 'red earth' or ochre was still in stock in July when 480 tons was on hand with a value of £3,199.

SHAKEMANTLE QUARRY

Following the closure of the Shakemantle Iron Mine in 1899, the site lay quiet until 1907 when it was purchased by Mr. Arthur Morgan, a director of H. Crawshay & Co. That November Morgan approached the Crown for terms and conditions upon which he might lease an old quarry adjacent to the iron mine site, presumably the one originally served by the southern siding at Shakemantle. He intended erecting plant on the old iron mine site to convert the stone into railway ballast and road metalling — areas in which Morgan had considerable interests. The Crown quoted a rent of £10 for the first year and £25 thereafter, merging into a royalty of 1½d per ton on all crushed stone supplied to railway companies for ballast and 3d per ton on all other stone. Although Morgan declined these terms, in 1911 the quarry was leased to Mr. W. D. Meredith, a Free Miner and colliery manager for H. Crawshay & Co. who had been used by them previously to obtain quarry leases. In this case it would appear that he was acting on behalf of Arthur Morgan whose renewed interest might be attributed to the sale of the quarry which, in September 1911, was assigned to the Basic Lime & Stone Co. Ltd., whose registered office was in Century Chambers, West Bute Street, Cardiff. It would appear that the company took the form of a syndicate headed by the local Forest of Dean Liberal MP, Mr. H. Webb.

With the commencement of work at the quarry, the Crown became worried that a track which they had previously used for taking timber from nearby woodlands would be seriously interfered with. Part of this track, including a tunnel, was on the formation of the old tramroad which had served the iron mine. In order to continue unhindered, the Crown proposed loading timber onto the railway at Shakemantle Siding. In October 1912 they received a letter from Basic Lime & Stone Co. which stated that 'the GW Co. would not allow your crane to travel over our siding, and as the GWR will not permit the timber to be loaded by labour provided by you, we shall be glad to know

(*PRIVATE AND NOT FOR PUBLICATION*)

GREAT WESTERN RAILWAY.

(*For use of the Railway Servants only*).

Notice No. 9390.

REGULATIONS FOR BLASTING AT SHAKEMANTLE, FOREST OF DEAN CON-TRACTING COMPANY AND GLOUCESTER COUNTY COUNCIL QUARRIES, SITUATED BETWEEN BULLO PILL AND RUSPIDGE STATIONS (FOREST OF DEAN BRANCH).

1. On and after April 5th, 1915, the following arrangements will be made for Blasting operations at these Quarries. Blasting operations must only be carried out under the sanction of the Signalman stationed at Eastern United Colliery Signal Box.

2. A disc, worded "Blasting Disc," will be in use, and except when in possession of the Quarry Foreman as authority to blast, it must be kept in the personal charge of the Signalman in the Signal Box.

A Porter or a Platelayer (as the case may be) will be appointed to convey the Disc from the Signal Box to the Foreman at the Quarry and after the shots have been fired the Disc will be handed back by the Foreman to the Porter or Platelayer who will examine the Line to see if any damage or obstruction has been caused and he will then return to the Signal Box, report to the Signalman as to the state of the Line and hand back the Disc.

3. When the blasting disc has been given to the appointed man for conveyance to Quarry Foreman, no train must be allowed to leave Eastern United Colliery Signal Box for Bullo Pill, nor from Bullo Pill for Eastern United, until the blasting disc has been returned to Signal Box and line reported clear.

4. Before the Signalman allows the blasting disc to leave his possession there must be no down train on its way from Bullo Pill to Eastern United Colliery Signal Box, but the blasting disc may be handed to the man appointed to receive it after an up train has passed Eastern United Signal Box, and is running between that box and Bullo Pill. If no Up train is running between Eastern United Colliery and Bullo Pill West, the "Obstruction" signal must be sent to Bullo Pill West, and the "Obstruction removed" signal must not be given until the blasting disc has been returned and line reported clear.

5. The time the blasting is to be carried out must be whilst the trains are running at their present times :—

   Morning—9-0 a.m. to 9-30 a.m.
   Mid-day—11-50 a.m. to 1-0 p.m.

6. The Signalman must be careful not to allow blasting to be carried out if it will interfere with the running of trains.

7. If the men engaged at the Quarry carry out any blasting operation without being in possession of the blasting disc, as provided in Clause 2, or if they in any way depart from the instructions or do anything to interfere with the safety of the line, or if they neglect to obey the orders given, the Signalman must report the circumstances to the Chief Inspector at Gloucester, who must immediately report the matter to the Divisional Superintendent.

8. Blasting must not be carried out before daylight or after dark, or during a fog or falling snow.

9. The wages of the man who conveys the disc from and to the Signal Box will be chargeable to the Quarry owners.

All concerned to note and arrange accordingly.

Acknowledge Receipt.

T. H. ROBERTS,

GLOUCESTER, MARCH 30TH, 1915. Divisional Superintendent.

250   CHANCE & BLAND, GLOUCESTER.   649

Facing page: Shakemantle Quarry and loading screens between the wars, with the northern connection to Shakemantle siding and its controlling ground frame (under the white painted wooden cover) in the foreground. The cave halfway up the quarry face was the remains of a tramroad tunnel. The ruined engine house to the right of the picture belonged to the Perseverance Iron Mine, again owned by Henry Crawshay. The private siding serving this mine had diverged through the fence on the right, almost opposite the gateway into the quarry. The smoke rising in the background to the right of the picture was probably from a lime kiln alongside the road to Soudley. The official notice above shows that the railway was well protected against the dangers of blasting by safety regulations, and the absence of any reports of damage indicate these worked well in practice. Local inhabitants were not so well served, however. People travelling along the Cinderford–Blakeney road were merely warned and allowed to proceed at their own risk. The Thomas family, who moved to the Crown cottage next to Perseverance around 1915, were even less fortunate, having to shelter indoors from the shower of rocks when warned that blasting was about to begin. Whenever the cottage roof was damaged, the Crown claimed compensation from the quarry owners. The cottage, formerly the Perseverance manager's house, was primitive by modern standards, having no electricity or mains water for drinking or washing. Candles and oil lamps provided the only light, whilst the Crown built a small reservoir for the family's use. This often ran dry, so water was collected in a tin bath from Cinderford Brook by Mr. and Mrs. Thomas, and this had to be done before a certain time in the morning, as Eastern United emptied its waste water into the stream once a day, causing a rush of dirty water down the valley. Needless to say, all water in the cottage was boiled!

Collection Ian Pope

Shakemantle Lime Kilns, Lower Ruspidge. 1202.

how you propose to get over the difficulty.' Several suggestions were made by the quarry co. including the provision of a platform and a short siding stemming from their own, or a separate siding outside the boundary gate of the quarry siding laid down at the expense of the railway company and thus subject to an annual charge. This latter proposal was unattractive to the Crown who would have much preferred to use their tenant's siding free of charge. The following month the quarry company wrote again insisting that if the Crown were to use their siding, then a separate loop siding would have to be provided as they were expecting to have a good deal of traffic passing to and fro and could not have the siding blocked by wagons awaiting the Crown's timber traffic. The Crown replied that they were not concerned over how the facilities were provided, but they *must* be and at no cost to them! In November the works manager at the quarry was instructed to make a loading bank, although no formal agreement had been reached over the use of the siding. The loading of the Crown timber appears to have been a problem as in December 1912 the GWR were said to be 'hard pressed for cranes' and it was not until September 1914 that the GWR agreed to the use of a crane on Shakemantle Siding — then three months later they changed their minds. In March 1915 the Crown, having received no assistance from the Basic Lime & Stone Co. in the provision of a loading facility, decided to give notice to the quarry company to quit the siding. The quarry company were already having difficulties of their own as, due to the war, they could not get enough wagons to send stone away. In June 1916 it was stated that the stone obtained from the quarry was not suitable for conversion to Basic material and in August 1916 the leases on the quarry were transferred to the Porthywaen Lime & Basic

Co. Ltd. of Oswestry. Arthur Morgan's interest in taking over the quarry early in 1920 reveals that the present lessee was not prepared to re-start the quarry. This suggests that it had been disused for a period, perhaps since 1915. In June it was stated that the company had no intention of re-opening the quarry 'if they can possibly help it'. Some work must have been contemplated in January 1922 when it was stated that a Mr. Negus at the quarry wanted to erect a hopper and elevators. He appears to have been one of the partners in the Porthywaen Lime Co. The question of loading timber on the Shakemantle Siding was raised again in 1924 when the Crown wanted to load some beech using a railway travelling crane. However, they were informed that the timber had to be loaded at either Soudley Siding or Ruspidge as the siding was not in a fit state for either engines or travelling cranes to pass over. By the end of December the siding had been put into repair (new keys having been the main items required) and it was safe for steam cranes to travel up to 70 yards inside the gate.

Porthywaen Lime worked the quarry fully and in 1930 the company was taken over by the Steetley Lime & Building Stone Co. who traded at Shakemantle as the Steetley Lime & Basic Slag Co. In July 1936, under the management of Mr. T. B. Rees, the company was anxious to tender for the supply of material for use in the construction of nearby sewage beds for the East Dean Rural District Council. There was apparently a large pile of suitable material alongside the siding at Shakemantle and it was felt that every assistance should be given by the GWR as the Porthywaen Lime Company were large customers of the railway at Porthywaen and other places.

The sewage beds were to be built to the south of Blue Rock tunnel and it was proposed that material brought from the quarry could be unloaded on a patch of firm level ground to the north of the tunnel and then carted around the outside of the spur of the hillside through which the tunnel passed. If the material was to be unloaded at this point, the haul on the branch would actually be less than 70 yards. The outcome of the proposal is not recorded, but a memo produced at the time in connection with these proposals reveals that the siding was served by the 10.00 a.m. ex-Eastern United Colliery which was booked to call at Shakemantle Siding with traffic picked up from the southern connection.

The Steetley Lime & Basic Slag Co. continued working the quarry until 1948, production having dropped off considerably during the last three years. The lease of the quarry was given up in 1949 and the private siding agreement was terminated on 29th September of that year, the siding having been last used in December 1948. The connections to the siding were spiked over on 13th June 1950 following abortive discussions over the removal of the quarry machinery which could not be done by road. Late in 1950 the land occupied by the siding was purchased by Messrs. T. W. Little & Sons Ltd, who intended developing

the quarry 'at an early date'. Discussion over reinstatement of the siding went on for over two years until finally, in June 1953, the decision was taken to recover both the North and South Ground Frames and the southern connection. The northern connection was not removed until 1962, by which time the quarry was owned by the Shakemantle Quarry Co. who proposed sending railway ballast out from the quarry, but this was overtaken by the closure of the branch.

PERSEVERANCE SIDING

This siding trailed from the down direction just beyond the northern connection to Shakemantle, passing through a gate to terminate alongside the iron mine buildings. It was provided at some date after 1860 and served the Perseverance Iron Mine which, as already mentioned (page 114), was worked in conjunction with the Findall Iron Mine. In later years the pit was worked by Henry Crawshay & Co. Ltd. with a cut-out being driven from the bottom of the Perseverance shaft to Shakemantle. The mine closed at the same time as Shakemantle. Whether ore was loaded here is

Looking back towards Soudley on 4th May 1964, showing the site of Perseverance siding which led off to the right through the gate opposite the northern connection to Shakemantle siding. Cinderford Brook bridge in the foreground had a steel girder span with rolled joists and timber floor. It had stone and brick abutments and a span of 12ft 6in on the square and 21ft on the skew. *A. K. Pope*

A closer view of the northern connection to Shakemantle Quarry, shown here in the 1950s after being abandoned. Empty wagons were put into the siding from 'down' trains, the engine not being allowed to pass the gate. When they had been loaded, they were gravitated to the south end of the siding for collection by 'up' trains. Crews remember that occasionally there were as many as seven wagons of stone for Bullo Docks where they were loaded into the *Finis* for shipment to Stonebench, a wharf on the Rivern Severn's east bank just below Gloucester.   *R. Dagley-Morris*

unknown, but coal would have formed an incoming traffic to feed the boilers for the pumping engine.

QUIDCHURCH SIDING

Stemming from Perseverance Siding, Quidchurch Siding was probably provided by the owner of the Quidchurch Colliery. Like Perseverance Siding, it was a gated single line and terminated at a loading bank. In 1825 Moses Teague joined forces with Messrs. Whitehouse and Montague as Whitehouse & Co. in order to work Quidchurch. As these gentlemen were connected with both the Cinderford Iron Works and Shakemantle Iron Mine, they may have intended working Quidchurch to supply coal to the other concerns. In the event, only Montague appears to have put up any capital and the partnership broke up in 1826. Montague continued alone but appears to have driven a level but not struck coal. Teague's involvement may have been as holder of the gale as in 1833 Quidchurch Colliery is listed as being worked by Messrs. Musgrave and Teague who surrendered the gale prior to 1844.

Quidchurch was re-galed on 17th December 1844 to James Beech of Ruspidge. A level at Quidchurch, situated in Staple Edge Wood, gave access to coal from the Trenchard vein and all unallotted veins above. The Coleford High Delf seam was also allotted in the form of all the old pillars left to the land side of Findall and Cooper's Level Collieries. By the 1850s it would appear that the level was owned by Mr. W. F. Corbett who was in arrears with his tramroad tolls. Despite this, he was given permission by the South

Wales Railway to erect a loading chute, but, with the conversion of the tramroad, Corbett became worried that in consequence of a deviation (made to ease the alignment), his colliery was left stranded from the railway. The South Wales Board advised him that he was quite welcome to make a siding connection but it would have to be at his own expense. Corbett may have formed the Quidchurch Colliery Co, which in 1858/9 was listed as having offices at Bullo Pill.

Being in the middle of the wood, the level was connected to the railway by a long tramway which ran down to the siding on an inclined plane. How long the siding remained in use is unknown but in 1869 it was reported that Quidchurch had closed soon after the opening of the broad gauge, probably prior to June 1866 when Quidchurch Colliery was said to be exhausted.

At this time it was held by Rev. John Wylde who also owned the unopened Extension and Emperor Gales. By 1873 Messrs. Lückes & Nash were the registered owners of the gale which in January 1881 was up for auction. The *Dean Forest Mercury* for 10th June 1887 gives details of a court case brought against Messrs. G. A. Robinson and William Aston, colliery manager, both of Manchester, by one William Niblett for the non-payment of wages at Quidchurch Colliery. It is possible that at this date the siding at Shakemantle was not being used. This siding and the tramway are still shown on the 25-inch Ordnance Survey for 1878, so perhaps there was still some activity at Quidchurch. The siding had been removed by 1900.

A train of tank wagons, bound for Berry Wiggins' depot at Whimsey, about to pass under the bridge carrying the Cinderford to Blakeney road over the branch. *A. K. Pope*

A closer view, taken 29th August 1961, of the check-railed 10-chain curve on the approach to Staple Edge Halt where the gradient eased from 1 in 45 to 1 in 71 past the colliery. The signal is part of the down home signal bracket for Eastern United Colliery signal box. The bridge was originally constructed with stone abutments, timber beams, and a timber and Barlow rail floor. It was reconstructed in 1918 with second-hand steel girders and brick parapets at a cost of £236.
Keith Allford

This view, taken from the bridge on 4th August 1947, shows the beginning of the goods loop installed in 1913. The gated entrance to the Eastern United Colliery features behind the signal. All freight trains having work to do at the colliery had to be put into the goods loop clear of the main line before any shunting commenced. Staple Edge quarry can be seen in the centre background.

L. E. Copeland

The gated entrance to the disused colliery on 8th June 1962.

Keith Allford

STAPLE EDGE HALT

Staple Edge Halt, photographed on 4th June 1909. On the hillside, just to the right of the nearest telegraph pole, work has commenced on the site of Eastern United Colliery as witnessed by a small group of workmen and some pit carts. Two of the cottages on the right were acquired by H. Crawshay & Co. at a cost of £350 from Frank Dykins. They were occupied by one Jonah Jackson and a Mr. Turley and when Dykins called in his mortgage, Jackson was said to be 'very much upset about it'. The other two cottages, mortgaged to Messrs. Bryant & Helps, were purchased for £300 and utilized as workshops once the colliery was started. With all the industry further upstream around Cinderford, the Cinderford Brook in the foreground did not always flow crystal clear! *Collection A. K. Pope*

STAPLE EDGE BRICKWORKS

It is likely that Staple Edge Brickworks were started about 1860 by Messrs. James Gollop and James Ridler of Lydney who traded as Gollop & Ridler. They were mainly colliery proprietors who also had a coal merchants business in Lydney under the style of Gollop, Ridler & Co.

Gollop and Ridler were the registered owners of Cooper's Level, Findall Mine Level and Wallsend gales together with the Quidchurch Stone Quarry. They took out a Crown lease to dig clay on 5th March 1860 but it was probably the presence of a good bed of fireclay overlying the Trenchard seam in the Findall gale which led to the establishment of the brickworks. The Crown granted a lease on 17th April 1860 to authorise the taking of this fireclay.

After the death of James Ridler on 30th August 1877, Gollop continued with Ridler's representatives until December 1880 at which time the partnership was dissolved. In October 1881 James Gollop formed a limited company, Gollop & Co. Ltd., which, incorporated on the third of that

month, had a capital of £25,000 in 2,500 £10 shares. The purchase price for the property, to be paid to Gollop, was £12,000 made up of £4,000 in fully paid up shares, £6,500 which was to be used to pay off a mortgage from the Gloucestershire Banking Co. taken out in February 1879, and £1,500 in cash.

The subscribers to the company were James Gollop, who described himself as a colliery proprietor, together with two other members of the family, Francis, a coal agent of Lydney, and Charles, gentleman of Lydney, who both held one share. Henry Rock, gentleman of Lydney, also held one share. The larger shareholders were William Wood and James Wintle Blanch, both mine and colliery proprietors, who held 100 and 50 shares respectively, whilst George Bedson, an iron master from Marple, Cheshire, held 100.

The property listed in the sale agreement included the collieries, the brickworks, several cottages, the Bell Inn at Ruspidge, and sixty-two railway wagons on hire from the

North Central Wagon Co. under a lease dated 15th June 1879. Gollop & Ridler had previously hired seventy 10-ton wagons from the Gloucester Wagon Co. under a 3 year lease dated 9th January 1872. We can safely assume that these wagons worked into the sidings at Staple Edge and Gollops' Siding on the Forest of Dean Central Railway at Howbeach, but, unfortunately, no details of the livery carried by the wagons have been discovered.

It would appear that insufficient shares were sold to discharge the mortgage and in September 1884 the company went into voluntary liquidation. This is probably the date that the brickworks was closed, although one source gives a date around 1880. Records for Cooper's Level, Findall and Wallsend show that during the late 1880s the registered owner was the Gloucestershire Banking Co.

The sidings into the brickworks (two are shown on the 1881 OS 25-inch map) were removed by 1900 and the site was cleared. It is possible that the most westerly of the two sidings was used also in conjunction with the Staple Edge Colliery (marked as 'air shaft' on the 1881 OS). This was started about 1866 by a Mr. Walmer but was surrendered by 1878. The Findall Level was also in this area.

EASTERN UNITED COLLIERY

The Eastern United Colliery gale was one of the seven areas into which the deep gales of the coalfield were amalgamated following the 1904 Dean Forest (Mines) Act. The No. 4 Group, as it was first known, comprised the following gales: United Deep No. 2, Emperor, Extension, and part of Central. The area contained six veins, estimated to contain 41,000,000 tons of coal which it was hoped would give the colliery a working life of 200 years if 200,000 tons were extracted annually. The principal seam, reputed to be 5ft thick, was the Coleford High Delf, a steam coal much in demand. The other seams in the gale were the No Coal, later to be worked from Lightmoor Colliery, the Brazilly, Yorkley, Whittington and the Trenchard. The Coleford High Delf lay between the Whittington and the Trenchard.

The gale was granted on 19th March 1906 to James Riley Brown and others forming a committee of Free Miners. They gave an option on the gale to a Mr. Wyatt, but things did not progress well in this direction. Wyatt had interests elsewhere in the Forest and was said to have been forming a company to work Eastern United and the New Bridge Engine gale at Nailbridge to the north of Cinderford. He was also to build a railway and 'do other wonderful things'! The Crown were not impressed and saw little hope of any of his schemes coming to fruition. Indeed, he was unable to come up with the £100 purchase price for Eastern. This may seem a small amount for the colliery but the Free Miners were also to receive one-sixth of the royalties paid to the Crown, the minimum being ½d per ton. This sum was shared out annually amongst the Free Miners.

The Crown were far more interested when Henry Crawshay & Co. Ltd. expressed interest in the gale. When Wyatt was unable to proceed with the purchase, the Committee of Free Miners offered the gale to Mr. R. C. Heyworth, a director of Henry Crawshay & Co. Ltd. In October 1907, Heyworth reported to the Board that he had the option to purchase until 1st December and that he would hand it over to the company if they agreed to pay the £100 before 21st November. By the end of the month, Mr. William Meredith, under manager at the company's nearby and highly successful Lightmoor Colliery, had produced a report on the prospects of the property. The owners of the Findall gale had also been asked if they would allow a level to be driven from their property to enable the working of Eastern United.

Evidently the report was satisfactory as it was decided to pay the £100 purchase price to William Meredith in his capacity of Free Miners representative which gave him a

The site of Eastern United Colliery, seen in early 1909 when work had begun on driving one of the new dipples, or adits. The purpose of the lower archway is unknown, but it might have had some connection with the original Findall Colliery or with the Staple Edge brickworks which had previously occupied the site.
Cty. Margery Oakey

Looking along the Cinderford road towards the lower end of Ruspidge village with the bridge over the FoD branch in the middle distance. Any disruption attracts attention as witnessed here, but no doubt the prospects of an extensive new colliery being thrust upon this little community ensured endless discussion. The parapets of the original road bridge over the branch can just be discerned on the right.

Courtesy Margery Oakey

foot in each camp! The payment did not commit Crawshays to work the gale, it merely gave them the option to do so. The matter of whether to invest or not in its development was to be put before the shareholders in February 1908. The gale was officially acquired by H. Crawshay & Co. Ltd. on 24th December 1907.

The work to persuade the Directorate, and probably the shareholders, began in January 1908 when William Meredith reported to the Board that as house coal seams in the Forest were rapidly becoming exhausted, the coal was getting much more expensive to work. He predicted that within a few years the Forest coalfield would undergo a considerable change with the companies working house coal seams transferring their attention to steam coal from the deeper measures. The Lydney & Crump Meadow Collieries Co. had already secured about 20 million tons of steam coal with the acquisition of Arthur & Edward Colliery, together with the rest of the new North Western United gale. They had also just purchased the Northern United gale which would give them another 20 million tons. The Western United gale was being opened by the Cannop Colliery Co. which expected large outputs in about six years. Meredith estimated that Lightmoor Colliery would last about 20 years as the main seams being worked were rapidly becoming exhausted, but, although its closure was threatened several times during the late 1920s and through

the 1930s, as things turned out, Lightmoor was kept at work until 1940.

Following Meredith's survey of the gale, it was decided that the best method of working the coal would be by driving two 'dipples', or adits, from the outcrop at Staple Edge, Ruspidge, through Cooper's Level gale (then in the hands of the Crown) and the old workings of Findall Colliery. The latter gale was in the possession of the Wallsend Colliery Co. whose chairman, Mr. Arthur Shaw, was approached by Crawshays to see what amount his company would require to give Crawshays the right to work through the gale. The initial offer was £750 but the price eventually settled upon for six acres of Findall gale plus the old Findall, or Walmer's shaft, was £1,000. Acquiring the Findall area and driving dipples avoided sinking shafts. The dipples could be driven from the outcrop into the Coleford High Delf seam where there was a good, solid, rock roof above the coal. About 44 yards above the Coleford High Delf lay the Whittington seam and about 40 yards above this was the Yorkley seam, on top of which lay water-bearing strata. Therefore, if a shaft had been sunk, it would have passed through this heavily watered area and involved pumping, but driving dipples avoided the water.

With the decision taken to drive dipples at Staple Edge, an area of surface land was required for associated buildings and railway sidings. The acquisition of land was completed by December 1908 and included four cottages already on the site which were purchased for £650.

Although it was originally intended to form a separate company to finance the venture, Crawshays decided to work it themselves and issued 6% debentures for £20,000. All were taken up by existing shareholders, the issue being over subscribed to the extent that the company could have raised twice the amount of capital.

Work began on the site on Whit Monday 1909 under the guidance of William Meredith who had been appointed certified manager of Eastern United as well as maintaining his post at Lightmoor. By August it was reported that work on the surface provisions was well under way.

Several items of equipment had been ordered prior to development work commencing, including two boilers and a stack from Messrs. Danks of Netherton, pumping plant from Messrs. Evans & Son, and a steel bridge to carry the colliery waste to the tip on the opposite side of the Ruspidge—Soudley Road. As already mentioned, the colliery itself was situated on the site of the old Findall Colliery which had started around 1866 and was worked by means of a pit, later known as Walmer's Shaft. The shaft was about 70 yards deep and the coal was brought out through a cut-out about 15 yards from the surface. Walmer's Shaft had since flooded to a depth of about 50 yards and work on de-watering it began in October 1909. Work on the new dipples evidently commenced soon afterwards and in December it was reported that the shaft was free of water and that the dipples had struck an old roadway of Findall Colliery. At the Board meeting of H. Crawshay & Co. Ltd. in January 1910, the Secretary reported that having got into the old workings, the thirty or so men working on the number one dipple believed that they should be presented by the company with some beer to celebrate the occasion! They were awarded up to two quarts each but told that it must be consumed off the works.

The *Dean Forest Mercury* for 20th August 1909 gave a description of the intended new works. There were to be two dipples, one on the north side of the old shaft and one on the south, about twenty-five yards apart. The north dipple was to be 8ft wide and 7ft high and used for

The mouth of one of the new dipples, with Mr. W. D. Meredith, the first manager, standing in the centre and Mr. C. J. Morgan, later to become manager, on the left.   *Courtesy Margery Oakey*

travelling and incidental work. The wider south dipple, 10ft wide and 7ft high, was to be used for the main haulage by means of an endless rope system, capable of bringing out 800 tons of coal per eight-hour day. The dip of the roadways was to be 1 in 4, gradually decreasing as the distance from the surface increased. The eventual haulage distance was 1,200 yards with the ropes travelling at a speed of 3½ miles per hour. The carts to be used were to carry from 10-15 cwt each. The haulage was to be powered by steam with a double horizontal engine geared 5 to 1, with 12in diameter cylinders and a 12in stroke. Haulage engines were supplied by Chas. D. Phillips in October 1909 but these may have been smaller ones used for the colliery development work. A winding engine was also to be placed above the old Walmer's Shaft 'for incidental purposes'. Pumping was to be electric, the generating station containing a Bellis and Morcom 2-crank, 2-cylinder, vertical enclosed engine capable of developing the necessary power to drive a 3-phase 400 kilowatt alternator. In March 1910 a small electric pumping plant was needed 'at once' at a cost of £500. In June £750 was authorised for steam duplication of the electrical plant. Two Lancashire boilers (a third was held in reserve), presumably those ordered from Messrs. Danks, were used during the work of opening up the colliery. It was anticipated that it would take about a year to reach the coal face 200 yards down the dipple, and while this work was in hand, developments continued on the surface.

Discussions with the GWR over the provision of railway accommodation had evidently begun during 1908, and by January 1909 it was reported that Meredith's plans of the arrangements had been accepted by the railway company, although the latter required a 'block end' for their brake van and 'a runaway safety switch'. A contemporary sketch plan shows a single siding trailing off the main line in the Bullo direction, with an extended headshunt towards Bilson. An agreement with Crawshays dated 4th January required the colliery to marshal wagons and vans intended for the Bullo direction separately from those for Bilson. Eastern United were charged 7s 6d per hour for any period in excess of 15 minutes spent picking up or dropping off wagons, or any period in excess of 30 minutes if both operations were required. By July 1910 no excess shunting had been recorded, a situation which prompted the Divisional Superintendent at Gloucester to instruct the goods guards at Bullo Pill to make statements of excess time for station master Thomas at Bilson.

In July 1909 application was made to the Crown for the necessary land on which to lay the sidings near Staple Edge Halt and the Board of Trade was also approached to sanction the commencement of the works. Both were granted and the work was reported as complete in September. The formal siding agreement with the GWR, dated 31st August, was for a single connection to the branch with minimal trackage inside the colliery, the GWR, having the power to order extra works if the outwards traffic averaged ten truck loads a day over a period of three consecutive calendar months, or at any time they required after the first three years. The new works were inspected by Colonel H. A. Yorke for the Board of Trade on 6th December 1909 and he reported as follows:

'The line is single and is worked on the electric train staff system.

'The points are operated from a ground frame containing 2 levers, which are locked by the key on the electric train staff.

By the time this picture was taken, probably mid-1910, development work was well in hand, with the lower end of Ruspidge beginning to take on a new look. The steel bridge from the colliery to the dirt mound was supplied by Messrs. A. D. Dawnay & Sons at a cost of £160 and erected late in 1909. The railings were boarded to protect the public from falling debris. The mouth of the South Dipple can just be seen on the colliery bank behind the nearest corrugated iron building. The curved roof structure housed two boilers supplied by Messrs. Danks of Netherton, who also erected the steel chimney stack. The initial private siding connection with the GWR is shown here with the colliery's own sidings obviously still in hand. The headframe and winding engine house on the hillside on the extreme left of the picture were erected over the old Findall shaft. The new brick-built weighbridge house seen through the bridge probably resulted from the quotation received from Messrs. Pooley in March 1910.

Collection A. K. Pope

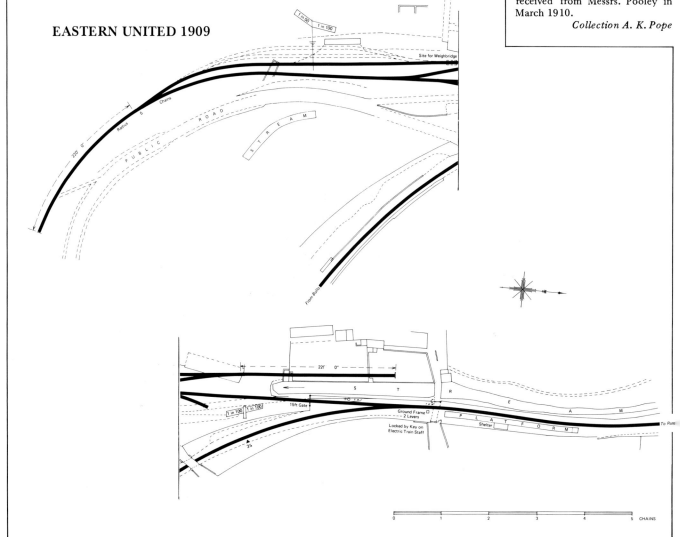

EASTERN UNITED 1909

General View, Ruspidge.

S.&Co.,Cin.

A postcard view of the scattered community of Ruspidge with typical Forest of Dean workmen's dwellings. Work at the colliery has progressed a little further including extra sidings. The brick building on the left with the central door housed the Bellis & Morcom generating plant whilst the two corrugated iron buildings probably housed the haulage engines used during development work. It would appear that coal was being loaded into railway wagons off the bridge to the dirt mound. As the dipples followed the coal seam, a certain amount of coal was produced quite early on, certainly some was being sold as early as September 1910. The plume of steam to the right of the colliery draws our attention to the railmotor just leaving Staple Edge Halt which was conveniently situated for the colliery but probably little used by the colliers. The Feathers public house, the first building on the left on the way into Ruspidge, was also well situated for the colliery.

Collection I. A. Pope

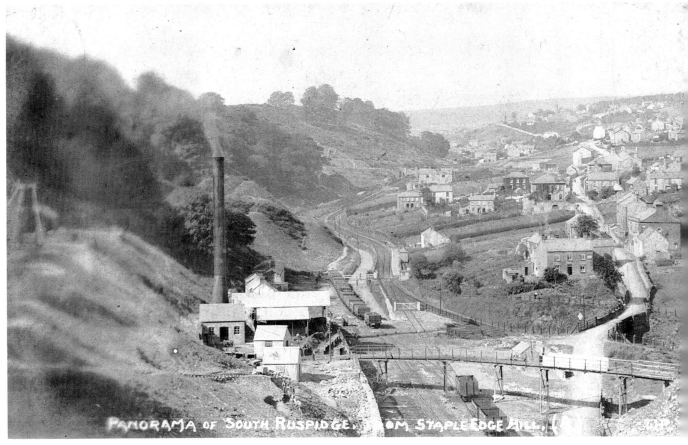

PANORAMA OF SOUTH RUSPIDGE, FROM STAPLE EDGE HILL.

'Owing to the steep gradient at this place it is necessary that all trains doing work at the siding shall have their engine at the lower end, and this the Company have agreed to do.'

The facilities provided at this time can be seen on the plan. It is interesting to note that neither plans nor early photographs show any screens, so it would appear that the wagons were loaded directly from the tubs passing over the bridge which led to the original waste tip. The runaway siding is another feature which cannot be detected in the early photos. The sidings and connections costing £225 sufficed until 1911 when the output exceeded the average of ten truck loads per day over a period of three months.

The first time that the Board minutes of Henry Crawshay & Co. Ltd. record sales of coal from Eastern United was September 1910 when 250 tons of small steam coal, at 6/3d per ton net, had been dispatched over eight weeks, at the rate of 30 tons per week, for Messrs. R. Thomas & Co. in wagons belonging to E. Jones & Son. Presumably this coal was destined for Lydney Tinplate Works. In October there was a further order for 2,500 tons to be delivered at the rate of 50 tons per week, but this time carried in the wagons of R. Thomas, although the order was still placed through E. Jones & Son. Other orders at this time were from the Dean Forest Coal Co. which, on behalf of Messrs. Ralph Preece & Co. of Hereford, ordered 200 tons of block coal for delivery over the next twelve months, and the Stonehouse Brick & Tile Co. for 1,000 tons of rough small over the following six months.

By the end of 1910 the colliery encountered the first of the geological problems that were to haunt it for several years. Having driven dipples through 200 yards of the Findall gale, when coal was cut in the south dipple, with a thickness of 4ft 6in, it only lasted for 10 yards before being pinched out by a washout where the coal, after being about 9ft thick, disappeared completely. The phenomenon was caused where a stream had cut through the marshy area while the deposits were being laid down, thus removing the organic material which later formed the coal. The great thickness of coal on the eastern side of the washout had resulted from being on the inside of a bend in the stream where more material was deposited due to the sluggish nature of the water. Roadways were driven off the main dipples northwards and southwards for distances of up to 1,000 yards and workings were opened out, but only barren ground was encountered apart from the area near the barrier which had to be left against the old Findall workings where the thickness of coal was 13ft. Meredith asked the Board whether they wanted him to go on driving the main dipples as well as driving out cross roads to win the coal. It was decided that he should go on with the main drivages and develop the colliery as quickly as possible. The output for the whole of 1910 was only 8,192 tons.

Crawshays had decided early on that as far as possible all coal from Eastern United should be sold direct to customers rather than through coal factors. Evidently, some wagons must have been lettered up for Eastern United prior to March 1911 when the question was raised of taking

PANORAMA OF SOUTH RUSPIDGE FROM STAPLE EDGE HILL. (B.)

thirty *more* wagons for the colliery. The Lincoln Wagon Co. offered to supply the wagons on a seven year purchase lease at £8 16s per wagon per annum, with the option of purchasing them on completion of the lease for 5/- each. The agreement was signed in April.

Coal sales seem to have continued steadily during 1911, the increased output leading the GWR to invoke the clause in the private siding agreement for the extension of the sidings. In order to carry this out, Crawshays had to purchase land to the east of the branch and convey it to the railway company, divert the Cinderford Brook and obtain authority to divert two footpaths crossing the line. The GWR's estimated cost of £2,803 included slewing the branch to make space for a loop siding and a new signal box, the amount being paid in three instalments, one prior to work commencing, one on completion and the final one after twelve months had elapsed. The cost was to be refunded to Crawshays in the form of a rebate on traffic charges for ten years, or, until the actual cost was covered.

Work on the sidings does not seem to have progressed very quickly, probably because Crawshays were reluctant to spend more money than necessary while the colliery was in difficulties. The main dipples were still being driven forward, the thickness of coal in the face of the southern heading being given as 3ft, whilst to the south of the heading it was between 3ft 6in and 4ft. It was not until September, however, that coal was struck in the north heading, coming in at 2ft 6in on the 21st, and it was June 1912 when plans were sent to the Board of Trade showing

A panoramic view of Ruspidge, produced as a pair of postcards, showing the course of the Forest of Dean branch passing the colliery. It was not until November 1911 that the East Dean Rural District Council's surveyor called the attention of H. Crawshay & Co. to the fact that their dirt mound was tipped over the council's main sewer leading from Cinderford to the outfall works at Soudley. Crawshays had constructed a culvert under the mound and it was thought that new pipes for the sewer could be put through this if the council would pay for the work and also an annual wayleave. Naturally, the council were not too keen on this and suggested that Crawshays should pay half the cost. Several upturned carts can be seen on top of the mound in the foreground, which is remembered locally as smoky, sulphurous and very unpleasant. Eastern United coal was reputed to be so easy to burn that a fire could be lit without using wood. The coal was not generally sold locally but the colliery charged local people for the privilege of picking coal from the waste tip. This was of poor quality and full of stones but found a ready market in the area as it was cheaper than coal from a merchant.

Collection I. A. Pope

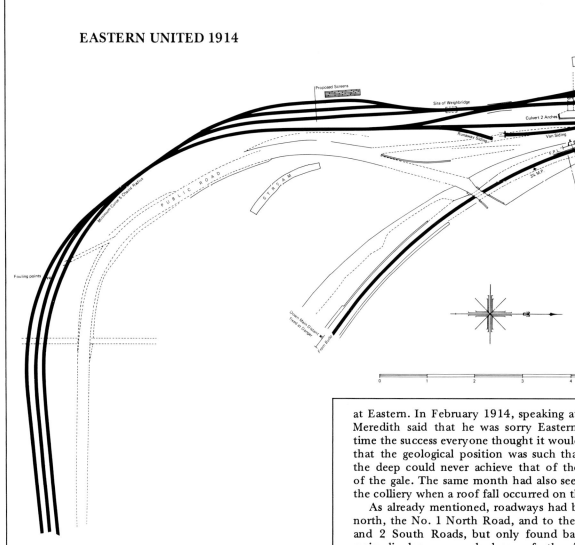

EASTERN UNITED 1914

the new proposals, and even then the company did not hurry, new screens not being ordered until September 1912. The works were reported as complete to the Railway Inspectorate in March 1914 and the necessary inspection was carried out by Colonel Von Donop:

'At Staple Edge Halt a new goods loop has been provided on the west side of the single line. The points and signals are worked from a new box containing a frame of 17 working levers and 4 spare.

'On account of the gradient on which the halt is situated it has been arranged that trains shall not be accepted simultaneously in both directions.

'Arrangements satisfactory.'

It would appear that the box and the loop were brought into use prior to Von Donop's inspection, both being in use in December 1913. The improvements to the colliery yard can be seen by reference to the 1914 track plan.

In April 1913 the new manager, Mr. Charles J. Morgan, reported that the colliery was 'doing very badly'. Morgan had been appointed in September 1912 with Mr. William Smith as under-manager, Meredith instead concentrating on Lightmoor, although he still continued to advise on matters

at Eastern. In February 1914, speaking at a local function, Meredith said that he was sorry Eastern was not at that time the success everyone thought it would be, pointing out that the geological position was such that development in the deep could never achieve that of the western portion of the gale. The same month had also seen two fatalities at the colliery when a roof fall occurred on the 5th.

As already mentioned, roadways had been driven to the north, the No. 1 North Road, and to the south, the Nos. 1 and 2 South Roads, but only found barren ground. The main dipples were pushed on a further 730 yards, also in barren ground, and other roadways were taken off. The Nos. 2 and 3 North and No. 3 South were pushed about 300 yards out but here the strata appeared to have been crushed and buckled, forming a series of rolls, or washouts, so that the coal was unworkable and development work was stopped. At the end of the main dipples, the Coleford High Delf, which had been about 18in thick, suddenly stopped against an upright face of rock.

In April 1914 quotations were invited from contractors to drive the dipples on as fast as possible for a further 300-400 yards. In June, Morgan was advocating the use of mechanical power in the form of rock drills to drive the headings faster. Morgan's report in July revealed that the pitching of the strata in the face of the dipple was still upright and that until it got into the normal position, 'it was impossible for anyone to say where the coal lay and whether we were in the right ground or not'. In the absence of coal, it had been decided to carry on driving the main dipples, with the south slightly ahead of the north, at the original inclination of 1 in 3 in the hope of finding the coal again. After 70 yards of driving through vertical rock, they came across a seam of coal 18in thick, then more vertical rock, and 50 yards further on heavy feeders of water were encountered.

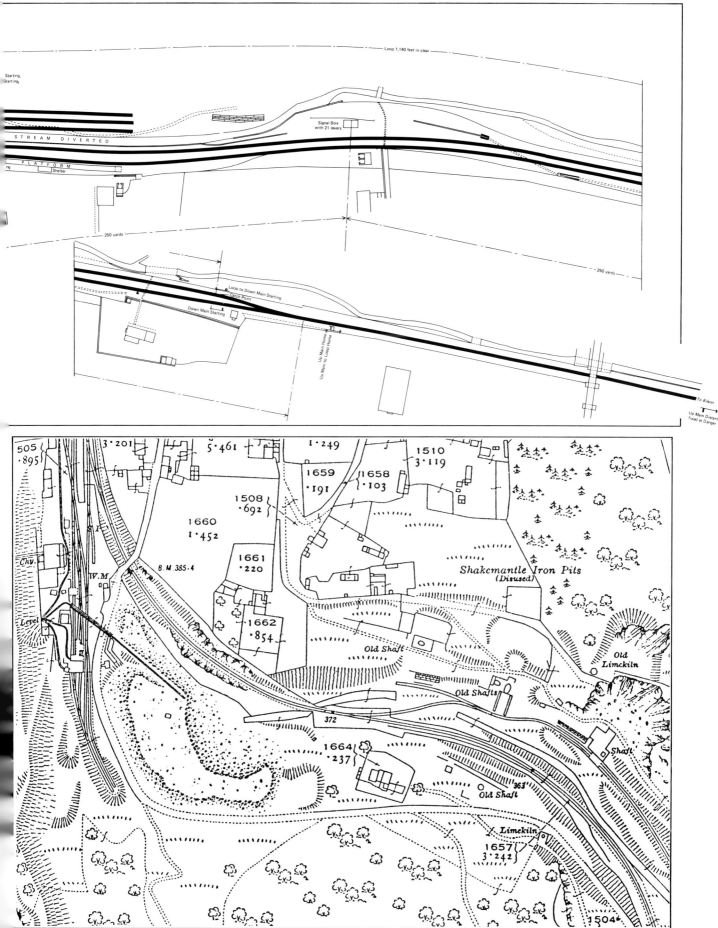

Loop 1,140 feet in clear

Starting,
Starting₂

STREAM DIVERTED

Signal Box
with 21 levers

PLATFORM
ng   Shelter

250 yards

250 yards

Loop to Down Main Starting
Catch Point

Down Main Starting

Up Main Home
Up Main to Loop Home

To Bilson
Up Main Distant
fixed at Danger

505
·895   3·201   5·461   1·249   1510
3·119

1659   1658
·191   ·103

1508
·692

1660
1·452

Chy.   B.M.385·4   1661
·220

W.M   Shakemantle Iron Pits
(Disused)

Level   1662
·854

Old Shaft

Old Limekiln

Old Shafts

372

Shaft

1664
·237

363

Old Shaft

Limekiln
1657
3·242

1504

Taken from 25-inch Ordnance Survey of 1922. Crown Copyright reserved.

The Geological Peculiarities of the Strata at Eastern United
taken from the Iron and Coal Trades Review, 21st January 1916.

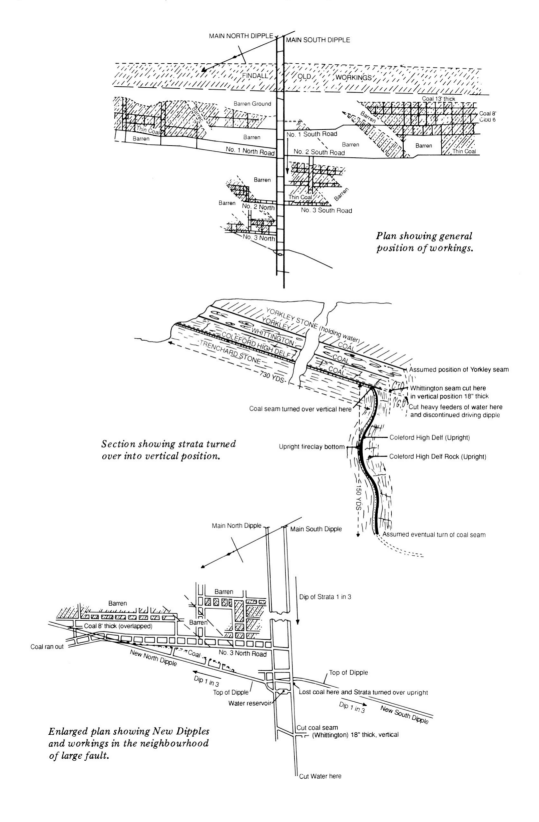

Plan showing general
position of workings.

Section showing strata turned
over into vertical position.

Enlarged plan showing New Dipples
and workings in the neighbourhood
of large fault.

The problems at Eastern were such that several other colliery managers were invited to inspect the situation, among them being T. H. Deakin of Parkend. The Deputy Gaveller, Forster-Brown, also gave the matter some thought and in October decided that Crawshays were not necessarily correct in assuming that the coal had gone up in an anticline, and suggested instead that if they had been driving along the top of an anticline, the coal would be below them. In January 1916 Charles Morgan presented a paper to the newly formed Forest of Dean branch of the National Association of Colliery Managers, giving the history of the development of the colliery and its difficulties. Later in the month it was reproduced in *The Iron and Coal Trades Review*, by which time the true geological position at the colliery had been established. When the coal ran out in the main dipples and the vertical wall of rock was encountered, it had, at first, been assumed that it was the underlying Trenchard rock, but it proved to be the overlying Coleford High Delf stone which, together with the seam, had been driven back under the original seam by some 10 yards. The Deputy Gaveller's theory had proved to be correct as the dipples had reached the Staple Edge Monocline where the coal had gone down about 200 yards vertically. In October it was reported that difficulties were being experienced in working the Coleford High Delf seam which, in November, was described as being 'irregular' and said to cover 1,945 acres. By this time the outlay had amounted to some £53,000 with the colliery losing about £10,000 per year. Meredith had reported that they were driving down a slope in the coal between the fireclay and the rock. The coal had every appearance of going down vertically and it was hoped by that means to get down to the true pitching of the coal. Two new dipples were driven, one to the north and one southwards, falling at 1 in 3 virtually at right-angles to the main dipples, but keeping to the fracture which proved to run at an angle of about 55° NE and SW. To the north the folding in the strata was so severe that several times the coal was found completely upside-down. By January 1916 the New North Dipple was down 400 yards (about 133 yards in vertical distance) and the New South Dipple 250 yards.

By November 1916 fortune had turned and it was said that the colliery was looking very well with 5ft of coal in the heading. The coal had levelled out and roadways were driven out westwards as far as the barrier of the gale from the new dipples which were down to the natural pitching of the coal.

In February 1917 the Chairman of Henry Crawshay & Co. expressed great satisfaction with the engineers and the way in which they had developed the colliery. Perhaps this was more a question of great relief that at last things looked brighter, although it was tempered by asking the manager why the bottom dipple was being driven on so slowly! By November 1918 output had reached 100 tons per day for the first time in eighteen months, but the colliery lost money again in December, due, it was said, to difficulties in overcoming water, and the interruption of Christmas holidays. The loss continued with expenditure exceeding receipts by £1,547 16s 6d in January.

Finance was on the agenda again in July 1918 when it was reported that the boilers were in a very bad state. The middle, or No. 2, boiler was being repaired by the British Arc Welding Co. at an eventual cost of £161 12s 8d. The No. 3 boiler required a total outlay of £232 5s 0d whilst No. 1 boiler needed attention to the tune of £525. The damage was caused by the water at Eastern, so, to alleviate the problem, the boiler feed water was taken from the pond at Lightmoor via a new pipeline. At the same time a new Lancashire boiler was ordered from Messrs. Galloway at a cost of £1,042.

By September the colliery was back in profit and in April 1919 it was announced that it was in a position to output 200-250 tons per day but there was not enough machinery to bring it to the surface. The following month it was decided to install another endless rope haulage system to enable the extra output to be achieved.

In May 1919 Mr. Arthur Morgan, one of the Directors of Henry Crawshay & Co., who lived at Abbotswood House,

An Eastern United 12-ton wagon photographed in January 1914, part of an order for twenty wagons placed with the Gloucester Railway Carriage & Wagon Co. Ltd. and numbered 354-373. The wagons were provided on seven years redemption hire at £16 5s 6d per wagon per year. Crawshays did not purchase many wagons from Gloucester and this is the only order directly recorded as being lettered 'Eastern United'. The first mention in Crawshays' minute books of wagons for Eastern United is in March 1911 when thirty wagons were ordered from the Lincoln Wagon Co. (see page 138). *GRC & W Co.*

asked if he could be connected to the Eastern United electricity supply to light his home. This was agreed to and it was also decided to run cables to W. D. Meredith's house, The Villa, at Ruspidge. This was accomplished by June and over the following years several more of Crawshays' properties were added to the pole route and supplied with power.

That June Eastern was threatened by the anticipated stoppage of the adjoining Wallsend Colliery. If pumping ceased, there was a risk that Eastern would be flooded once Wallsend had filled with water. In July it was decided that if Wallsend Colliery could be acquired in conjunction with the other collieries similarly threatened, then Crawshays would spend up to £5,000 in doing so. In the event, Wallsend was purchased jointly with the Park Colliery Co., owners of Norchard Colliery near Lydney, and Richard Thomas & Co. A new company, Howbeech Collieries Ltd., was set up to work the colliery.

In July Charles Morgan stated that things were difficult at the colliery as he could not get sufficient men. He was hoping that once the new machinery arrived (this had been on order since the previous September) he could maintain an output of 500 tons per day, although he doubted that the existing screening plant could cope. September saw an inrush of water which nearly overcame the pumping plant. Virtually all the available power from the generating plant was absorbed to the extent that there was nothing left to power the haulages. This spurred the management into visiting both Messrs. Mather & Platt and Bellis & Morcom to hurry along the new generating plant which was on order. They met with success and the following month the plant was being installed. A sheerleg, which broke as the new armature was being lifted into place, caused damage and further delay.

By December the underground haulages had been converted from direct to endless rope systems, thereby allowing a quicker movement of the tubs which were clipped onto a continually moving rope instead of being marshalled into 'journeys'. For the half-year concerned, the colliery lost £14,799, so it no doubt came as a relief to the directors when Charles Morgan reported in January 1920 that he wanted just a few more months to get the colliery back in order.

The question of the screens arose again in March 1920 when the 'elaborate' screening arrangements were cited as unsatisfactory. Only 'Block' and 'Through' coal was being produced and there was a breakdown almost every week. The screens were of the shaker variety where the coal passed over a grid of woven iron netting which was shaken by a small steam engine or electric motor via eccentrics. The size of hole in the grid increased through the screens so that the dirt and small coal fell through first, and the varying grades followed in order. It was felt that the grades of coal being output at Eastern would be better produced over a bar screen where the coal slid down a number of bars placed side by side, the distance between them determining the size of coal produced. This system, which was an older design, was also the cheapest as no means of shaking the screens was required. The Board ordered plans to be drawn up and obtained quotations, but it is not known whether the work was carried out. If it was, the problem was not resolved as in October 1922 it was again said that improvements were necessary. This time it was thought that the answer lay in adding travelling picking belts where stone and dirt could be removed by

hand after the coal had been graded through the screens. Again it is not known if this was done, but it is unlikely to have been carried out at once as the matter of reconstructing the screens was raised again in August 1923 when it was left to Arthur Morgan to do so 'when considered necessary'.

The inadequacy of the screens was probably highlighted by the increased output from the colliery, and the siding provision was also put under considerable pressure. In July 1921 the GWR began pressing for increased payment for siding maintenance and in September also wanted to impose a charge of 25 shillings per hour for the time their engine was engaged in shunting at Eastern in excess of the 15 minutes allowed in the siding agreement for putting in or taking out traffic, and 30 minutes if both operations were performed. Crawshays told the GWR that they would not pay any such charge and that the railway must take their engine out of the colliery yard at the expiration of the allotted time. The effect of this on traffic is unthinkable and in December Arthur Morgan reported on a meeting at Paddington at which it was agreed that any maintenance charges would be waived and that a nominal £1 per month would be charged for extra shunting. After a visit to Eastern by GWR officials in February 1923, it was decided that the charge would be dropped completely.

Connection to the electrical supply provided by the West Gloucestershire Power Company from their power station at Norchard near Lydney (see *The Severn & Wye Railway, Vol. 1*, Pope, How & Karau, Wild Swan, 1983) was a considerable improvement. The purchase of electrical current instead of generating their own had been under discussion since 1921, when it was considered that a supply might be obtained from the Hereford Corporation. Negotiations had previously been opened with the new West Gloucestershire Power Co. after a quote had been obtained in September 1922, and it was found that Eastern could generate its own power more cheaply. In February 1924 the Power Co. reduced the rate quoted and an agreement to take their current was signed in May. By October all of the necessary plant was in place; one of Eastern's generating sets (Sissons) was sold off, the second being kept as a standby.

In February 1925 Charles Morgan was promoted to assist the Managing Director, Arthur Morgan, and handled most of the commercial matters. The manager's post at Eastern was filled by an under-manager from Lightmoor, P. K. D. Trotter. One of his first tasks was to begin the opening up of the south side of the colliery from the South Dipple. Previously all development work and coal-getting had been concentrated on the north side towards the boundary with the undeveloped Northern United gale, due to the easier geological ground for winning coal.

In March Trotter suggested that a steam brake be fitted to the haulage engine on the South Dipple for safety purposes as this was the engine by which the men were conveyed in and out. However, in May the Mines Inspector condemned the entire haulage for the conveyance of men. A new haulage was consequently ordered from the Uskside Engineering Co. of Newport during December for the sum of £1,000.

Also in December Arthur Morgan said that he would like to see the colliery further developed by the provision of additional siding accommodation, increasing the electrical plant and by opening up the south side. He believed that these measures would make Eastern United a first class

Eastern United Colliery, Ruspidge, Nr. Cinderford. 1190

The area around the mouths of the dipples c.1924, showing the original screening arrangements enabling wagons to be loaded on two roads. The wagons visible here belong to the Dean Forest Coal Co., Crawshays' Lightmoor Colliery and Baldwins of Bristol. The screens were in line with the north dipple mouth in front of the building housing the dipple haulage engine. The hip-roofed brick building on the left housed the steam winding engine for haulage on the south dipple from which a journey of carts is emerging. The building work in progress to the right of the screens was for the enlargement of the power house, probably to take electrical switchgear and distribution boards connected with the use of electricity supplied by the West Gloucestershire Power Co. rather than electricity generated on site. The corrugated iron building alongside the power house accommodated the boilers. This picture provides another view of the headframe over the old Findall, later known as Walmer's shaft, on the bank above the buildings, together with a small fan house, used to ventilate the underground workings, and the winding engine house. *Collection N. Parkhouse*

colliery, second to none in the district, although works of such scope would cost a large sum of money.

Trotter's period as manager ended in January 1926, when he resigned in order to move to London and manage a branch of his family's business. The Directors were sorry to see him go but wished him well in his chosen new career. In his place they appointed Mr. W. E. ('Ted') Oakey who had also been an under-manager at Lightmoor. He was strongly recommended for his new post by W. D. Meredith as he knew the district and got on well with the men. Ted Oakey was born in Cinderford and began work at Foxes Bridge Colliery. He studied for his manager's certificate at Wigan before returning to Lightmoor. He had a brother Oliver who also became a colliery manager in the Forest, having charge of Cannop after J. J. Joynes.

It was not long after Ted Oakey's appointment in February that he was pitched into the problem of managing the colliery during the General Strike. It would appear that, due to the regard in which the company was held by the men and their personal friendship with both Meredith and Oakey through sporting and Free Mining activities, not all of them came out on strike and some who did so returned to work very quickly. No coal was worked during June but

the horses remained underground and in consequence had to be exercised regularly. Those who remained were employed on this task and in keeping the roadways clear and in good order ready for a resumption of work. In July it was reported that 'some few men' had returned to work at Eastern, and on the 22nd it was hoped that five or six truckloads of coal would be got away. Despite the resumption of coal-winning, and consequent income from coal sales, the colliery lost £479 9s 6d in July. Money did not come in instantly as the majority of sales were on 30 days terms. By 26th August, 356 men were back at work, but the management were not prepared to start a second shift again at that stage as the men would have to go to and from work in the dark, risking intimidation and perhaps worse from other colliers still on strike. The threat had receded by mid-September, when 554 men were working, and the second shift was reintroduced. The difficulty then was sharing out the coal produced amongst the factors who were clamouring for it. It was decided that the fairest system was a percentage basis according to how much trade the factor did with the colliery prior to the strike.

Unfortunately, Crawshays' minute books do not reveal either the tonnage of coal produced or the average profit

A similar view to that on the previous page but taken after the enlarged power house had been completed. Whilst the boiler house alongside had been extended, it would appear that this was a temporary measure; perhaps one of the boilers was moved to give room for the growing power house, but once the use of electricity was well established, a boiler was removed. It would seem that one boiler was always kept in steam, probably as an emergency back-up. Beyond the bridge to the waste tip a journey of carts can be seen at the mouth of the north dipple. The chimney to the left of this was for exhaust steam from the winding engine whilst the taller stack to the right of the power house provided the draught for the boilers.

Courtesy Margery Oakey

per ton for Eastern at this period. What is certain is that the colliery was making record profits which enabled the development cost of the colliery to be written off. From soon after the start of the colliery, the amount of money expended in development was recorded as a running total in the minutes. Once coal was produced at the colliery, the value of sales was deducted from the development cost, so the total does not reflect the full amount spent on opening up the works. The maximum sum recorded was in July 1922 when £96,474 12s 9d stood against the colliery. By January 1926 coal sales had reduced this figure to £58,400 and it then reduced steadily until in September it stood at £41,463. After this, with the money coming in from coal sold both during and after the strike, it tumbled down and was totally cleared by December, after which the colliery was making money for the company.

Although the months after the strike were a boom time in terms of the profit made, the situation was not to last, and difficult times were ahead for Eastern United as with many other collieries. One of the first indicators came in February 1927 when it was reported that the Cannop Coal Co. intended to break away from the Steam Coal Collieries Association in the Forest and sell their coal free from any control. It was anticipated that they would offer coal for as little as 14 shillings per ton as opposed to the usual 18 shillings. It was therefore decided by Crawshays that if Cannop took this step, then they would reduce their prices to a slightly lower figure rather than lose any orders. As the coal was easily sold at the higher figure, it was felt that Cannop were giving the customers four shillings unnecessarily. After several meetings of the Association, they managed to persuade the Cannop management to stay their hand for a while but the problem was not going to go away.

The question of the difficulties encountered in shunting the sidings at Eastern came up again in March when Sir Felix Pole, General Manager of the GWR and a friend of

Arthur Morgan, together with a group of GWR officers from Gloucester, examined the site at Eastern. Their attention was focused at the south end of the sidings where it was decided a connection could be made to the branch. Plans were drawn up at once and available in time for Crawshays' board meeting the following month together with an estimate of the cost. Although during the visit Pole had intimated that the GWR would bear the expense of the alterations, they now wanted Crawshays to contribute two-thirds of the estimated £12,000. After some haggling, the railway reduced their demand to £5,000 but this was also rejected, Crawshays seeing £2,000 as their maximum contribution. The railway countered, a Mr. Ford claiming that the GWR had done more for Eastern than for any other colliery on their system and pointing out that if his proposals were not accepted, then a charge of 17s 6d per hour would have to be made for shunting beyond the agreed time. The proposed siding scheme was fully explained by Mr. W. D. Meredith who pointed out that, although it offered a perfect system, it involved the expense of moving the screens to the site of the boilers which would therefore also have to be re-sited. With the prospect of such a massive upheaval and expenditure, it is no wonder that Crawshays were not prepared to proceed with the scheme, especially when the Board considered that a large proportion of the expenditure would go on straightening the Forest of Dean branch to the benefit of the Great Western. In early May 1927 Arthur Morgan visited Paddington to explain that they would make their own arrangements to provide the accommodation required under the siding agreement and that this would be done by extending the empty wagon roads at the south end.

At the same time as applying to the Crown for the land to extend the sidings, Crawshays sought extra space for tipping ground. The area between the Cinderford–Blakeney road and the Cinderford Brook had become full, and after a meeting with the Deputy Surveyor, it was decided that a

A group of the colliery's office staff standing in front of two wagons belonging to Lowell Baldwin & Co. This company, formed soon after the First World War, were factors and became large customers both at Eastern United and Lightmoor. The company was reconstructed in 1921 as a limited liability company with a capital of £40,000. The tall figure, third from the left, is Lowell Baldwin himself.

M. Buffrey

patch of ground to the south of the colliery at the top of Staple Edge hill could be used. The work on extending the sidings, at an estimated cost of £2,000, and on the new tip space, were in hand by the end of May.

The sales of steam coal came onto the agenda again in May when it was reported that the Cannop Coal Co. had forced the price of coal down unnecessarily. They had brought the price of small steam coal down from 16s 6d per ton to 15 shillings and of large steam from 23 shillings to 18 shillings a ton. Cannop apparently took the view that the coal was too dear for the country and wanted to give other industries a chance — a rather philanthropic attitude not necessarily in the best interests of other collieries in the district.

When the annual accounts for Eastern for 1926-7 were published in July they showed a profit of £74,824 of which £10,000 was set aside for future developments. Work was continuing on opening up the south side of the colliery and, although Meredith thought it would take two years to get down to the coal, Arthur Morgan expressed the view that every effort must be made to reach it in twelve months. Opening up the south side would mean that the output of the colliery could be doubled and the cost of production decreased. It was hoped that in two years the output of the colliery would reach 1,500 tons daily, at which point Crawshays would be in a position to deal with any cutting of prices by firms such as Cannop. Despite undercutting by other companies, Eastern often won contracts at higher prices than its competitors due to customer loyalty and to hard bargaining on the part of Arthur Morgan. Customers in the first category included the likes of Messrs. Cadbury Bros., who took Eastern United coal for use in their factory at Frampton on Severn.

Another blow to Eastern's coal sales was the introduction of new railway rates from 1st January 1928. These were on a fixed mileage basis which gave an edge to collieries such as Norchard, Princess Royal and Parkend as they were situated closer to many of the markets. This advantage amounted to between 6d and 9d a ton, so the main factors trading with Eastern wanted to know how they were going to deal with the question. Arthur Morgan responded by informing the railway company that he was going to allow the factors the difference in the rates and then deduct the sum from the railway carriage account. He hoped this would bring matters to a head and in a flat rate being introduced for all Forest collieries.

The output returns for Eastern United make their first appearance in the minute books in March 1928 when it is recorded that the figures for February were:

Average cost of getting one ton of coal		13s 2.66d
Average selling price per ton		14s 9.45d
Average profit per ton		1s 6.79d
Sales:		
Large coal	7,880 ton 0 cwt	
Small coal	8,600 ton 11 cwt	
Total	16,480 ton 11 cwt	

The figures remained at about these levels until June, when the cost sheets for the previous month revealed that the colliery had made a loss of £886 9s 0d. This brought an immediate directive from the board that Oakey must economise at Eastern as far as possible 'without detriment to the colliery'. The following month the position was even worse with a loss of £1,310 12s 11d, although the figures for the previous year published at the same time revealed a profit at Eastern for 1927-8 of £6,604 8s 5d before deductions. The monthly losses at Eastern continued until a profit of £333 was returned for October. This was probably due to a reduction in the wages bill, but Crawshays' chairman, Capt. Creagh, wanted to see them further reduced. One hindrance to output at Eastern was the shortage of pit carts, and Oakey was promised an extra 50 or even 100 if he could show a profit of £1,000 in one month. This dangled carrot had the desired effect as the profit returned on November output was £1,044, but Arthur Morgan did not live up to his promise and ordered only 25 new carts, adding that with the new provision he would like to see the output increased by a further 100 tons per day as it had dropped off. Oakey replied that he had been watching the situation very closely and believed that there had been some cases of deliberate hindrance to output in the form of 'unexplained breakages' probably due to the fact that he had had to reduce wages throughout the pit. Three men were dismissed as a result of the manager's observations and he hoped that this would bring an end to the problems.

Also in December 1928 an order was placed with the Norton Hardy Co. for a new set of screens for producing four grades of coal. At a price of £2,100, they were supposed to be completed within two months. The order had been prompted by further complaints about the quality of Eastern United coal, Arthur Morgan admitting that the existing screens were probably the worst in the Forest!

By January 1929 trade had taken an upturn and the three working shifts were reintroduced at Eastern. The three shifts were the morning, evening and night and thus in the Forest afternoons did not exist! It was hoped that once the system was fully operational, it would result in an additional 200 tons a day being raised, although an extra half dozen ponies would be required underground to enable this to be achieved. From January through to May, profits of over £1,000 were achieved each month, the highest being £1,640 in the first month. By April the new screens were well advanced with men from the colliery working overtime and weekends to get them finished. However, the short boom did not last and in June a loss of £668 was incurred due, in the main, to working short time. Presumably, the three-shift system had been dropped. Profitability returned the following month and was again over £1,000 in September, and in October over £2,500.

Coal output had increased during the 1920s; in 1920 itself 58,038 tons were brought to the surface and by 1930 this had increased to 239,749 tons. In 1929 over 200,000 tons were put onto the railway which, under an agreement reached with the GWR, entitled the colliery to a penny per ton rebate on its traffic charges. This was agreed to, partially to help offset the difference in the railway rates between Eastern and the other Forest steam coal collieries, but, unfortunately, in April 1930, a letter was received from the GWR's Chief Goods Manager withdrawing the special rates as they were illegal.

In March 1930 it was reported that about 60 tons of coal a week were being drawn out of the South Dipple and development work on that side of the colliery was continuing with an eye to the future. It was predicted that the available coal on the north side had a life of only ten or

The loaded wagon sidings, sometime between 1926 and 1932. Whilst in this view the wagons are berthed according to size of coal, this was rare. During the summer months, when loaded wagons were held in the sidings awaiting an order, it was common for wagons labelled outwards to be scattered about the sidings, thus involving much work with the stationary haulage engine, situated in the brick building directly above the Cinderford Brook, or the railway company's locomotive to pull them out. Wagons in the sidings which can be identified on the original postcard belong to William H. James, a Cinderford coal factor; Renwick Wilton, West Country coal factors; the Dean Forest Coal Co., and Eastern United. The single wagon on the left of the view was on the 'country sales', or landsales, siding alongside the colliery. The row of cottages, which predated the colliery, can be seen on the right. Converted for colliery use, they housed a carpenter's shop, paint shop and blacksmith's shop. The fitting shop was in the taller portion and electricians in the far end. The incline in front of them was used by timber carts, etc. worked by horses up to the dipple entrances. Waste tipping between the Cinderford to Blakeney road and the Forest of Dean branch ceased during the mid-1930s and an incline was built up the hillside in the background to take the waste material away.

Collection Ian Pope

A slightly later view taken from the hillside above the colliery. This photograph, used in a booklet entitled *Fine Forest of Dean Coal*, dates from about 1934 and shows the new loading screens, to the left of which the tub route emerged. From here tubs were either sent straight on to the waste tip or empty back down to the dipple mouth via a 180° curve, passing through the cart shed for inspection, and in the foreground, the empty wagon roads curving sharply around alongside the road.

This picture also provides a glimpse of the West Gloucestershire Power Company's transformer which was installed in 1924 on the bank in the foreground. It would appear that two 500 KVA transformers were initially installed, but they proved unreliable in operation. In August 1926 the No. 1 transformer failed and the steam generating set was brought back into use. This may not have been the first failure as the 'repeated breakdowns' referred to in Crawshays' minutes made the management rather hesitant about electrifying Lightmoor Colliery which would also utilise the Eastern transformers. The No. 1 transformer was returned to its makers, Messrs. Johnson & Phillips, for repair. It was returned during September but failed again after less than 48 hours, and was sent back to its makers. In October it was decided that a third transformer would be desirable and at the same time a duplicate cable from the transformers to the Eastern power house was ordered as a safety measure. In January 1927 the No. 1 transformer was reported to have been returned to the colliery where it failed again after five hours running! In February it was decided to order a 1,000 KVA transformer from Messrs. Johnson & Phillips and a further twelve months guarantee was negotiated on all three. The problem with the two original transformers seems to have been solved by March when Mr. Oakey reported that he was satisfied that the transformers and electrical equipment was generally efficient. With the delivery of the 1,000 KVA transformer, the two 500s were put to run in parallel, again with satisfactory results.

The two small buildings between the transformer and the empty wagon roads housed a haulage engine, used for moving wagons about the yard, and behind is the empty wagon weighbridge provided in 1921. All empty wagons into the colliery were internally inspected to ensure that no foreign bodies were buried under the coal when the wagon passed through the screens. The fuss created when a sackful of tins was discovered when a wagon was being unloaded at its destination is still remembered today. Wagons owned by Crawshays also had their running gear inspected and, if necessary, repairs were carried out by workmen summoned from the wagon repair shops at Lightmoor Colliery. For a small consideration they would also repair wagons belonging to others!

Collection Ian Pope

The c.1926-built screens feature again in this view showing coal being loaded via a belt, after grading, into a Baldwin wagon. By the 1930s, the Bristol-based Baldwin Company, formed by two brothers after the First World War, had become one of Eastern United's larger customers, as were Renwick Wilton and Charringtons. All three firms were coal factors. The 'duff', or dust coal, was taken to paper mills at Keynsham. The 'creeper' on the cart route can be seen to the right of the screens. After emerging from the dipple mouth, a journey of carts was unhitched from the haulage cable by a 'lander' who ran alongside the journey. Once the brake was applied on the haulage engine, the cable went slack and was unhitched from the journey, which continued on its way over a weighbridge. Here each cart was checked by a checkweighman so that the colliers responsible for filling it would be paid their dues. The journey, still moving from the momentum gained from the haulage up the dipple, passed onto the 'creeper', where dogs engaged on the cart axles and hauled them up to the screens where the carts were emptied in a rotary tippler onto the jigger belts. Carts full of waste were taken straight through the tippler and up the dirt mound.

Courtesy Margery Oakey

twelve years unless the Northern United gale, which at the time was undeveloped, could be acquired and worked. A barrier of coal 11½ chains wide had to be left on the northern boundary of Eastern as protection from water in Northern. Crawshays were hoping to work Northern United in connection with the Cannop Coal Co. which, if things worked out, would pump all of the water and leave dry coal in the gale for Crawshays. It would also allow for the working of the coal in the Eastern United barrier. The full history of Northern United is detailed later.

The question of siding accommodation at the colliery arose again in November 1930 when, to hold the number of wagons required for the Eastern traffic, the GWR were contemplating putting three sidings in at Bullo at an estimated cost of £3,500 of which they expected Crawshays to contribute half or, alternatively, to pay 10% of £1,750 a year for ten years. Neither option met with any favour and it was decided that, as all the colliery needed was a sufficient daily quota of wagons put into the colliery, it was up to the factors to pay for the sidings if they wanted a special selection of empty wagons. The matter continued to be discussed until April 1932 when the GWR decided to let the question rest until further difficulties over wagon supply arose.

The winning of contracts was concerning the management again in October 1932 after Cannop Colliery had installed a dry-cleaning plant for their coal. Serious thought was given to installing one at Eastern in order to compete, but on the other hand, Cannop were compelled to sell their dry-cleaned coal for at least one shilling per ton above the going rate.

The outlook for Eastern was good, if only the necessary trade could be found, but the introduction of a nationwide Government instituted quota system in the Forest soon proved a further handicap. In December Eastern United was forced to lie idle for upwards of a week because the quarter's quota was exhausted, but unfortunately the period corresponded with a patch when the company had ample orders to keep the colliery at full work. Protests were made to the Forest of Dean Executive Board about the quota for Eastern, which was based on output figures for 1929. The company also complained about being fined 2s 6d per ton on the excess produced in the last quarter as they had already almost exhausted their allocation for the current quarter. The quota, or standard tonnage, could be transferred from one colliery to another and the Forest of Dean Coal Owners Association had agreed that this should be done freely, but the colliery with the largest amount of unused quota, 7-8,000 tons, was Cannop, and a request to them for the transfer of 2,000 tons met with an offer to sell it for 6d per ton. One of the hindrances to successful negotiations was that Henry Crawshay & Co. had left the local association, so it was decided to rejoin as it might be useful to them. In June 1933 representatives of all colliery owners in the district, except Cannop, held a meeting at which it was decided to apply to the Government for additional standard tonnage for the whole district. It was also decided that Parkend Deep Navigation would transfer about 1,500 tons to Crawshays, and that Crawshays should pay the £19 5s 0d fine imposed for excess production and rejoin the Coal Owners Association to fight their case from the inside. At an executive board meeting Cannop maintained their attitude towards their quota and decided to allocate just 60% of the standard tonnage for the next quarter. For Eastern United this meant that only 2½ days

per week could be worked at a time when they were producing 1,000 tons a day. Cannop, which was only working two days a week at the time, were trying to make things uncomfortable for everyone else and were cutting prices drastically in order to get business. One contract in particular, the Ross Gas Co., which had always been supplied by Eastern United, were quite happily paying 20s 11d per ton for large coal. Cannop now quoted 17s 6d per ton and were warned off by Crawshays who made it clear that if they took the contract then Crawshays would not respect any business reserved for Cannop. In July 1934 it transpired that Cannop had applied to increase their quota by a further 5,000 tons, to which everyone objected, and the matter went to arbitration where their application was turned down.

In October 1934 it was thought that the installation of a coal crushing plant at Eastern would prove an advantage in enabling them to compete with Cannop and Princess Royal collieries, which already had similar equipment. It seems that customers wanted coal 'about 7in cube' and were prepared to pay the same rate for it as for large coal. However, it was difficult to keep up with the flow of orders for small coal when the colliery was only working three or four days a week, and when about 35% of the coal produced was large. On days when the colliery was not working ('play days'), the cost to the company was anything from £100 to £120. Even if all of the large coal was crushed, the difference in price would only amount to about £75 a day. Further enquiries revealed that only about 15% of the large coal was in fact over 7in in size and it was thought that this could be dealt with by the installation of a plate in the screens with a 7in mesh, which was already on order. Nevertheless, the board decided that further enquiries should be made about the cost of crushing plant. In November it was suggested that a wagon load of coal should be sent to each of the firms producing coal breakers in order that tests could be made to find the most suitable equipment. In December a representative of the Nortons Tividale Co., makers of the screens, went down to Eastern to inspect the site and asked that 20 cwts of coal be sent for testing purposes, and in January the expenditure of £900-£1,000 on a breaker was authorised.

This was not the only alteration to be carried out to the screens at the time as consideration was being given to the problems posed by a big fall for the coal when loading. At first, Nortons Tividale suggested an arrangement of rubber bands to reduce the fall, but then came up with the idea of a pulsating jib for the loading of the large coal and nuts. The cost per jib was £140, and in February 1935 it was decided to install one as an experiment. However, the jib idea was abandoned in March as the belt could not be raised sufficiently to extract the small coal, and so the rubber bands were reintroduced. These were in use in April but still the drop of 18in was too great and 6in was more desirable. It was not until August that it was decided to obtain a new loading belt for the large coal and reduce the drop to 9in. In the same month it was reported that the coal breaker was in use and helping to avoid the congestion of stocks. This must have eased the situation, as in July coal sales had been poor and loaded wagons awaiting an order from a customer had been stabled on sidings around the area (see page 21).

In April 1936 Messrs. Lowell Baldwin Ltd., one of the largest coal factors trading at Eastern, complained that they had lost at least £150 due to the inability of Eastern United

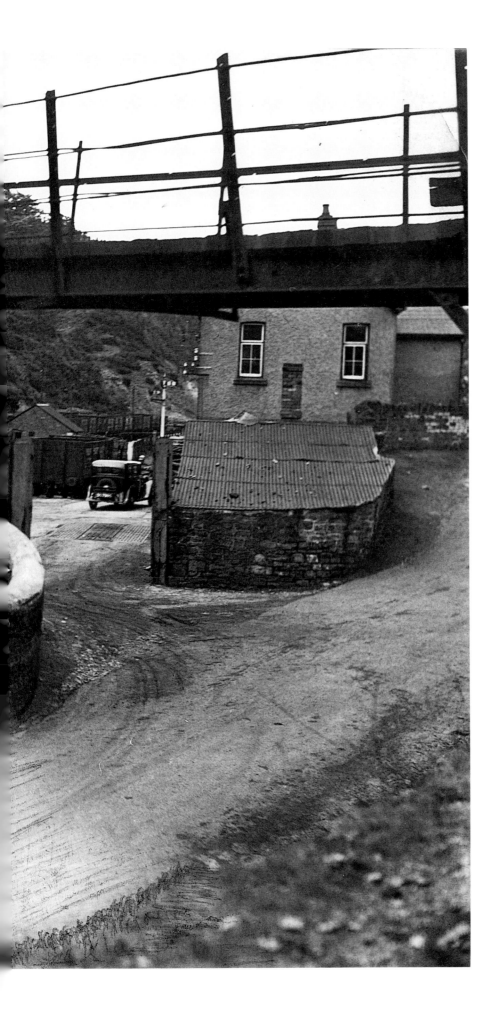

A view through the colliery gate into the yard c.1935, showing how the bridge, which led to the original dirt mound, had been cut off where it crossed the sidings, and the usual scattering of bicycles left by colliers who cycled to work. The front of the enlarged power house can be seen on the left, with the boiler now alongside. The lean-to on the boiler house in front of the power house contained a donkey pump to feed water into the boilers. Steps descended from the hole in the retaining wall, leading to, it is believed, a pump which took water from the colliery's drainage outfall which led into the Cinderford Brook. The retaining wall was also the place where the 'Butties' stood to pay out their men. The large building in front of the cottages was the chaff house where feed for the ponies was kept. A sawmill was also housed in part of this building. Prior to its erection c.1930, chaff was brought down daily from Lightmoor Colliery by horse and cart. Lorries and carts collecting coal for local delivery were loaded direct from the side of the screens or from wagons on the 'country sales' siding in front of the offices. Sometimes wagons for local trade or workmen's coal were unloaded elsewhere in the yard if there was time to complete the work between trains serving the colliery, and if time ran short, they were unloaded from both sides. The lorry weighbridge can be seen just inside the colliery gate.

Courtesy Margery Oakey

Looking over the colliery fence from the Blakeney to Cinderford road in the late 1930s. The extension to the screens housed a crusher which was added c.1935/6. Large coal was difficult to dispose of, so the crusher was installed to reduce the large lumps to a more saleable size, in an attempt to increase sales during the summer months. Selling coal during the summer was a cut-throat business with a reduction of only a halfpenny per ton being sufficient to capture an order from a rival colliery. If coal could not be sold, the colliery would come to a stand and during the summer only two days a week might be worked. The other days were known as 'play days' and were signalled by blowing the colliery hooter at a set time on the previous day.

Courtesy Margery Oakey

to accept their empty wagons for loading during a recent busy trade period. As Baldwins were such good customers, it was decided to send £100 compensation. In May a letter arrived from the Gloucester District Goods Manager of the GWR, Mr. Calloway, stating that the difficulty of stabling loaded wagons from Eastern had become acute and that the railway company would be obliged to charge 6d per wagon per day after the stipulated free period. Further, they would only accept wagons up to the limit of their accommodation and reserved the right to give notice at any time that no more wagons could be accepted. This worried Crawshays and a suggestion was laid before the Board that three or four sidings could be laid on the site of the Cast House which would provide accommodation for about fifty loaded wagons at a cost, it was thought, of about £2,000.

When in July 1937 the GWR announced that they were not prepared to go on shunting at Eastern free of charge, it was calculated that it would cost Crawshays some £1,000 a year if a charge were made. At the same time the GWR, who had been studying plans for the sidings at the Cast House, came up with a price of £14,685 of which they would pay £7,450, leaving Crawshays to contribute £7,235 which could be spread over seven years.

Crawshays contemplated extending the existing loaded sidings northwards into an old quarry which had been used to provide stone for both surface and underground works at the colliery, but these ideas appear to have been shelved when the problems of gaining access to the site for the removal of spoil, etc., was considered. It would have constituted a serious block to traffic at certain times so the idea was dropped.

Returning to happenings at the colliery, in February 1938 a ballot had been held at the colliery to decide the future of the 'butty system'. Under this arrangement, a contractor and his mate, or butty, agreed with the colliery management to work a certain area of coal for a certain price. They won the coal, loaded it into a tub at the coal face and brought into their workplace any materials necessary for the support of the roof. These materials were supplied by the colliery but had to be taken from the pit top, or 'bank' by the contractor. If two shifts were being worked, then the contractor took one and his butty the other. They were usually assisted by an additional man and a boy.

The colliery owners paid the contractor for the amount of coal brought to the surface on a fortnightly basis and it was up to the contractor how the money was divided amongst his team. Whilst most were probably fair, some kept the largest portion to themselves. Of course, in taking an area or portion of the coal face, the contractors did not know whether the coal would be easy to work or whether it would disappear within a couple of yards due to faulting. If no coal was being produced then no money was forthcoming and weeks of toil could go unrewarded. At times like this, and during the summers when the trade was slack, it was the men employed by the contractor who were laid off as there was normally enough work to keep the contractor going.

The colliery company itself employed very few men directly, those concerned being mainly involved in the maintenance of the colliery and 'ripping', or opening out, roadways and haulage roads.

The result of the ballot was only 54 in favour and an overwhelming 279 against the butty system, which was abolished at Eastern in March. It was replaced with the 'share-up system' but the colliers did not take to it and their discontent affected output. Under the old system there were 180 buttymen in some 60 coal places. They were responsible supervisors who reported happenings to the manager, but now there was no one responsible. It was

The rear of the screens during the Second World War, showing a variety of wagons going underneath. The steel-bodied tubs on the creeper above were first introduced at Eastern in October 1929.
Collection A. K. Pope

2021 class pannier tank No. 2153 engaged in pulling out loaded wagons from the colliery during the 1940s. Loco crews remember the difficulty in getting wagons out of the yard when vehicles labelled outwards could be scattered about in the loaded sidings and only a few wagons could be pulled out at a time.　*J. James*

The 200 road, one of the main roadways equipped with steel arches and overhead electric light.

Courtesy Margery Oakey

A group of ponies underground.
Cty. Margery Oakey

A. B. Clifford (left) and Alf Hodges leaning on a cart at an underground junction. The 'dagger' attached to the rear coupling of the cart was a safety device designed to arrest any wagon running away back down a dipple if the haulage cable broke.
Cty. Margery Oakey

A journey coming up Hale's Train Road on the north side of the colliery and passing through a brattice cloth doorway which aided ventilation. Men who transferred from Eastern to Crawshays' Northern United Colliery were used to a good rock roof like the one shown here. They were always wary of Northern's looser roof. Northern men who came to Eastern believed they stood less chance of surviving the collapse of a solid rock roof.
Cty. Margery Oakey

158

Alf Hodges and Ron Addis seen in a roadway in April 1955.
Courtesy Margery Oakey

Tom Davies at the top of two underground inclines on the south side of the colliery.
Courtesy Margery Oakey

An electric pump in Cooper's pump house with its attendant switchgear behind.
Cty. Margery Oakey

This view, taken in June 1928, was probably close to the coal face with water being directed via the pipe to a sump, from where it was pumped to the surface.
Courtesy Margery Oakey

A group of colliers and a distinguished visitor in Worsfold's Heading. From left to right are J. Worsfold, Sir J. Worthington, Askwith, W. D. Meredith (Crawshays' senior colliery manager) and A. Worsfold. The heading being driven through rock to open up new areas was probably named after these two Worsfolds who were responsible for driving the heading.
Courtesy Margery Oakey

Another view taken in April 1955.   *Cty. Margery Oakey*

Ventilation doors at the top of the endless haulage road in the north side of the colliery. The doors were opened to allow the passage of journeys of carts but closed to divert air through other parts of the colliery, thus ensuring a regulated supply of fresh air throughout the workings. There were doors of this nature all over the underground system, often tended by door boys — young lads employed to open them for a journey to pass through.
Cty. Margery Oakey

feared that the discontent would lead to a strike, but eventually everyone settled down to the new system.

A further jolt came in October 1938 when the Executive Board considered amending the central selling scheme so that, instead of purchasing the entire colliery coal stock in wagons in sidings, they would only take the grades they wanted to meet demand. This meant that the colliery had to hold stocks of unwanted grades, which would have meant great difficulties at Eastern and may have produced a stimulus for the Cast House sidings scheme on which no work had been done. Work started soon after February 1939 when the GWR came up with a scheme to reduce costs by 50%. The new works were designed to accommodate 133 wagons and involved the extension of Cullamore Bridge, which once carried a tramroad from Lightmoor Colliery but had since been used only as a footbridge. Some of the work was done by Crawshays, and in August 1939 it was reported that good progress was being made with the sidings and some of the colliery fitting staff were involved in the work.

In September progress was held up awaiting the removal of a permanent way hut and the railway fence, but this had been done by October and in November the GWR laid in three sets of points at the north end of the layout. The following month saw two sets of points fixed at the south end and one siding was completed in January 1940. However, all worked stopped in February as the war had considerably altered the situation. Instead of problems in storing loaded wagons, difficulties were now being encountered in getting sufficient empty wagons. On several occasions during November and December 1939, wagon shortages led to the colliery being idle; indeed, on 5th December when only 45 out of 75 wagons required were delivered, the colliery had to 'play for the day'. The trouble was caused by the wartime pooling arrangements and a visit by the Managing Director, Mr. F. N. Washbourn, to Paddington ensured a good supply being diverted to the Forest of Dean. November and December 1940 saw further

As mentioned in the text, the underground workings at Eastern were beset with geological problems, with the coal ofter disappearing. Here workmen are seen driving a roadway through the rock in search of the Coleford High Delf seam which has been thrown out of its usual position by the movement of the earth. The men were wearing respirators to protect themselves from the stone dust. Coal dust was not a particular problem in the Forest as it was often too wet to be thrown up while being cut. The majority of coal was also cut by hand, a much less dusty operation than using a machine. *Courtesy Margery Oakey*

wagon shortages, but the cause this time was the bombing of vital junctions.

In January 1941 it was reported that £900 had been paid to the GWR for the work on the Cast House sidings and that a similar amount was now due, but as there was no longer any need to stable wagons, the sidings were offered for the use of the railway or the Government. In the event, they were not used by either, nor by the colliery, so the GWR waived the annual maintenance charge and it was not until July 1942 that a siding agreement was signed, at which time the actual cost of the work was put at £1,870. The full scheme was never completed.

To aid production, the first coal-cutting machine, a Hopkinson Minor, had been installed in February 1939 but it did not halt the decline in production which had started in 1938 following a record year in 1937. The start of the Second World War brought new problems for Eastern. Firstly, men began leaving the colliery to work in munition factories where the pay was higher and, secondly, absenteeism became rife. By April 1940 the number of

colliers was down from 450 to 294, but, with the impending closure of Lightmoor Colliery, some men transferred to Eastern, thus easing the situation.

Life for the men was improved when a temporary canteen was opened on the outface on 12th September 1941. On the opening day 720 pies were sold but facilities were not available to make hot tea. A permanent canteen was opened on 3rd July 1942. It was built on land acquired from the Steetley Basic Co. on the opposite side of the Cinderford—Blakeney road and it was intended to extend the buildings to provide pit-head baths in the future.

In March 1942 the under-manager, William Smith, retired at the age of 76. He had been employed by Crawshays since 1887.

In November 1944 a debate began over proving the coal in the 250 acres of ground on the south side of the main dipple. In the early years, headings were driven between the dipple entrance and the No. 2 South Road (see page 138), but found mainly barren ground. Further headings driven on down the dipple were stopped after 10 chains because of

A main roadway with an end-loading conveyor which brought coal from the face for loading into railborne carts. The manager, Ted Oakey, is leaning on the right of the conveyor in this view taken on the day he retired, 30th April 1956.

Courtesy Margery Oakey

These pit-head baths, built on the far side of the Forest of Dean branch and the Cinderford–Blakeney road, were opened on 17th February 1951. The slate roof in the foreground belonged to the colliery office. The edge of Shakemantle Quarry can just be discerned on the extreme right of this view and the cutting of the FoD branch in the right foreground.

Dean Forest Newspapers

A glimpse into the colliery yard in April 1955 with the offices prominent in the left foreground. The men were paid out in the lean-to on the right-hand end. *Cty. Margery Oakey*

FIG. 1: OUTPUT AND PROFIT/LOSS ACCOUNTS

Year	Output	Cumulative Expenditure	Coal Sold	Loss	Profit
1910	8,192	£13,599 11 3			
1911		£16,978 7 2	£7,326 6 5		
1912		£24,819 14 2	£19,586 6 11		
1913	61,801	£37,883 6 1	£28,147 6 11		
1914	45,691	£38,781 15 1	£25,678 12 11		
1915	29,217	In June 1915 it was decided to		£6,095 7 10	
1916	19,752	place whole of loss or outlay on		£2,702 19 2	
1917	19,258	Eastern to the debit of profit or		£11,964 19 10	
1918	35,791	loss account as a loss.		£5,328 16 9	
1919	46,660				£2,038 15 9
1920	58,038			£10,578 17 11	
1921	34,646			£8,631 0 1	
1922	74,146			£1,887 6 4	
1923	138,148				£11,607 18 2
1924	134,600				£17,986 14 8
1925	105,642				£10,049 4 1
1926	115,357				£9,103 14 3
1927	173,085				£62,368 5 6
1928	184,192				£6,414 16 9
1929	221,839				£4,425 7 11
1930	239,747				£21,433 6 10
1931	206,899				£22,893 6 2
1932	197,864				£18,816 16 2
1933	203,001				£16,988 1 0
1934	223,179				£20,319 16 1
1935	255,187				£23,376 4 10
1936	268,533				£37,776 2 1
1937	283,666	Thereafter merged with Northern United Colliery			
1938	234,479				
1939	226,029				
1940	217,107				
1941	197,140				
1942	195,298				
1943	191,799				
1944	178,781				
1945	162,349				
1946	168,524				
1947	171,601				
1948	169,210				
1949	158,107				
1950	134,959				
1951	144,834				
1952	150,882				
1953	141,841				
1954	119,471				
1955	112,187				

the high cost weighed against the likelihood of barren ground. A lot of coal still lay untouched in the vertical strata where it was 13-15ft thick for a depth of 200 yards throughout the area of Eastern United. This would yield thousands of tons of coal; the only problem was working it in the steep pitching. The company were in something of a quandary over whether or not to prove the coal with the impending nationalisation of the coal industry. Crawshays did not want to spend their money proving something which would be of benefit to others, yet they did not want to be accused of hiding the true reserves.

By March 1945 both Eastern and Northern United were working towards each other in the barrier of coal between the two collieries, and thought was given to co-ordinating the work. It was agreed that Eastern should work the majority and that a small barrier would be left to hold back water from Northern, thus making an underground connection impracticable.

By 1946 all major decisions at the colliery had to be sanctioned by the Coal Board and in December Eastern's manager, Ted Oakey, was reminded that he was to get all available coal from underground before midnight of the 31st to ensure that it stood to the credit of Crawshays. The company was also anxious that cut coal, won at Crawshays' expense, did not pass to the National Coal Board.

On 1st January 1947, ownership of Eastern became vested in the National Coal Board, but output had peaked ten years earlier, and by now the colliery had seen its best days.

Eastern's production costs rose with the combination of declining production, geological difficulties and the amount of water which had to be pumped out of the workings. Pumping gear capable of handling 4,000 gallons per hour had been installed to deal with the water problem but the deposits of coal were the real weakness. With an average thickness of only 3ft 6in, they were too thin, often faulted and broken. This meant that a promising seam could

The main colliery entrance, again seen in April 1955, with the board proclaiming Eastern United as part of the National Coal Board's South Western Division.
Courtesy Margery Oakey

Looking over towards the colliery from the end of the platform of Staple Edge Halt during the mid 1950s. On arrival at Eastern, a train of empties ran into the loop on the right. It then reversed through the GWR boundary gates and into the short siding beyond where the brake van was left. After drawing forward, the empties were propelled hard up into the empties sidings. Then, because of the restricted headshunt, the loaded wagons were collected from the loaded sidings in groups of 6-8 wagons at a time and formed up onto the brake van, which had presumably been gravitated out. When the whole train had been assembled, it was propelled hard against the gradient of the loop where, once the engine was clear of the colliery exit, brakes were hastily pinned down. Once this had been achieved, it was quite usual to be held there for half an hour or so before being signalled away for the descent to Bullo. The cinder foot crossing was used by the few colliers who travelled to work on the train.

M. Rees

Harry Furber at Eastern with his shunter's pole.
M. Rees

suddenly disappear and not be found again until after several days unproductive work. At times the angle of the coal was so steep that it was both slow and laborious to win.

In an attempt to find more workable coal, new headings were driven in the direction of Blakeney, with 14ft high roadways, steel archways and electric locomotives for haulage. When a good seam was found, the future seemed bright and Eastern was regarded as the best pit in the Forest. The end, however, came suddenly.

Following a production meeting held in Cinderford to discuss the best way to work the new reserves, several of the men walked into the town centre only to be met by a newspaper placard pronouncing 'Eastern United to Close'. This was a severe shock to the men, but the colliery closed as from 30th January 1959.

A description of the colliery in its latter days appeared in the *Dean Forest Mercury:*

'Eastern United runs all the way from Ruspidge to Parkend, a matter of several miles, while the North side reaches nearly to Northern United.

'The men sit on the hard sides of the metal trucks and the motor, unwinding its cable from the drum, allows them to run into the steep tunnel. Above it is a signal wire, by pulling on which it is possible to call an immediate halt. And in the walls at intervals of ten yards are manholes designed to give a safe refuge if things go wrong. The early part of the descent is electrically lit and weird fungoid growths can be seen hanging eerily from the timbers, but very soon the light bulbs cease and only the individual lamps of the men lessen, but do not defeat, the utter blackness.

'The first tunnel runs down for 800 yards and then there is another slope of 700 yards. Thence the tracks lead off to the coal faces, most of them carrrying lines for the trucks. The longest road is now equipped with 50 hp electric locomotives, battery powered and capable of moving heavy loads . . . Conveyor belts move the coal from the face to the trucks, the moving surface fabricated at great expense from fire proof material. And although some of the coal was won by hand right up to the end, much of the work of the pick and shovel had been eliminated. Mechanical cutters burrowed into the seams and a great deal came down when the face was blasted. Strong flail-like arms forced and shovelled the lumps onto an elevator and thence it passed to the belts and trucks.

'Steel arches had replaced the wooden pit props.'

About 80 men were retained for the underground salvage which was completed by August. Their hearts were not in the job and much machinery and equipment was left underground when the mouths of the two dipples were finally blocked up, leaving the dark warren, where 900 men had once been employed, silent and deserted.

The Forest railmotor pulling away from Staple Edge Halt on its way to Cinderford on 6th July 1946.   *L. E. Copeland*

A Newnham-bound railmotor at Staple Edge Halt on 4th August 1947. The retaining walls either side of the Cinderford brook were built in 1913 when the water course was diverted in connection with the new goods loop.

L. E. Copeland

In the years around 1957 the FoD branch was often worked by a pannier tank with a couple of pensioned-off main line coaches instead of the usual auto-trains. Here a Cinderford bound train is seen leaving Staple Edge Halt and about to pass Eastern United Colliery signal box.

D. Gardner

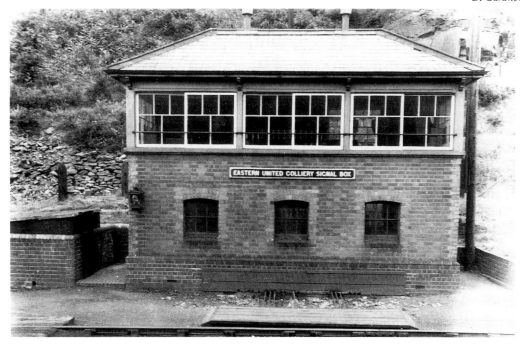

Eastern United Colliery signal box, shown here on 13th June 1933, became a source of dispute between Crawshays and the GWR when in October 1914 an account for £53 6s 7d was received for six months up-keep of the new box. The GWR had originally asked for £98 which Crawshays considered far too much so the Board expressed great satisfaction that the secretary had already been successful in getting the amount reduced! In January 1915 another account was received from the GWR for the sum of £39 9s 10d for the period up to 31st December 1914 but, as no further communication had been received over the previous demand, nothing was done about this one. It was not until June 1915 that a letter was received from Mr. C. A. Roberts, Chief Goods Manager of the GWR, with amended terms. Although it was agreed to pay £88 6s 7d together with £35 per half-year for the upkeep of the box (the next half-year was to be considered due on 30th June, and would continue until such time as the railway provided switching out apparatus in the box), this was not the end of the matter, for in July 1916 there were still problems over the signal box. It seems that a meeting had been held with a Great Western official, which was described as being 'most unpleasant', and no decision had been arrived at. Presumably the problem was still over payments, but no more details are recorded.

L. E. Copeland

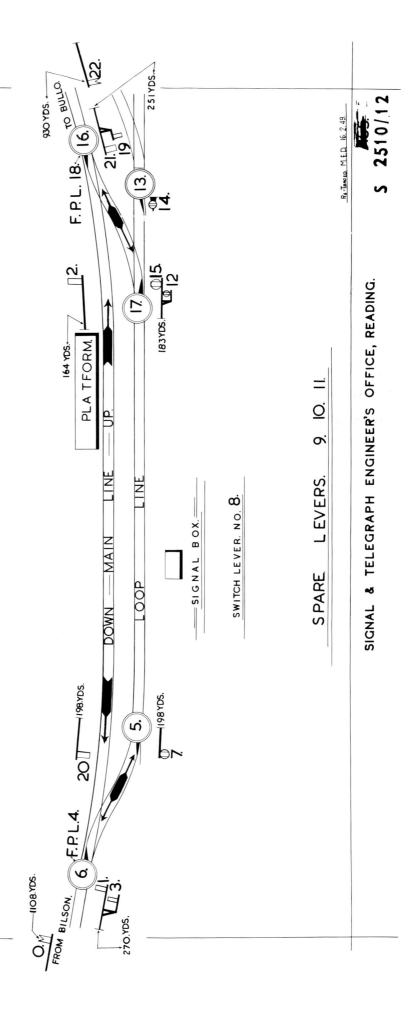

EASTERN UNITED COLLIERY.

PLATFORM.

DOWN — MAIN — LINE — UP.

LOOP — LINE

SIGNAL BOX.

SWITCH LEVER. NO. 8.

SPARE LEVERS.   9.   10.   11.

SIGNAL & TELEGRAPH ENGINEER'S OFFICE, READING.

Re-Traced. M.E.D. 16.2.49.

S 2510/12

F.P.L. 18.

TO BULLO.

930 YDS.

251 YDS.

164 YDS.

183 YDS.

198.YDS.

198 YDS.

F.P.L. 4.

FROM BILSON.

O.M

1108. YDS.

270.YDS.

A later view of Eastern United Colliery signal box, its lamp hut and coal store, on 8th June 1962. The timbered area in the foreground was a trolley run-off point. The two sets of single line token exchange apparatus, one for each direction of travel on the main line, were rarely used because the signal box was switched 'out of circuit' for most of the time. *Keith Allford*

The interior of the signal box on 4th April 1962 showing the token instrument for the section to Bullo West box. The short handle is No. 8 lever, which worked the electrical switching between long and short section token working — 'switching out'. The lever frame was extended (in connection with the installation of the Cast House sidings?) from 21 to 23 levers, numbered 0—22. *Keith Allford*

The northern end of the passing loop at Eastern United Colliery on 8th June 1962. The empty track bed on the left is the remains of the Cast House sidings provided in 1940 but never used (see page 159).

Keith Allford

The course of the old tramroad across the top of Cullamore Bridge, leading to Lightmoor Colliery which can be seen on the horizon. After removal of the tramroad the route was used daily by a horse and cart bringing feedstuff to the Eastern United horses from Lightmoor prior to the erection of the chaff house at Eastern. *L. E. Copeland*

MEERBROOK SIDING

In March 1857 the South Wales Board received a letter from Henry Crawshay requesting permission to remove the points and siding at his Cinderford ironworks and re-lay them to serve Meerbrook Quarry. This was agreed to and a rate of 6d per ton was levied on stone from the quarry up the line together with 'the usual charges for stone to Bullo'. In his submission to the Board, Crawshay said that 200-300 tons might be taken which suggests that, initially at least, the stone was to be used for a specific purpose, probably at the ironworks. The length of time that the siding remained in use is unknown but it had been removed by 1902.

Some of the Cast House sidings were still in situ when this picture was taken from Cullamore Bridge on 6th July 1946. The site of Meerbrook siding was obliterated by the provision of Eastern United loop. *L. E. Copeland*

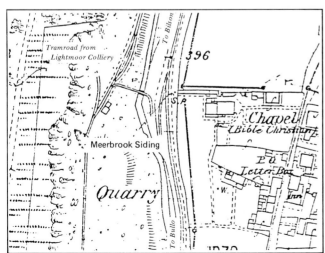

Taken from 25-inch Ordnance Survey for 1878. Crown Copyright reserved.

Two more views of Cullamore Bridge, again taken on 6th July 1946. The original timber beams of the span over the FoD branch were replaced with second-hand girders in December 1923, Henry Crawshay & Co. contributing £10 towards the cost. There is a local story that a horse fell off the bridge and was killed by the fall. Being too heavy to haul back up, it was buried where it lay. The lower view shows sidings on the Cast House site passing through Cullamore Bridge.

L. E. Copeland

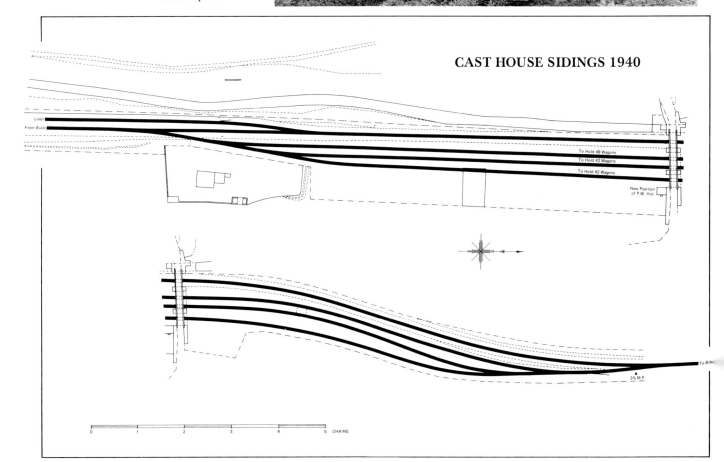

CAST HOUSE SIDINGS 1940

Loop
From Bullo

To Hold 48 Wagons
To Hold 42 Wagons
To Hold 42 Wagons

New Position of P.W. Hut

To Bilson

3¼ M.P.

0   1   2   3   4   5   CHAINS

An earlier postcard view of Ruspidge as seen from Little Staple Edge. The cast house can be seen on the right of the picture, beyond Cullamore Bridge. *Collection N. Parkhouse*

Ponies from Eastern United in a meadow alongside the railway, just south of Cullamore Bridge. In 1913 the Cast House was being used to stable ponies used at the colliery. *Courtesy Margery Oakey*

Looking north from alongside the course of Lightmoor Colliery tramroad in the late 1950s, with a two-coach train approaching the Ruspidge down distant signal. *Don Gardener*

This shaded approach to Ruspidge level crossing, seen on 8th June 1962, was at the top of a 1 in 58 climb which levelled out through the station.

Keith Allford

On the same occasion, looking in the opposite direction down the bank from Ruspidge level crossing, with the Eastern United up distant in the foreground. It was unusual for a 'worked' distant signal to be provided on a single line on the GWR; 'fixed' at caution was the rule. At Eastern United working distants were provided because the box was usually switched out and all trains then ran on the 'straight line', requiring no special reduction of speed. In fact the distant signals could *only* be pulled off when the box was switched out. *Keith Allford*

Ruspidge station, 4 miles 5 chains from Bullo, looking towards Cinderford in June 1922. A 'lock up warehouse and crane' were authorised for 'the Cinderford Station' in April 1866 for an estimated £65. Subsequently, in April 1878, £60 was authorised for a (replacement?) crane. Officially called Cinderford station, the locals apparently referred to it as Cinderford Bridge station, as confirmed in the local paper of 12th November 1886 which reported 'Early yesterday morning an engine from Bullo ran into the railway gates at Cinderford Bridge Station and made matchwood of them'. When a 'new goods station for Cinderford' was opened on 1st December 1884 at Whimsey Sidings (see Volume 2), it was named Cinderford and 'the present Cinderford station' became 'Ruspidge'. When the line was upgraded for passenger traffic in 1906-7, the existing station and platform at Ruspidge was adapted for passenger use, the goods office being converted into a waiting room. The goods accounts at Ruspidge, which included traffic dealt with at Soudley furnace crossing, Soudley siding, Shakemantle and Eastern United Colliery, were transferred to Bilson Junction from 1st March 1910. The lamp in the foreground may have been the one moved in March 1910 to 'a more convenient position'.

H. J. Patterson Rutherford

RUSPIDGE HALT

The former goods office in use as a booking office and waiting room, equipped with both railway and public telephones. The corrugated iron lamp shed can just be seen at the far end of the building. Prior to the upgrading of the line in 1906-7 and the resignalling necessary for the introduction of passenger services, the Forest of Dean branch was worked by train staff and ticket with two sections, Bullo—Ruspidge and Ruspidge—Bilson, the staffs being square, painted blue, and round, painted white, respectively. The 1895 working rules stated that every down train from Bilson had to stop at Ruspidge to pin down brakes. Trains had to draw down to Ruspidge as soon as they were ready to leave Bilson and had received the train staff or ticket. They had to stop at Ruspidge clear of the level crossing and wait for instructions from the station master or officer in charge to start for Bullo. The 'pick-up' was allowed to leave without 'line clear' as it had to call at the intermediate sidings but had to stop dead 150 yards outside the Branch Home Signal at Bullo. The load was not to exceed twenty wagons from Ruspidge. 'Line clear' could not be given for any train to leave Ruspidge within twenty-five minutes of any up passenger train being due to pass Bullo. *Collection A. K. Pope*

The 3-lever ground frame on the platform controlled the Up and Down distants and gate bolts. This picture shows the frame manned by porter Cyril Dymond in the 1930s.
Collection A. K. Pope

178

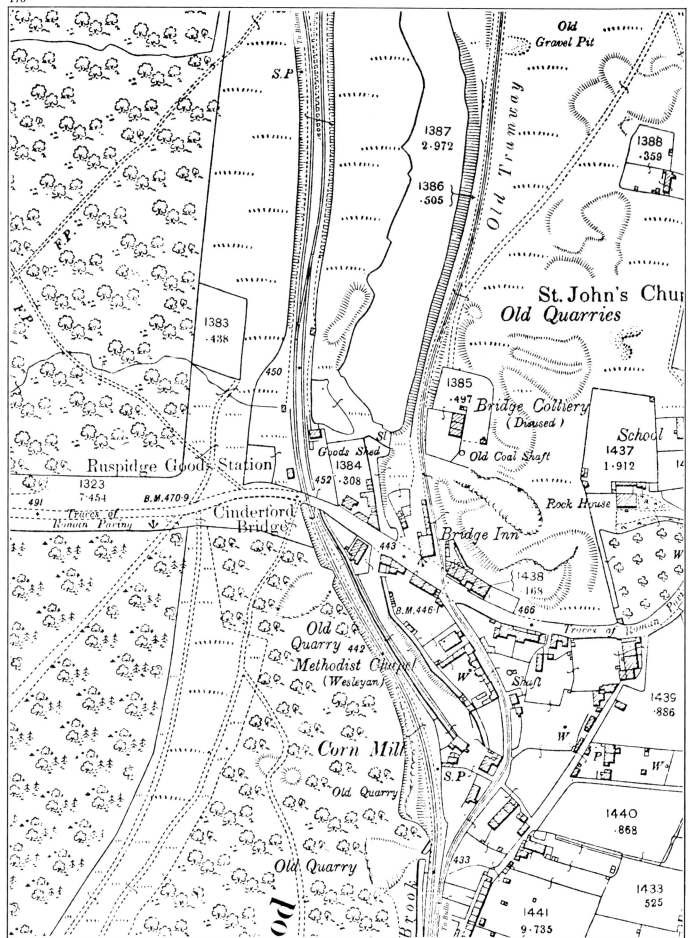

Taken from 25-inch Ordnance Survey of 1902. Crown Copyright reserved.

Local people leaving the train
which had just arrived from
Newnham on 24th August 1946.
L. E. Copeland

Guard Fred Tarling with a brake
stick on the platform at Ruspidge.
Collection A. K. Pope

Cinderford Bridge

CDD. 24

A 1950s postcard view over the level crossing, looking along the road from Speech House to Littledean through the area known as Cinderford Bridge, some of the earliest settlement in the area. Ruspidge is off to the right; Cinderford Bridge itself, over Cinderford Brook, is just beyond the garage, and the course of the old tramroad ran behind the Bridge Inn on the corner. The large house amongst the trees at the top of the hill was the Villa, the residence of several of Crawshays' employees.

Collection I. A. Pope

The entrance gates to Ruspidge goods yard feature on the right of this 1960s picture of a train of Berry Wiggins tankers crossing the road on the way to the depot at Whimsey. *A. K. Pope*

On Wednesday, 11th March 1959, 24-year old Gareth Jones found the brakes didn't hold on his 1939 car which he was driving down the hill towards Cinderford Bridge. "I could see that I should have hit either one of the side pillars or the middle of the gate itself. I chose the centre of the gate . . . I found myself on the line and about 30 yards to my right I saw the goods train coming." According to Harry Trigg, the fireman on No. 8701, the shout from his driver, Bill McOwen, for brakes and sand prompted him to look out of the cab in time to see the driver of the stranded car returning to lock his vehicle! The accident delayed the train for one hour. *Dean Forest Mercury*

Ruspidge station on 12th July 1956.

H. C. Casserley

The stone building at the end of the platform was part of the original provision at Ruspidge, but its purpose is unknown.

D. Clayton

Taken a few minutes after the picture on page 179, this view shows the railmotor receding into the distance on its way to Cinderford. The ballast siding had been situated on the trackbed alongside the running line, veering away to the right through the cutting apparent in the distance above the roof of the platelayers' hut. The connection to the goods siding (facing towards Bilson) dated from 1939, prior to which access had been via the ballast siding, or 'Ballast Hole' as it was known by loco crews. The goods siding was generally served two or three times a week. The point was worked locally from a ground frame released by the token for the section and not from the lever frame on the platform.

L. E. Copeland

CINDERFORD BRIDGE COLLIERY

It has not been established when work commenced on this gale. Prior to 1838 it was held by Moses Teague, possibly in conjunction with the Cinderford Iron Works further north, but whether any coal was won is uncertain. By March 1841 Teague had died and the concern was bought by James Cowmeadow who was also working Addis Hill Colliery and had an interest in Tormentor Colliery.

In September 1842 Cowmeadow applied to enclose one and a half acres of ground on which to store timber and erect pay and other offices, stables, smiths, carpenters and other workshops. To support his need for the buildings, he pointed out that the pay office was necessary as, following the Act which forbade the practice of paying colliers in public houses or beer shops and stopped the employment of women in mines, he had to have a paying-out point. The sketch map which he supplied to the Crown delineating the area of ground he required also showed Cinderford Bridge Pit 'now being sunk down to the coal', suggesting that little work had previously been done on the gale; certainly no coal was being won from this point.

In June 1843 Cowmeadow was granted the right to work the adjacent Celestial Colliery in order to continue the Cinderford Bridge Colliery in the Coleford High Delf vein south-westward as far as the north-east boundary of the Findall Mine Level.

By April 1848, after Cowmeadow's death, the Crown was pressing his widow Elizabeth for the payment of rent arrears. She pointed out that they still owed her £10 for a pit which her husband had sunk at the Crown's request to see if any coal had been worked under the proposed site of St. John's Church c.1842-3. The Deputy Surveyor had not been content with just sinking a shaft near to the site, but had a heading driven a short distance, which, according to Elizabeth Cowmeadow, made the sum due more like £20!

The gale was disposed of to a Mr. Wagstaff who, in May 1854, applied to build a broad gauge siding off the South Wales Railway's Forest of Dean branch. This was to curve away from the branch in a south-easterly direction, crossing the end of the pond which once served Soudley ironworks, and then divide into two sidings before reaching the pit, crossing a remaining portion of the tramroad on the level. A Mr. Crawshay, who claimed ownership of the mill (Cinderford Mill) below the pond, objected, claiming that

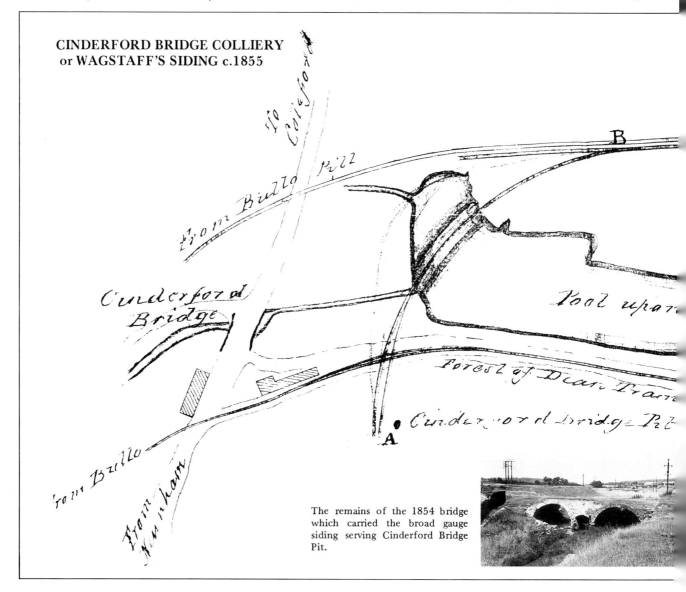

CINDERFORD BRIDGE COLLIERY or WAGSTAFF'S SIDING c.1855

The remains of the 1854 bridge which carried the broad gauge siding serving Cinderford Bridge Pit.

The centre of this 1930s [?] view from behind Ruspidge Halt features the colliery manager's house, now converted to 'Wagstaff House'. The broad gauge siding serving Cinderford Bridge Colliery had curved away from the running line to terminate in the vicinity of the ramshackle yard. St. John's Church is on the skyline.
Collection A. K. Pope

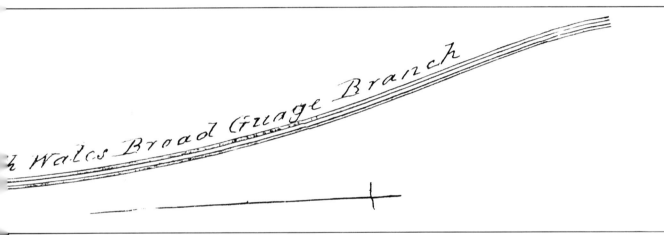

by putting an embankment across the end of the pond, the works of the Cinderford Iron Co. would be liable to flooding.

The mill building and wheel had formerly been conected with old workings on Cinderford Bridge and were used for drying coal. A lease and licence to convert the building into a corn mill was granted to a Thomas Brace in 1819. The pond was made by the Cinderford Iron Co. circa 1826 by constructing a dam about a quarter of a mile below an existing one. The mill was purchased by Moses Teague and subsequently by the Cinderford Iron Co., not by Crawshay alone. At this time the mill had two sets of stones of about 4ft diameter.

By June 1856 the Cinderford Iron Co. and Wagstaff had come to an agreement over the siding which, it would appear, was built soon afterwards. Correspondence from Wagstaff at this time is on paper headed 'Cinderford Collieries Office' at 36 Cannon Street, London.

Problems with Cinderford Mill arose again in September 1857 when the mill building, which by this time belonged to the Crown, and the mill house, which still belonged to the Iron Co., were damaged by subsidence from Cinderford Bridge. Wagstaff appeared in court as the defendant in an action brought by Stephen Allaway on behalf of the Iron Co. who successfully sued him for the damage to the buildings.

Wagstaff was not only having problems with the Iron Co. Early in 1858 his pump broke which stopped him winning coal. Claiming that he had spent about £28,000 on the works, he attempted to persuade the Crown to reduce his arrears of dead rent. It seems he owed £115 and on 3rd April that year it was reported to the Crown that the bailiffs were in at Cinderford Bridge.

A sale of plant and equipment was arranged for 6th April, the notice reading:

'Sale of railway plant engine machinery of Cinderford and Bilson Green Collieries. Included were 19 Adams and Co. Registered Railway Coal Trucks, Muck Waggon, 22 Coal Trams, 40 Pit Carts, 3 Working Pit Engines (complete), 5 Weighing Machines, Wire Guides and Ropes, Large and Small Crabs, Ropes and Chains, Railway Plates, Pullies, Working Tools, New and Old Iron Blacksmiths Forges and Stock, 4 Sets of Harness, Horse Cloths and other valuable Effects.'

The Bilson Green Colliery mentioned was the Old Leather Pit.

However, the debt for which a distress order had been issued was paid, so the sale did not proceed, but the debt to the Crown was not settled and continued to grow until in June 1859 it had reached £149. This was broken down as follows:

On the Cinderford Bridge Gale	£105 0 0
On the Celestial Steam Coal Gale	1 10 0
On the Richard Whites Gale	37 10 0
On the Whites Delight Gale	5 0 0

It would appear that Wagstaff may have gained an interest in the last two gales mentioned around 1855 but details are unknown. The only property on which goods were available for sale under a distress order was at Cinderford Bridge.

A sale was arranged for 30th August 1860 at 'Bridge End Colliery' where there was 'one engine, two boilers, crab etc. etc.' and at the 'Garden Pit', south of Cinderford Bridge Pit, was 'one engine, one boiler etc. etc.' The sale, however, was abandoned when Wagstaff deposited his bond with the Gaveller. It was also stated at this time that Wagstaff was about to lease the Moseley Green New Engine gale on Moseley Green from a Mr. Corbett. The lease of this colliery may have had something to do with the fact that Wagstaff was chairman of the Forest of Dean Central Railway Co. Ltd. which was building its line between Awre Junction on the South Wales Railway and Howbeech which was just south of Moseley Green.

Wagstaff's financial problems were coming to a head. In August 1862 it was reported that Messrs. Child & Co. had lent Wagstaff £1,000 in January 1858 secured against his properties. In January 1861 Wagstaff was adjudged a bankrupt and on 29th August 1861 an order for the sale of his properties was issued. It was pointed out that the total purchase monies which did not exceed £900 did not even pay off the capital of the debt.

The next period in the history of the gale is rather hazy. It is likely that the sale went through and that the purchaser was a Mr. John Vincent. In August 1862 there was a renewal of a lease to a Peter Plumley. By August 1876 Vincent wished to surrender the gale if it could not be disposed of. A schedule of the machinery included:

> Winding Engine: single cylinder horizontal of 60 hp. [The cylinder was 16in diameter by 5ft stroke. It had a 10ft flywheel and two 8ft diameter flat wire rope drums working first motion.]
> Pumping Engine: details as per the winding engine but with a 4ft spur wheel and an 8ft cog wheel with crank motion connected by rod to a 'T' bob. [The engines were stated to have been erected about 1855 and in work for about five years. Both were in a fair state of repair.]
> Boilers: Three egg-ended, two 29ft x 5ft, other 27ft x 5ft — all in a good state of preservation.
> Pit Framing: Single pit headframing with 9ft sheaf. A single deck cage in iron and wood. Two 3½in flat wire ropes, one 100 yards in length, the other 140 yards. Round 1¼in wrought iron pit guides. A counter balance wheel 9in in diameter. 150 yards of tram plate (underground) of about 24 lbs per yard. [The pit framing and the cage were reported as rotten.]
> Colliery Sidings: old GWR broad gauge laid without sleepers. A broad gauge 24 ton weighing machine by Pooley's. A switch and crossing. [The siding consisted of about 4 chains double road and 1 ch 50 links of single. The weighing machine was apparently 'much out of repair'.]
> Buildings: Carpenters shop, blacksmiths shop, offices and engine house [all of which had a slated roof].

These buildings, which were mostly under one roof, were in a dilapidated condition. The office was being used by a person named Marfell as a dwelling house. The range of buildings eventually became known as Wagstaff House and was probably built under a Crown licence dated 11th August 1854, when Wagstaff applied for an area of land to build a dwelling house with stables and offices.

The old tramroad course behind the Bridge Inn, with Cinderford Bridge Pit building in the background.
B. Baxter, cty. Railway & Canal Historical Society

It was observed that there were no trams or tools belonging to the colliery as they had been disposed of some years before. The shoots for tipping small coal into railway wagons had rotted away although the walls themselves were still in good condition.

It would appear that the sale was not arranged as both Cinderford Bridge and the Celestial Steam Coal gales were forfeited to the Crown in February 1878.

The gale was re-granted on 11th June 1906 to a Henry Fox and nine others. They had originally applied for the re-grant in February 1878 immediately after the forfeiture. On 14th July 1906 they assigned the gale to William Llewellyn Davies and P. Evans. It would appear that Evans assigned his interest to a Hugh Harries. In February 1914 they were granted a reduction in the dead rent from £20 to £10 per year on the grounds that the gale was mostly covered by houses and that it contained large quantities of water. Some work was probably being carried out at this time using a pit sunk opposite the Forge Hammer Inn at the end of Victoria Street. However, they recently had to pay heavily for surface damage caused by subsidence.

In April 1916 there was a conveyance from Hugh Harries to James Harries who in November 1919 also gained William L. Davies's interest in the concern. What work was done on the gale is unknown and it was surrendered on 11th June 1926. The Deputy Gaveller decided that it would not be re-advertised due to the amount of housing on the surface above, but, despite the fact that no advertisement appeared in the local press, a Charles Jenkins successfully applied and held the gale until 23rd February 1929.

There were 891 applications for a re-grant of the gale in May 1929.

CINDERFORD IRONWORKS

When erected in 1795, the furnace at Cinderford was the first in the Forest to use coke for smelting iron. Behind the concern at this date were Thomas Teague, George Teague and George Martin, who had invested about £3,000 to build the works. Unusually, the site they chose was not against the side of a hill, which would make charging such a furnace so much easier. Instead an incline was built to take the raw materials to the furnace top. Furthermore, no authority was sought for the erection of the works, yet despite several attempts by the Crown to get the work stopped, construction went ahead. It would appear that the furnace was first blown in about 1797 but, as with several other furnaces in the Forest, a high output could not be achieved with a make of only about twenty tons per week, although the quality of the iron made was said to be high. According to Nicholls in *Iron Making in the Forest of Dean*, published in 1866, a Mr. Bishop, who was later connected with the ironworks, believed the low total was occasioned by the 'rude and insufficient character of their arrangements'. Moses Teague, writing in 1827, put the problem down to the nature of local iron ore and the unsuitability of the local coal for coking. Whatever the cause, the works could not compete with other iron-making districts and the furnace was blown-out in 1806.

The ironworks lay idle and decaying until July 1827 when the Office of Woods received a letter from Moses Teague, the nephew of Thomas and George, seeking permission to 're-establish and extend the ironworks at Cinderford'. This time the Crown willingly granted the land required by Teague, especially as it was of no value to them for growing trees! Teague set up the Cinderford Iron Company in partnership with William Montague of Gloucester and Messrs. Church and Fraser, and they were later joined by William Bishop (mentioned above) who acted as clerk to the company.

During reconstruction Teague persuaded William Crawshay to invest in the concern, although he did not become a partner. Crawshay also began investing in other iron and coal concerns in the Forest from this date as witnessed by Shakemantle Iron Mine (page 120). The furnace was re-started in November 1829 with Moses Teague acting as manager, but it was not a very auspicious time for iron making as the market was very depressed, which resulted in the furnace being blown-out again by October 1832. However, the company was not deterred and in November Crawshay journeyed up from Wales to watch the setting out of the site for a second furnace.

In addition to extending the works, the Cinderford Iron Company itself was re-structured in 1834, with William Allaway, owner of tinplate works at Lydbrook, and John Pearce joining Teague, Montague and Crawshay in a new partnership which retained the old company name. By 1837 a large proportion of the output from the furnaces appears to have been going to the Lydbrook tinplate works and, with Allaway's son William in charge at Cinderford, Crawshay was concerned that some 'creative accounting' was going on. He and several other of the partners would have preferred another of Allaway's sons, Stephen, to be in charge at Cinderford, but this was not readily agreed to and Crawshay and Teague were looking to be released from the partnership. The crisis seems to have blown over, especially when a Mr. James Broad was appointed manager, a post he was to hold for the next twenty years.

In 1837 Crawshay bought up the shares of Pearce and Montague, who held two-twentieths each, thus giving him a half share in the works with Allaway. Crawshay had been giving the financial benefits from three-twentieths of his share to Moses Teague and continued to do so until Teague's death in 1847.

A third furnace at the works had been started in 1836 and was in production by 1840, when it is recorded that there were three blast furnaces together with a 54in blowing engine. From 1838 the annual output of iron was around 12,000 tons.

The works continued under the ownership of Crawshay and Allaway and the management of Broad until 1847, when William Crawshay sent his son Henry to the Forest to manage his interests. As this involved overseeing the furnaces, iron mines and collieries owned by William, it is likely that Henry's position was more as a general manager with Broad continuing as furnace works manager. In one way Henry being sent to the Forest was a form of banishment for marrying a serving girl, an arrangement never recognised by the family. Whatever the reasons behind his coming to the Forest, Henry set about the job he had been given with considerable energy. He improved and enlarged many of the Crawshay concerns, William Crawshay commenting in 1861 that Henry's pits, engines and collieries were 'the most perfect in the kingdom'.

When, in 1854, the Forest of Dean branch was opened as a railway, the furnaces were connected via a siding from Cinderford (Ruspidge). Crawshay also built a private railway between the furnaces and Lightmoor Colliery which, opening in 1854, was connected to the Forest of Dean line at Bilson. One broad gauge 0—6—0, supplied by the Neath Abbey Ironworks, is known to have worked on the line bringing coal from Lightmoor for use at the furnaces. As already mentioned, Crawshays had a private tramroad which was used to bring iron ore from the Buckshaft and St. Annall's Iron Mines, although, as this was a very rich ore, it had to be mixed with an inferior type brought from the western side of the Forest around Bream where Crawshays held several other iron gales. This ore was brought via the Severn & Wye tramroad to the interchange point at Churchway where the tramroad wagons were loaded onto broad gauge flat wagons, or 'runners', for carriage to the ironworks. This interchange facility appears to have been provided in 1867 prior to which date the tramroad was retained for through communication.

Despite Henry being regarded as something of an outcast by the family, his father obviously retained a soft spot for his son and, in 1854, William transferred his 50% interest in the furnaces to Henry and another period of expansion began. A fourth furnace was added c.1856/7, together with a new blast engine. It was probably in connection with these building works that Crawshay approached the South Wales Railway for the removal of the siding and connection to the ironworks for re-use at Meerbrook Quarry (see page 171). This work appears to have been carried out, so it is likely that traffic to and from the ironworks went via the Lightmoor Railway, interchange being effected with the Forest of Dean branch at Bilson. The siding from Ruspidge may have been reinstated in 1861 when the GWR put in a siding off the start of it to take out cinders generated by the furnaces for use as ballast, although it may not have the works directly off the Forest of Dean branch may have

Cinderford Ironworks in the 1890s, probably towards the end of its working life, with a large stock of pig iron stacked around the yard and on the wharves. The cylindrical steel structure was the furnace built by Messrs. Fielding & Platt in 1880. An interesting selection of GWR wagons and several tramroad wagons can be seen amongst the stacks of pig iron.   *Collection A. K. Pope*

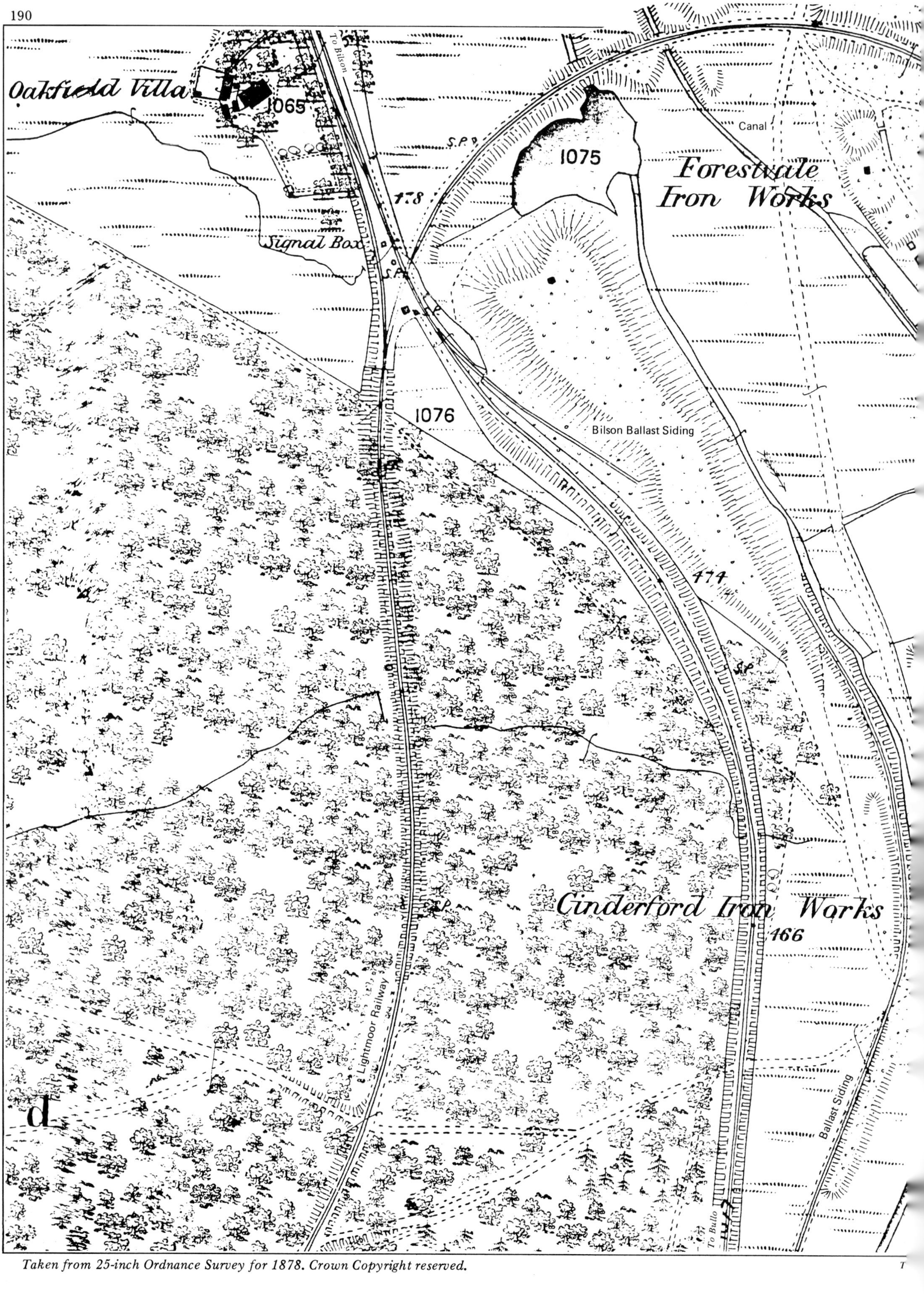
To Bilson
Oakfield Villa
1065
S.P.
178
Signal Box
S.P.
1075
Canal
Forestvale
Iron Works
1076
Bilson Ballast Siding
174
S.P.
S.P.
Cinderford Iron Works
166
Lightmoor Railway
d
To Bullo
Ballast Siding

Taken from 25-inch Ordnance Survey for 1878. Crown Copyright reserved.

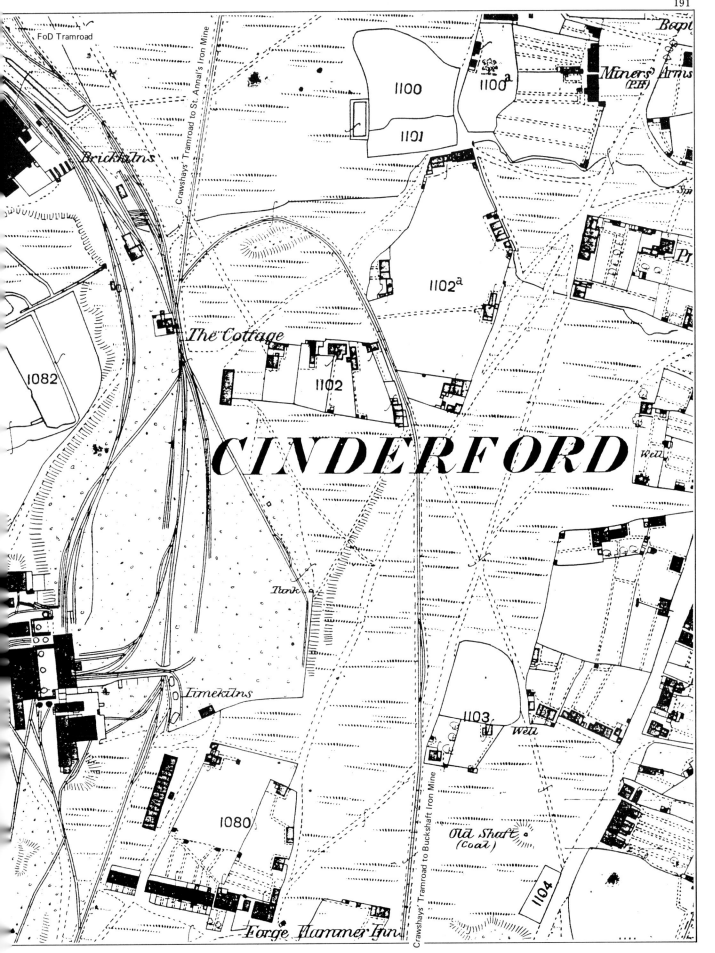

FoD Tramroad

Brickkilns

Crawshays' Tramroad to St. Annal's Iron Mine

1100

1100ᵃ

Miners' Arms
(P.H.)

1101

1082

The Cottage

1102ᵃ

1102

Well

CINDERFORD

Tank

Limekilns

1103

Well

1080

Old Shaft
(Coal)

1104

Crawshays' Tramroad to Buckshaft Iron Mine

Forge Hammer Inn

been restored until May 1870 — again this cannot be confirmed. Another possible date for the reinstatement of the siding is May 1878 when an agreement was taken out with Henry, Edwin and William Crawshay which mentioned a junction and 'part of siding laid down some years since'. The first edition Ordnance Survey already referred to shows a line coming from Ruspidge and splitting into two sidings terminating either side of a loading wharf for interchange with the internal ironworks tramroads.

In 1862 Henry Crawshay bought out Stephen Allaway's holding in the works for the sum of £50,000. Stephen had gained his interest upon the death of his father c.1850 and continued trading as the Cinderford Iron Company, at first with William Crawshay and then with Henry. In March 1862 Henry Crawshay issued a circular which stated that in future the works would be carried on by him alone as 'The Cinderford Iron Works'.

The *Mining Journal* for December 1866 reported that of the four furnaces only three were in use. At the No. 4 furnace 800 tons were made per month whilst output from the other two was about 600 tons each. The iron was sent mainly to Wales with Messrs. Banks & Co. of Pontyminster, near Risca, being large customers. Trade was 'very brisk' and heavy orders continued to come in. The furnacemen had plenty of employment and were 'generally a contented class of men'. Another source, also dated 1866, gives the dimensions of the four furnaces as height 43ft, breadth 14ft, that of the hearth being 6ft, the average make being 500 tons per week of the 'finest hot-blast iron'.

Throughout the late 1870s the works, like others in the Forest, were struggling financially due to competition from other districts, but, unlike the furnaces at Soudley and Parkend, which were blown-out in 1877, Cinderford was kept going by the personal intervention of Henry Crawshay who injected some of his own money to keep it going.

Henry Crawshay died in 1879 but the works continued under the name 'Henry Crawshay & Co.' and in 1880 two of the furnaces were being replaced by one of a more modern design, with two stoves to Cowper's Patent, said to be different from the system adopted at Soudley (see page 92). The work, entrusted to Messrs. Fielding & Platt of Gloucester, was completed but the furnace served only a relatively short life. Like others in the Forest, the works was hit by developments elsewhere, including the siting of ironworks close to ports to take advantage of cheaper foreign ore being imported.

By 1889 production was already down to 300 tons per week. At this time the works manager was John Yorke Jarrett who seems to have come to Cinderford Ironworks after the closure of the works at Soudley. Soon only one furnace was in blast and that was not working to full capacity. In May 1890 it was decided at a Board meeting to continue the current make of iron until the existing stock of coke, about 3,522 tons, was exhausted and then review the situation.

In February 1891 coke was only being bought 'from hand to mouth'. By October 1892, when repairs were needed to the furnace, it was decided that no active steps would be taken in this direction. Quotes were obtained for the work including £1,000 for relining the furnace by Harper & Moore of Stourbridge, and £500 for repairs to the stoves. The furnace continued to work for a while longer and the question of repairs was deferred once again in December

1893. A large injection of capital was needed, together with the possible introduction of steel production, but Crawshays were unable to finance it. In February 1894 overtures were made to the Dowlais Iron Co., who had interests in iron mines in the Forest, to purchase the ironworks and Crawshays' iron mines but nothing came of this. The state of affairs at the works could not continue and in March 1894 it was decided that the annual loss of about £3,000 at the furnaces, together with the £4,000 needed for repairs, could no longer be incurred. It was resolved that in the interests of all concerned the furnaces should be blown out with all speed. When notices of closure were issued, the men immediately offered to take a 10% reduction in pay, but the problems were more extensive and the works shut down on 9th April. In June 1894 it was reported that there were still 5,457 tons of pig iron in stock. It was not until November that it was decided that the ironworks would be sold off by auction. In January 1898 the tender of Messrs. Clements & Dix for £2,055 was accepted for the plant. Also sold off were thirty old coke wagons which, with the closing of the works, were no longer required. The site was soon cleared, the last chimney being thrown in May 1901. The large heap of slag and cinders which remained had already proved lucrative and would continue to be so for several years to come.

OUTPUT FIGURES: CINDERFORD IRONWORKS 1890-94

Month	Average production cost	Average selling price	Profit	Loss	Sales	Make	Stock
Jan. 90	59/6	74/3	14/9		544	1100	
Feb. 90	61/1½	74/6	13/4½		370		
Apl. 90	59/10	71/6	11/8		360	1000	4432
May 90	59/3	69/6	10/3		127		
June 90	59/3	69/5½	10/2½		272		
Aug. 90	59/3	54/3		5/0	848		
Sept. 90	56/2¼	56/3	¾		1637		
Oct. 90	55/1	56/7	1/6		625		
Dec. 90	54/6	56/7¾	2/1¾		978		
Jan. 91	54/4	54/3½		½	802		
Feb. 91	54/4	53/8½		7½	975		
Mar. 91	52/5	52/0		5	1036		
Apl. 91	52/9	57/9	5/0		1035		
June 91	52/0	52/8	8		n/a		
Aug. 91	56/2¾	52/1¾		3/1	989		
Sept. 91	55/9½	49/11½		5/10	1789		
Oct. 91	52/3½	49/10½		2/5	1637		
Nov. 91	52/11	49/8¼		3/2¾	1469		
Jan. 92	54/10¾	51/0		4/10¾	917		
Feb. 92	53/7	51/4¼		2/2¾	1173		
Mar. 92	52/1½	50/1		2/0½	1127		
Apl. 92	50/4	50/9	5		1007		5262
May 92	51/8	50/10		10	1065		
Sept. 92	53/7	51/4¼		2/3¾	n/a		4530
Nov. 92	54/0½	51/5		2/7½	913¾		
Dec. 92					nil		
Jan. 93	53/0½	49/4¾		3/7¾	854		
Mar. 93	51/5	50/10½		6½	876		
Apl. 93	50/10	50/10¼	¼		624		
May 93	50/9	48/7¼		2/1¾	601		
June 93	51/2	49/4		1/10	826		
July 93	51/4	47/10		3/6	922		
Aug. 93	51/6½	49/1½		2/5	776		
Sept. 93	51/5¾	49/1½		2/4¼	818		
Nov. 93	51/7¼	49/1¾		2/5½	919		
Jan. 94	53/11¾	49/5		4/6¾			
Feb. 94	53/6	49/2¼		4/3¾	1155		
Mar. 94	Furnaces blown out	48/0			2249		6446
May 94		47/4½			913		5457
July 94		48/2¾			830		
Sept. 94		47/10½			558		
Oct. 94		48/6¾			450		

PANORAMA OF CINDERFORD, FROM THE VALLEY ROAD. (D).   WP. 148

The remains of Cinderford Ironworks and the workers' terraced houses viewed from a slag tip, perhaps not the most obvious subject for a local postcard. The slag siding ran into this area from the right.

Collection A. K. Pope

RUSPIDGE BALLAST SIDING

In June 1861 the GWR requested permission from the Crown to lay down a temporary siding to take away a heap of ballast in the form of cinders purchased from H. Crawshay & Co. This was the refuse from the various boilers and processes within the ironworks, the tips extending along the western side of the Cinderford Brook to the north-west of the works, the extremes of the tip being defined by the brook, the Forest of Dean branch and the curve of the Lightmoor Railway.

The siding, which extended from Ruspidge to Lightmoor Crossing, was originally sanctioned for two years (until June 1863) but it is not clear whether it was ever removed, as it is shown on the first edition 25-inch Ordnance Survey of 1879. The 1863 Working Timetable allowed for ballast trains from Cinderford to Cheltenham running along the South Wales main line 'between all Trains Up and Down during the night'.

In March 1897 the GWR extended the 'ballast siding at Ruspidge' which had been used for the last four years; then in June the siding came to the notice of the Crown when Mr. David of David & Sant, quarry owners, inquired if the Crown had any slag heaps to dispose of. He must have had his eyes on the old ironworks tip as questions began to be asked within the Deputy Gaveller's office and the Office of Woods as to who actually owned it. It was on Crown land for which no rent was paid and thus the Crown felt that they could legitimately charge a royalty on its removal. It was then discovered that the Cinderford Crushing Co. were

sending 'many tons daily' away from the tip using a siding laid on the course of the GWR's temporary 1861 siding.

Arthur Morgan's Cinderford Crushing Co. specialised in blast furnace slag and was later to remove some from the Soudley Ironworks site, as already mentioned on page 96. The company sold crushed slag, screened and unscreened, and ashes to the GWR which, in 1895 for example, had awarded contracts for slag for the Newport and Hereford divisions. Slag was also sold for use in producing concrete. The Cinderford tip had been purchased by the Crushing Co. in June 1892 for the sum of £20 from Henry Crawshay & Co. although when the Crown inquired as to how long the Crushing Co. had been in possession, the year 1895 was mentioned!

The Crown decided that a rental for the siding, which as far as they were aware had been removed in 1863, was due from the Crushing Co. together with a royalty for every ton taken. The licence for the siding was set at £1 per annum. In November 1897 it was thought that the slag would take 2-3 years to remove but it was not until September 1902 that the work was finished, the siding removed and the ground restored. It is possible that ash and cinders may also have been loaded on the Crushing Co.'s siding around the turn of the century, when Arthur Latham was working heaps around the Forest Vale ironworks site.

This was not the end of debris removal from the ironworks site as on 22nd August 1924 the East Dean District Council gave permission to Arthur Morgan to lay a line across Valley Road at a point about 350 yards from the Crump Meadow Colliery office 'to convert slag from Old Furnaces for material or ballast for use on railways'. Considerable plant was to be built and it was expected that about twenty people would be employed. On 17th August 1925 Arthur Morgan signed a private siding agreement with the GWR which on 6th June 1925 issued instructions for 'Ballast Siding Ruspidge'.

Special Instructions to be Observed for Working of Ballast Trains between Bullo Pill and Ruspidge, Forest of Dean Branch

The existing disused Siding on the Cinderford side of Ruspidge Station has been extended, and a loop provided capable of holding 30 wagons and van, leading into two dead end sidings — one to hold 15 wagons and the other to hold 20 wagons — for the purpose of obtaining ballast which will be worked from the site by Ballast Trains to points beyond Bullo Pill.

The trains, which will consist of vacuum fitted hopper wagons, will ordinarily work between Bullo Pill and Ruspidge as under:

Empty train	arr.	dep.
Bullo Pill		5.5 p.m.
Ruspidge Sdg.	5.25 p.m.	

Loaded train	arr.	dep.
Ruspidge Sdg.		6.20 p.m.
Stop Board		6.27 p.m.
Bullo Pill	6.40 p.m.	

Whilst the Ballast train is locked in the Siding at Ruspidge the empties must be berthed in the dead end Sidings, and the loaded wagons formed in the train.

Ruspidge is a non-Staff Station and the connection to the Siding there is locked by a key on the Electric Train Staff when Eastern United Signal Box is in circuit and Electric Train Token when the Block Section is between Bullo Pill and Bilson Junction.

The train on arrival at Ruspidge will be met by a Porter Signalman from Bilson Junction, and the Driver must hand the Electric Train Token or Staff to him to unlock the Ground Frame. The train will then be drawn into the Siding, and after it is inside and clear of the points the Porter Signalman must lock the train in — satisfying himself that everything is in order — and at once proceed with the Electric Train Token or Staff to Bilson Junction where he must hand it to the Signalman, informing him that the whole of the train (with tail lamp attached) has been locked in the Siding at Ruspidge.

On receipt of the Electric Train Token or Staff and the Porter Signalman's assurance that everything is in order, the Signalman at Bilson Junction must replace the Electric Train Token or Staff in the Instrument and send the 'Train out of Section' signal to the Box in the rear.

After the 5.37 p.m. Rail Motor ex Newnham has arrived at Bilson Junction, the Signalman must ask 'Is line clear' for the loaded Ballast Train to leave Ruspidge for Bullo Pill and when accepted, withdraw the Electric Train Token or Staff which he must hand to the Porter Signalman to take to Ruspidge. The Porter Signalman must unlock the points and let the train out of

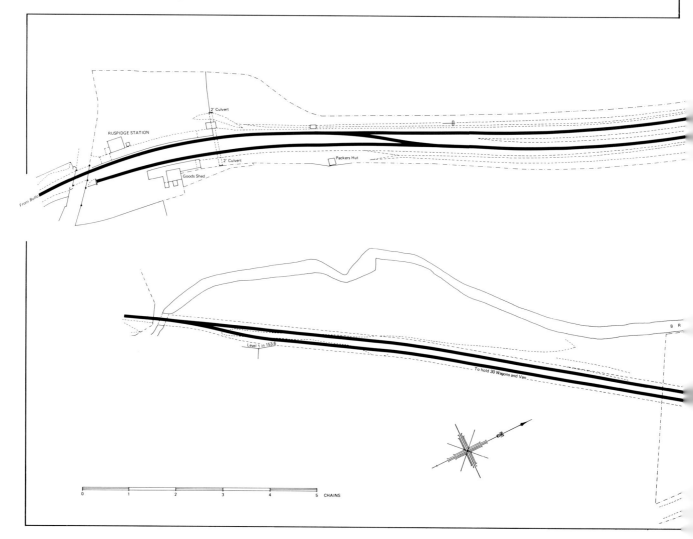

Whitchapel Row is said to have once been stables. The back of this row of workers' cottages features in the middle of the view on page 193. This is Valley Road which occupies the site of the sidings into the works, as seen on page 188.

Collection A. K. Pope

RUSPIDGE HALT & BALLAST SIDING 1925

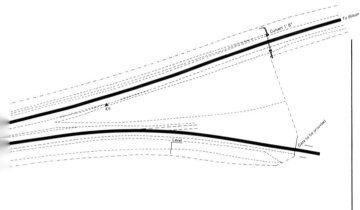

the Siding, and after he has again placed the points in their normal position he must hand the Electric Train Token or Staff to the Driver, and the train will then proceed to Bullo Pill. The Porter Signalman must then immediately advise the Bilson Junction Signalman by telephone that the train is leaving, and the Signalman must then send 'Train entering Section' signal to Bullo Pill.

In the event of the Ballast Train not being ready to leave Ruspidge at its booked time, the Guard must so inform the Porter at Ruspidge, who must at once inform the Bilson Junction Signalman to prevent the latter asking 'Line Clear' for the Ballast Train at that time; in which case similar arrangements as outlined above must be made for the Ballast Train to leave Ruspidge after the 6.48 p.m. Rail Motor ex Bilson Junction has cleared Bullo Pill.

Under no circumstances must engines pass the crusher in the dead end Siding at which point an Engine Notice Board is being erected.

Manuscript notices will be issued announcing when the Ballast Trains will pass.

S. Morris. Div. Supt.

It is not clear how long Arthur Morgan's traffic had continued but it was not until the weekend of 26th and 27th February 1939 that Ruspidge Goods Ground Frame was moved 30 yards nearer Bilson in consequence of the removal of the redundant siding. The connection had faced the down direction but the new point connecting with the remaining goods siding faced the up direction.

Cinderford from Beachtree Hill.

This panorama features most of the trackbed of the ballast siding, which ran from Ruspidge station, just off the right of the picture, to the site of the ironworks which was situated in the area on the left-hand side of the print.

Collection A. K. Pope

Heading away from Ruspidge, the gradient eased to 1 in 201, then successive shorter stretches of 1 in 66, 149, 99, 178 and 475 before entering Bilson Junction at 1 in 1280. The back of Whitechapel Row is featured on the right. *A. K. Pope*

A train of empties for Northern United in the early 1960s, passing the trees featured in the previous view. *A. K. Pope*

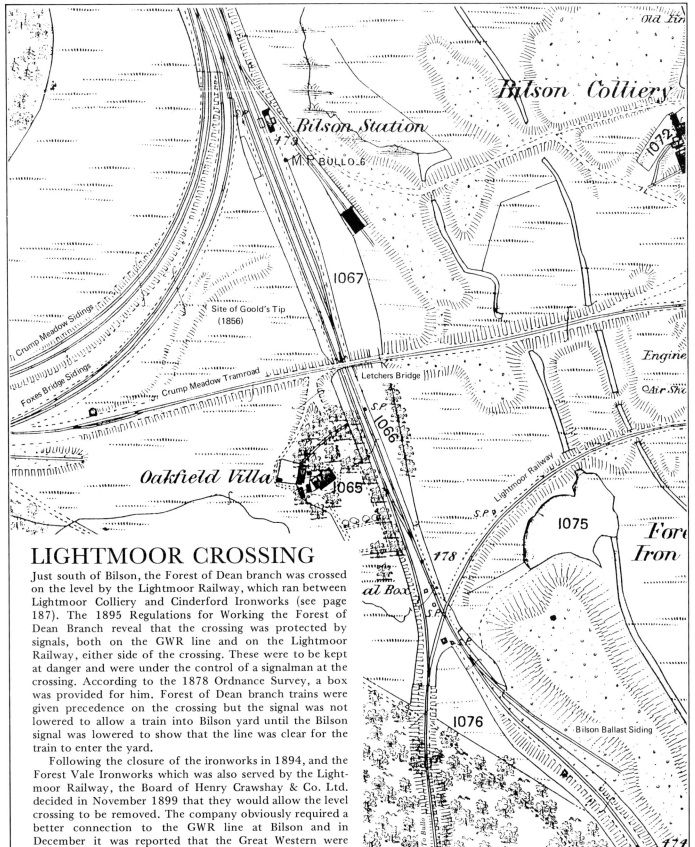

LIGHTMOOR CROSSING

Just south of Bilson, the Forest of Dean branch was crossed on the level by the Lightmoor Railway, which ran between Lightmoor Colliery and Cinderford Ironworks (see page 187). The 1895 Regulations for Working the Forest of Dean Branch reveal that the crossing was protected by signals, both on the GWR line and on the Lightmoor Railway, either side of the crossing. These were to be kept at danger and were under the control of a signalman at the crossing. According to the 1878 Ordnance Survey, a box was provided for him. Forest of Dean branch trains were given precedence on the crossing but the signal was not lowered to allow a train into Bilson yard until the Bilson signal was lowered to show that the line was clear for the train to enter the yard.

Following the closure of the ironworks in 1894, and the Forest Vale Ironworks which was also served by the Lightmoor Railway, the Board of Henry Crawshay & Co. Ltd. decided in November 1899 that they would allow the level crossing to be removed. The company obviously required a better connection to the GWR line at Bilson and in December it was reported that the Great Western were willing to put in the 'necessary siding for the conduct of Crawshays' traffic', and that the old crossing and the sidings at Bilson could be taken out. It therefore seems reasonable to assume that the two sidings running alongside the branch towards Bilson yard date from this time.

BILSON BALLAST SIDING

Little is known of this siding which was also provided to take ballast from the ironworks tip. The siding was removed by 1902.

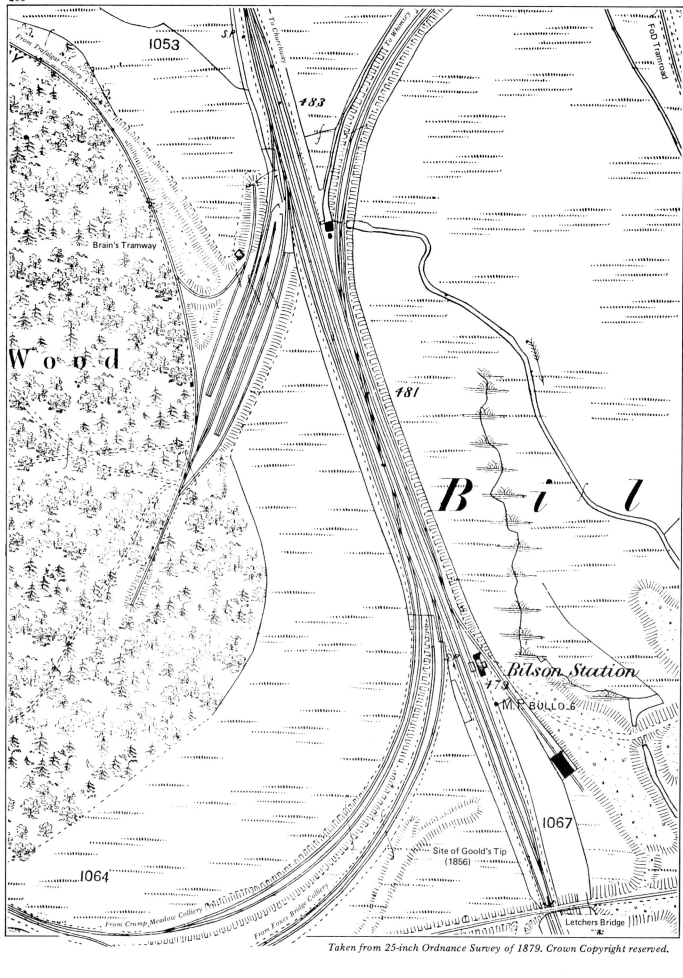

From Trafalgar Colliery

1053

S.P.

To Churchway

To Whimsey

FoD Tramroad

Brain's Tramway

483

Wood

481

B i l

Bilson Station

473

M.P. BULLO 6

1064

1067

Site of Goold's Tip
(1856)

From Crump Meadow Colliery

From Foxes Bridge Colliery

Letchers Bridge

Taken from 25-inch Ordnance Survey of 1879. Crown Copyright reserved.

BILSON

Bilson Halt temporarily served the town of Cinderford from 3rd August 1907 until the opening of the Bilson loop (to allow trains to run into the S & W station closer to the town) on 6th April 1908. It remained in unadvertised use (see page 14) and was only finally removed in 1944. One driver remembers 'a couple of hundred people on the platform' for the workmen's train. The gate on the left of this 1922 view closed across the private Lightmoor Railway. *H. J. Patterson Rutherford*

Bilson effectively formed the end of the Forest of Dean branch, as the two lines which diverged at the northern end of Bilson yard were known as the Churchway branch and the Whimsey, or Cinderford, branch. The junction was formed at a spacious site on Bilson Green and sidings were provided for the marshalling of trains. Later, several colliery lines joined the Great Western here and thus Bilson Junction became the focus of much activity.

Unfortunately, no track plans of the site during the broad gauge period have yet been discovered but it is known that in 1856 there were no colliery sidings running into the yard. A branch of the tramroad between the Crump Meadow and the Bilson Collieries, both of which belonged to the Bilson & Crump Meadow Collieries Co. of Mr. Aaron Goold, ran to the western side of Bilson yard and terminated at a tip. Goold had contacted the South Wales Railway board in January 1854 to ask for a branch from Crump Meadow to the new railway to avoid inconvenience to his pits when the tramroad was superseded. Brunel was instructed to prepare plans and the branch was agreed to on condition that Goold guaranteed a tonnage of 40,000 tons a year. In August 1855 Messrs. Tredwell, one of the contractors building the Forest of Dean branch, submitted their account for the construction of sidings 'into Goold's pit'; this may have referred to the siding on the western edge of Bilson yard under the tip. In September 1856 Messrs. A. and F. W. Goold were granted

permission to put in a siding in connection with their Bilson-Prospect Colliery. Whilst this may refer to a siding off the original tramroad, which was retained through Cinderford, it just might have been for the siding on the eastern side of Bilson yard which features on the first edition 25-inch Ordnance Survey as passing through a structure of some kind. The purpose of this siding and nature of the structure is unknown but it may have been for coal loading from Bilson Colliery.

In March 1857, when Goold was trying to persuade the SWR to discontinue the charge of 3d per ton for the use of tips at Bullo, the Board resolved to reduce the charge to 1d per ton depending 'on the outcome of the refusal of Goold to complete his sidings at Bilson in accordance with plan'. The following month he was requesting permission to put 'the Bilson & Crump Meadow Co.'s branch to Bilson inside the [South Wales] Co.'s fence.' This undoubtedly refers to a broad gauge branch from the colliery to Bilson yard built under a Crown licence granted to Goold and John Heyworth on 7th June 1855. The branch was certainly not completed in 1856. The South Wales minutes record that the branch was 'likely to interfere with the ground prepared for such additional sidings as may be required' and proposed an extension of their sidings at £80 which Mr. Goold should then build his tips alongside'. The SWR minutes for 15th November 1861 record that a siding was authorised at Bilson for the sum of £170 because the

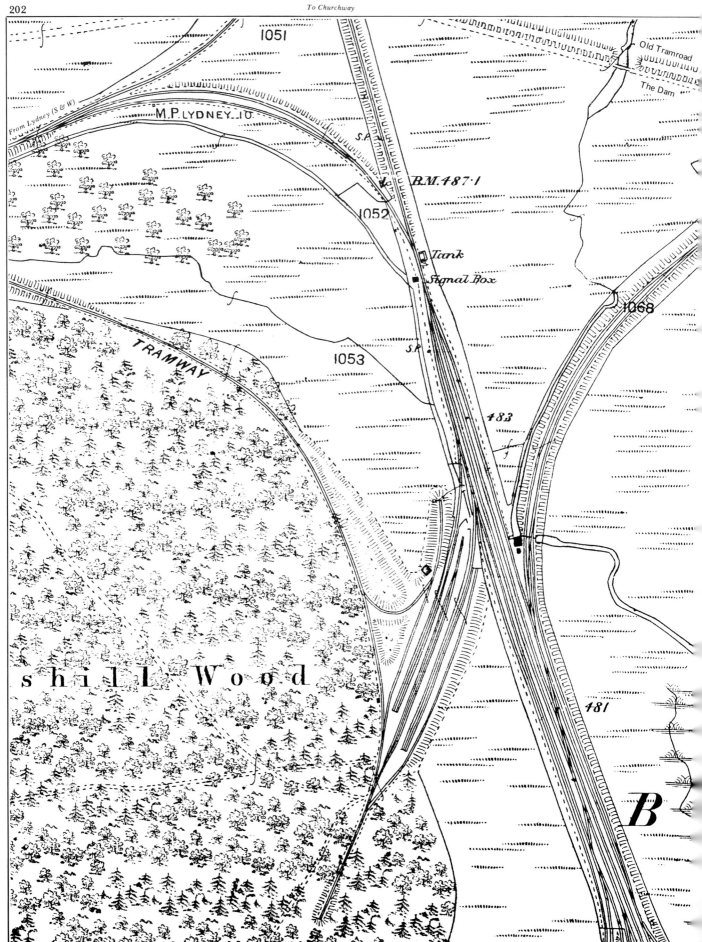

1051

Old Tramroad

The Dam

From Lydney (S & W)

M.P. LYDNEY. 10

S.P.

B.M.487·1

1052

Tank

Signal Box

S.P.

1053

1068

483

TRAMWAY

481

s h i l l   W o o d

B

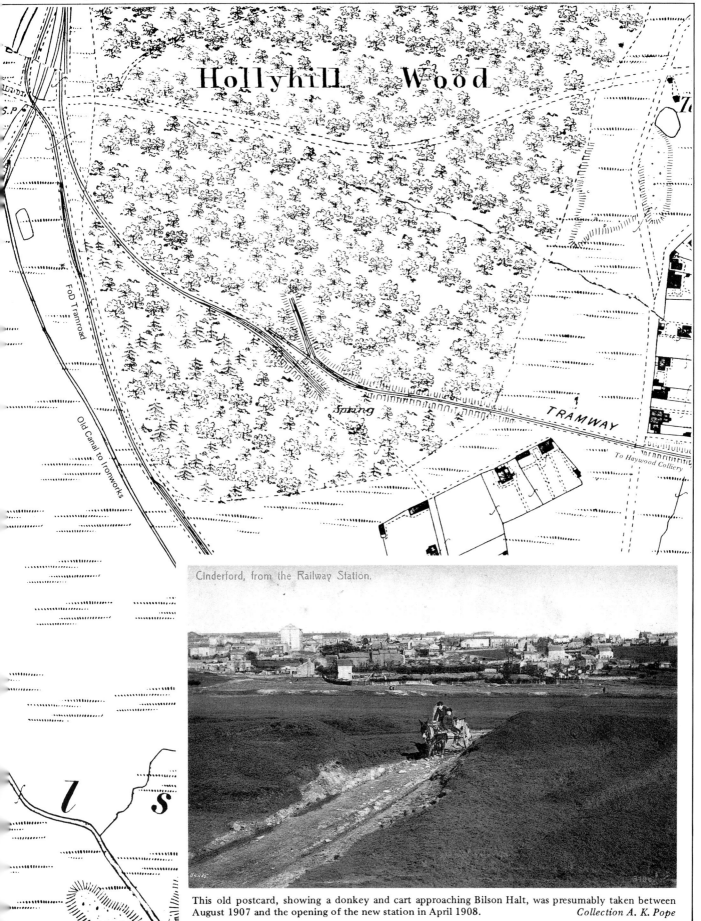

Cinderford, from the Railway Station.

This old postcard, showing a donkey and cart approaching Bilson Halt, was presumably taken between August 1907 and the opening of the new station in April 1908.

Collection A. K. Pope

General View of Cinderford.

General View, Cinderford.

railway company had been compelled to use Mr. Goold's siding 'at inconvenience to him of which he complains'. As with much of the early history of Bilson, it is not clear which siding this refers to, but it may be the one under the tip for Crump Meadow Colliery, suggesting that the sidings from the colliery were as yet incomplete. Although the broad gauge layout of the sidings is unknown, it was probably little different from the standard gauge arrangement shown on the first edition Ordnance Survey of 1878.

SWR minutes for 26th August 1859 record the receipt of a letter from Cornelius Brain proposing a branch from Trafalgar Colliery to Bilson. As he estimated that it would be two years before he would be ready to send coal to market, it was decided that points for a siding would only be provided when he was 'ready for traffic or at once if Mr. Brain pays'! Plans were obviously drawn up by October 1861 when Brain objected to the point at which his branch was to join at Bilson. He feared that because it was further north than the Crump Meadow connection, he would have to pay a greater railway toll! However, he was assured that he would be charged the same rate as his competitors. On 30th May 1862 Brain obtained a licence from the Crown for a 'road or tramway 15ft broad' and built a 2ft 7½in gauge line, known as Brain's Tramway, from which coal was tipped direct into broad gauge wagons.

In 1862 a public goods station was opened at Bilson and it seems likely that the structures in the middle of the yard date from this time. The provision of goods facilities at Bilson undoubtedly reflects the growth of Cinderford which was occurring at this time, the settlement having spread across the hillside, the areas known as Littledean, Woodside and Bilson now assuming greater importance than Cinderford Bridge. To oversee the goods station and the whole line, a station master was appointed at Bilson.

Further to all this, some time around 1868, rope-worked broad gauge inclined sidings were also laid to connect the new Foxes Bridge Colliery with the Forest of Dean branch at Bilson, the new sidings curving in from the west adjacent to the Crump Meadow connections.

It seems likely that Bilson Goods station was superseded by the opening of the new and more commodious goods station further north at Whimsey in 1884, and in 1890 it appears that a branch off Brain's Tramway, connecting it

with Bilson yard, was closed, the Trafalgar exchange sidings presumably being removed soon afterwards.

The 1895 Working Regulations give some details of the operation of Bilson yard. As well as the station master, there was also a head shunter and a centre signalman. The latter suggests that as well as the signal boxes at the Lightmoor Crossing and at the north end of Bilson yard, which controlled the Churchway branch and the junction with the Severn & Wye Railway, there was a box in the yard itself.

An accident report in the Dean Forest Mercury for 4th March 1887 mentions William James, a shunter at Bilson, who was killed when he fell off the steps of the engine while shunting wagons into the Lightmoor siding. James had been employed for about three months and was aged 19. One of the witnesses at the inquest was Joseph Williams, a number taker at Bilson.

The introduction of the FoD passenger service in 1907 brought about further expansion at Bilson which incorporated the junction of the new Cinderford loop line. This connected with an eastwards extension of the Severn & Wye Joint Railway, which had crossed the GWR lines north of Bilson Junction to reach the new GWR and S & W Joint Committee station at Cinderford in 1900.

The new arrangement, which presumably included provision of the signal box, diverted passenger trains over two new passenger lines built along the eastern edge of the existing layout, behind the former goods offices. The left-hand track connected with the existing Whimsey line and was used by passenger trains for Drybrook, whilst the right-hand track ran parallel for a while before climbing away on a curved embankment to join the new extension line at Cinderford Junction.

As the Cinderford loop was still under construction when passenger services commenced on 3rd August 1907, a (temporary?) halt opened to the south of Letchers Bridge bearing a nameboard proclaiming 'Bilson for Cinderford'. Equipped with two corrugated iron pagoda style shelters, Bilson Halt was used by colliers travelling to Crump Meadow, Foxes Bridge and Lightmoor collieries. When the new loop was eventually opened on 6th April 1908, Bilson Halt was simultaneously officially closed. In fact it seems most likely that it continued in use for colliers but this is unconfirmed. The halt was reopened on 2nd April 1917 and

General View of Cinderford.

A panoramic view of Cinderford c.1910, looking westwards, provides a rare view of the inclined tracks descending from Crump Meadow and Foxes Bridge Collieries into Bilson yard. The nearest one is Crump Meadow's gravity-worked line (by this time the second one for Crump ended by the gate in the GWR boundary) whilst behind is the rope-worked incline from Foxes Bridge — the triangular braced posts between the tracks guided the haulage rope. Wagons from these collieries were let down as far as the gate by colliery employees and pulled into the yard by the GW engine. The back of the signal box features in the centre of this composite view which also shows the Crump Meadow tramroad in place across Letchers Bridge.   *Collection I. A. Pope*

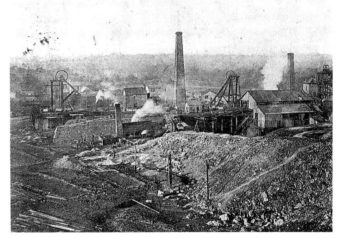

Crump Meadow Colliery, Cinderford.

Crump Meadow Colliery.

closed again on 1st October 1920, but thereafter staff remember it remained in unadvertised use and even appeared in official timetable alterations in March 1930.

From 1907 Bilson Junction was staffed by a station master, goods clerk, two signalmen, later three when Eastern United Box opened, two railmotor conductors, two signal porters, and one signal porter (S & W Jt assisting). Bilson was also responsible for staff at other locations on the line such as porters at Steam Mills and Whimsey. It is evident that, from this time at least, the station master here effectively controlled the line, but whether this control passed to Cinderford when the service was extended in 1908 is not known. A handwritten journal entitled 'Duties of Staff, Special Regulations, etc. at Bilson Junction' has survived and provides a detailed list of staff duties. It is believed to date from the start of the passenger service in 1907 with later additions and amendments, and because it gives an unusual insight, the following extracts are quoted:

DUTIES OF STAFF

Stationmaster [Originally A. E. Thomas, then C. J. Rees, T. E. R. Morris, M. Parry]
To have charge of all stores and stationery, see they are economically used, and to keep under lock and key what is not actually in use. To inspect daily the Offices, Boxes and see that everything is in proper order. To take charge of all Rail Motor tickets, issuing them to conductors as required. To enforce discipline amongst the staff and to report at once all disobedience of orders and any absence from duty or neglect. To see that the uniform staff appear in their uniform when on duty and they are at all times neat and clean. To examine the signals occasionally and satisfy himself that they

Foxes Bridge Colliery, showing the top of the rope-worked incline which led down to Bilson Yard. Both of these collieries will be covered in *The Severn & Wye Railway Vol. 4.*

Looking south from Letchers Bridge after the removal of the Lightmoor Railway, which continued beyond the sidings on the right. When the Lightmoor Railway was in use, the colliery company's engine brought loaded wagons into these sidings, uncoupled and whistled for permission to draw forward into the yard. After receiving a hand signal, it drew forward near the signal box where it waited while a GWR engine backed over the crossover to collect the wagons from the Lightmoor sidings and pull them into the yard. The Lightmoor engine then returned to pick up empties left in the other siding and take them up to the colliery. Bilson Platform had been situated on the left of the running line at the beginning of the curve.

L. E. Copeland

Lightmoor Colliery, again really part of the story of the S & W Mineral Loop to be covered in *The Severn & Wye Railway Vol. 4.* Collection A. K. Pope

work properly and that the lamps are kept clean. To enforce civility to the public on the part of staff at all times. To be responsible for the accurate preparation of all returns, for their being rendered when due. To close cash book 4.10 p.m. [later 2.30] daily and make up cash, handling cash bag to Stationmaster at Ruspidge Station [later Cinderford] same evening for despatch next morning [later 'same day'] to Newport in travelling safe per 7.25 a.m. [later 6.15 p.m.] ex Cinderford, and see that all books are entered up regularly, that all correspondence is attended to regularly and promptly, replies sent and that receipts are obtained from the consignees for all goods and parcels delivered to them. To pay particular attention to all special train notices, circulars or instruc-

tions of any kind issued from the chief officer and see that the staff under him do the same. To be responsible for the entire work of the station and see that it is carried out efficiently and that those under him regularly and faithfully discharge the duties allotted to them.

Goods Clerk [Originally Bertram H. Holder, then J. Horner?, John W. Boyd, Herbert Bull, B. Morris (sequence not proven)]
Make out invoices and record them in books daily, also enter up the other books relating to the traffic and compile the monthly accounts, to assist in the general duties of the office. To check conductors' slips with tickets and excess notes when they pay in daily, enter up booking clerks' train book, proof book and render

The Lightmoor Railway's Peckett 0—4—0ST, works No. 906 of 1902.   *H. G. W. Household*

passenger accounts, also returns to Divisional Superintendent's Office *including return of passengers carried over loop line to and from S & W Jt.* [* to * later crossed out] Make out weekly coal returns and goods and passenger revenues, also monthly returns of coal ex Eastern United and Foxes Bridge Collieries. Pay all cash daily to Stationmaster at 4.10 p.m. [later 2.30 p.m.] To check charges of inwards invoices & enter up books relative to same. Compile ledger accounts and register deductions and deal with correspondence respecting the entries, also general correspondence. Do advising concerning crippled wagons and confirm weights to firms who do not weigh their own traffic. Promptly attend to telephone instruments when no other member of the staff is available.

Signalman No. 3 Station Box [J. H. May]

On duty at 5.00 a.m. to 3.00 p.m. [later 1.00 p.m.]
Alternate week on duty at 11.40 a.m. to 9.40 a.m., Thurs 12.40 p.m. to 10.40 p.m., Saturdays 1.15 p.m. to 11.15 p.m.
Duties per list supplied from Divisional Inspector and posted in Signal Box, dated 31/7/07. Relieved by Signalman No. 4. Change hours of duty each alternate week with Signalman No. 4.

Signalman No. 4 Station Box [H. Canning, then W. J. Locke]

On duty at 11.40 a.m. to 9.40 p.m., Thurs 12.40 a.m. to 10.40 p.m., Saturdays 1.15 p.m. to 11.15 p.m. [later 1.00 p.m. to 9.00 p.m.]
Attend to GWR and S & W Jt. trains at the transfer junction. Duties as per list dated August 1st 1907, issued by Divisional Inspector and posted up in signal box. To relieve Signalman No. 3 each alternate

week. Assist as required, enter up and check Ruspidge wagon books, record weights and relieve clerk to dinner 1.00 p.m. to 2.00 p.m.

Signalman No. 5 Eastern United Box [F. H. (later W. C.) Waters]

On duty 5.00 a.m. to 3.00 p.m. [later 8.30 a.m. to 6.30 p.m., then 9.00 a.m. to 5.00 p.m.]
Duties as per list supplied from Divisional Inspector and posted in signal box dated Feb. 25th/14. Relieved by Signalman No. 6. Change hours of duty each alternate week with Signalman No. 6. To fetch in Signal Lamps after workmen's car has cleared Bilson Jc. 6.10 a.m. except during months of October, November, December, January and February when the work must be done according to necessity and train service. To register time engine enters Colliery Siding and time it returns. Take numbers and other particulars of wagon sheets and ropes put off and picked up, ascertain information which may be required from Colliery Coy. until late turn man comes on duty. To clean and trim all signal lamps and Staple Edge Halt lamps.

Signalman No. 6 Eastern United Box [W. J. Locke]

[Note apparently dated 12/10/15 states 'Dispensed with, only one man at Eastern' and description of duties crossed through.]
On duty 11.40 a.m. to 9.40 p.m., Thursdays 12.40 a.m. to 10.40 p.m., Saturdays 1.15 p.m. to 11.15 p.m.
Duties as per list supplied from Divisional Inspector and posted in signal box dated Feb 25th/14.
Change hours of duty each alternate week with Signalman No. 5 and deal with Down Distant Signal Lamp, clean Soudley Halt and

The site of Lightmoor Crossing where the Lightmoor Railway crossed the Forest of Dean branch on the level on its way to Cinderford Ironworks. This picture, taken on 26th August 1950, shows wagons on the remains of the Lightmoor exchange sidings. *John Norris*

Letchers Bridge, looking north into Bilson yard on 27th June 1948, with the running line on the right and two Lightmoor sidings on the left. Letchers Bridge, originally with timber beams and floor, was reconstructed in 1924 at a cost of £496. A second opening in the embankment had existed to the right of this view (seen on page 16). It was originally intended that a line should be put through the opening for use by passenger trains, thus giving a direct connection. The bridge was removed and the opening filled in June 1924.

L. E. Copeland

trim lamps ready for conductor to light, post bills in shelter and distribute handbills in Soudley. Clean Staple Edge Halt, light lamps at dusk and extinguish them after last car, post bills in shelter and distribute handbills in Staple Edge. Register time engine enters Colliery siding and time it returns. Take numbers and other particulars of trucks, ropes, sheets put off and picked up, put ropes ready to go forward in station truck daily and sheets ready to go forward in sheet truck Mondays, Wednesdays and Fridays. Ascertain information which may be required from Colliery Coy . . . [remainder illegible]

Rail Motor Conductor No. 5 [W. G. Harris, then Miss H. M. Bullock, S. R. Churchill, also J. M. Hills, J. W. Laxton (sequence uncertain)]
On duty 5.20 a.m. Off duty 3.20 p.m. [later 1.20 p.m.] Pay in cash 3.00 p.m. [later 1.20 p.m.] daily. To take charge of motor trains as per service book and special notices issued, until relieved by conductor No. 6 [later 7]. To issue tickets to passengers joining cars at halts, to enforce the Company's regulations relating to the behaviour of passengers, to see he has always sufficient change and supply of tickets before starting a trip, to obtain supply of the Company's publications and see that the publicity boxes on the cars are well supplied. To render journals to Divisional Superintendent punctually, to pay in cash at Bilson Jcn office at 3.00 p.m., change hours of duty each alternate week with conductor No. 6 [later 7]. To keep cars clean when in charge of same and sweep out cars daily at Drybrook from 9.30 a.m. to 10.00 a.m. *Parcels for Cinderford GW per 8.00 p.m. ex Newnham to be locked in Whimsey shelter on the 8.46 p.m. trip ex Drybrook. Also on Thursdays and Saturdays parcels per 9.34 p.m. ex Newnham to be locked in Whimsey shelter per 10.23 p.m. trip ex Drybrook*. [NB section * to * crossed out with the comment 'Now dealt with at Cinderford'.] To count passengers carried over loop, keeping separate records of those travelling to Cinderford only, travelling through Cinderford and joining car at Cinderford and render return of same weekly to Stationmaster. To confer with enginemen as to not stopping at Bullo Pill for water so as to avoid delaying main line trains. Not to allow passengers to alight or join cars at any place other than the halts or station platforms. To assist as required at Bilson Jcn office, also to clean and trim lamps at Drybrook Halt,

clean shelter and post bills [later deleted], removing same when out of date. Additional note – Trailers not to be loose shunted.

Rail Motor Conductor No. 6 [S. R. Churchill, later J. M. Hill, W. G. Harris, J. W. Laxton]
On duty 11.30 a.m. to 9.30 p.m. [later 10.00 a.m. to 8.00 p.m., then 12.30 a.m. to 8.30 p.m.] Thursdays 12.30 p.m. to 10.30 p.m., Saturdays 12.50 p.m. to 10.50 p.m. [later 12.30 p.m. to 10.30 p.m.]. To pay in cash at Bilson Office when coming on duty viz cash taken on cars the previous evening. To clean cars at Drybrook between 12.15 p.m. and 12.50 p.m. and at other times when necessary. Light lamps at Drybrook Halt and extinguish lamps upon last trip daily at Drybrook, Nailbridge, Whimsey, Staple Edge, Soudley, Bullo Cross and Ruddle Road. To render journals daily to Superintendent when in charge of car. To change hours of duty with Conductor No. 5 each alternate week and to perform the duties shewn under that heading. To send memo to Bilson Jcn office of bills out of date, bare timebill boards, defects or any irregularity at halts. Assist as required at Bilson office particularly in respect of literature for publication in the neighbourhood, and supply cars each morning and during the day as required, also see the current timebooks are exhibited in cars. Additional notes – The trailers not to be loose shunted. To prepare Bilson Jcn and Ruspidge coal abstracts and register weight invoices in Despatch Books. Each conductor to render to Stationmaster Bilson Jcn on Mondays a return in following form for Newspaper Parcels for halts between Whimsey and Drybrook. Date, From, To, Rate, No. of newspapers, Rly. Charge, Remarks.

Signal Porter No. 7 [H. Close, later A. G. Butler, W. A. Pitman, D. Coles (sequence not clear)]
On duty 5.00 a.m. to 4.00 p.m. [later 8.00 a.m. to 5.00 p.m.]
Change hours and duties each alternate week with signal porter No. 8 [later crossed out]. To open gates at Ruspidge Crossing for passing 5.10 a.m. auto engine ex Bullo Pill and work workmen's car as assistant conductor. To clean weighing office [later crossed out], attend to ground hand points during shunting operations, and also Ground Frame for goods trains leaving Bilson yard for Cinderford and Speedwell and also upon their returning to Bilson.

To relieve at S & W Jct cabin [later crossed out]. To take numbers of wagons forwarded and received, collect and fold all sheets and ropes, make out stock return for Wagon Inspector daily, giving particulars of rolling stock on hand and required. To record all trucks, ropes and sheets received and forwarded to collieries. Make out wagon returns at end of month, responsible for cleanliness of urinal and W.C., weighbridge and goods office, Bilson Halt, and to light fires. Check goods, enter up delivery books, check entries with invoices. Accompany 8.30 a.m. and 1.5 p.m. goods on Drybrook Branch. To attend to siding points, when required to open and close colliery siding gates, attend to yard lamps and telephone when possible.

Signal Porter No. 8 [A. G. Butler, later H. Close, W. A. Pitman]
On duty 7.50 a.m. to 6.50 p.m. [later 9.00 a.m. to 5.00 p.m.] Saturdays 10.15 a.m. to 9.15 p.m. [later 9.10 a.m. to 8.10 p.m.] Change hours and duties each alternate week with signal porter No. 7 [later crossed out]. Attend to signals and points at S & W Jc Cabin as required and in yard during shunting operations. Accompany 9.15 a.m. goods ex Bilson Jcn and record trucks in and out Eastern United Colliery Sidings also Shakemantle Siding [all later crossed out] and obtain signatures for traffic. Record numbers of trucks received and forwarded in evening and check all inwards and outwards traffic with invoices. Assist to fold sheets and ropes, take particulars of same, also trucks handed to and received from collieries. Advise consignees of traffic on hand. Open gates before using colliery sidings and close gates when not required for trucks to pass through to collieries or vice versa. Attend to yard lamps for lighting shunting operations. Label trucks as required and insert routes on all labels to foreign lines. Visit Lightmoor, Foxes Bridge and Crump Meadow collieries daily (except Saturdays) between 10.10 a.m. and 11.40 a.m. for purpose of obtaining signatures for traffic and particulars of Railway wagons, sheets and ropes on hand at each place. When signal porter No. 9 cannot come to Bilson Jcn to perform the duties allotted to that man, to work as assistant conductor *on 10.15 a.m. car ex Cinderford and later cars* as required. [* to * later crossed out] Assist generally in office.

Signal Porter No. 9 [H. Joyce, later A. King, A. W. Woodward]
S & W Jt Signal Porter who comes to Bilson Jcn to assist.
[Later note – 'Dispensed with Jan 1/17']
Late Turn – On duty 10.40 a.m. to 3.30 p.m. [later 4.00 p.m.], Thursdays 1.40 p.m. to 3.30 p.m., Saturdays 1.55 p.m. to 3.30 p.m. [later 11.45 a.m. to 4.00 p.m.]
Early Turn – On duty 11.25 a.m. [later 11.15 a.m.] to 4.30 p.m., Thursdays 2.45 p.m. to 4.30 p.m., Saturdays 3.00 p.m. [later 1.35 p.m.] to 4.30 p.m.
To relieve Signal Porters No. 7 and 8 as required, put out signal lamps, assist to fold sheets and ropes as required and prepare Bilson Jcn. [later Bilson & Ruspidge] coal abstracts. [Later note – 'Performed by late duty Conductor from Jan 1/17']

INSTRUCTIONS AS TO THE RECEIPT AND REMITTANCE OF CASH AT BILSON STATION

1. The names of persons at this station who are authorised to receive cash from the public on the Company's account are as follows.
   A. E. Thomas, Stationmaster [later C. J. Rees, T. F. R. Morris]
   B. H. Holder, Clerk [later J. W. Boyd]
   C. J. Williamson, Stationmaster, Ruspidge Goods [later P. Mills]
   R. Fear, Gateman, Soudley [later C. Rowbottom]
   Any trader or other person tendering cash to a member of the staff whose name is not shown above must be referred to one of the persons authorised to receive it.

2. The cash books at this station are closed at 4.00 p.m. The cash is made up at 4.00 p.m. and remitted daily in the following manner in accordance with the instructions of the Chief Cashier viz.
   By 7.25 a.m. [later 6.15 p.m. Jt train] car ex Cinderford thence to Newport per 7.33 a.m. from Gloucester [later via Lydney].

Bilson yard, viewed from Letchers Bridge on 26th August 1932, with spare auto-trailer No. 29 on 'the car siding'. Before (or during) the 1920s, four trailers had been kept at Bilson, then just two vehicles, one for the passenger service and one for the workmen's service and to act as a spare (see above). During the 1930s they were usually left overnight in the bay at Newnham and in later years they were kept at Lydney. As the safe at Bilson Junction had been broken into on several occasions, the 'motor car' takings were put in a locker below the instruments in the signal box. From left to right, the lines were: Lightmoor empties road (immediately in front of box); the bi-directional running line through to Churchway; 'the run-round' siding; the running line to Whimsey; and on the right the running line to Cinderford Joint. The two sidings on the left in the far distance were formerly connected to the Crump Meadow and Foxes Bridge Collieries, and the embankment running across the horizon carried the S & W's Cinderford Extension. The irregular boundary on the right marked the site of the siding and unidentified building shown on the 1878 Ordnance Survey. Signalman Hedley Woodward recalled a slightly different procedure to that described on page 209. He said the box would open at 4.15 a.m. (presumably 1920s/30s onwards) in time to release the single line token to allow a light engine to be sent from Bullo. On arrival, it would draw out the passenger trailer and shunt this clear. The loco would then bring out the workmen's trailer (which had been cleaned first) and return the passenger trailer to the siding for cleaning. The loco and workmen's trailer would then proceed to Drybrook Halt and work the workmen's train from there to Eastern United. The loco and trailer would then return to Bilson where the workmen's trailer would be exchanged for the (now clean) passenger trailer to work the first passenger service. In the afternoon the loco would return to Bilson to exchange trailers again and would work the return workmen's train from Eastern United to Drybrook Halt, sometimes picking up a van of bananas at Bilson for Whimsey. *L. E. Copeland*

Continued on page 214

Whilst the inspecting officer for the BoT didn't describe the signal box as new on his visit to inspect the FoD branch for the introduction of passenger services in 1907, it seems likely that it was installed only shortly beforehand in preparation for the associated modifications to the track layout. This picture was taken on 19th June 1933.

L. E. Copeland

A similar view taken much later, on 26th August 1964, showing the
arrival of 2—6—2T No. 4564 with the 11.55 a.m. goods from Bullo
Pill, and 0—6—0PT No. 8749 in 'the run-round' with a train of coal
from Northern United Colliery. *Rev. D. A. Tipper*

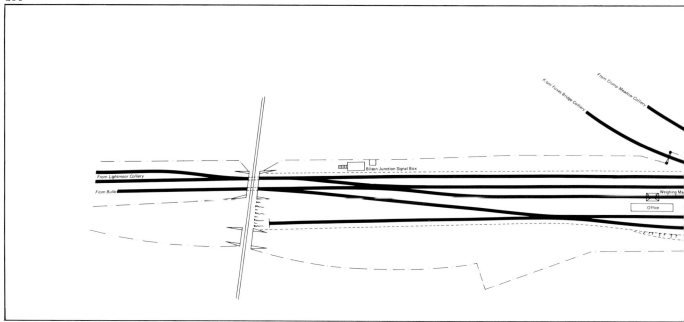

INSTRUCTIONS TO STATIONMASTERS AS TO THE RECEIPT & REMITTANCE OF COMPANY'S CASH

1. A form has recently been prepared and sent to me giving the names of the staff at each station who are authorised to receive cash from the public and this form has been returned to the station and must be kept in the station duty book in the office available at all times, indexed for easy reference and corrected from time to time as circumstances require.

2. Care must be taken that some person named on the list is on duty at all hours at which the station is open for Business. Any person tendering cash in respect of the Coy's Business to a member of the staff whose namee does not appear on the certified list must be referred to one of the persons authorised to receive money.

3. In respect of amounts received from the public at the station at the time of forwarding or delivering of Goods traffic a receipt must be given from book No. 296 and the counterfoil carefully filled up.

4. For amounts collected by the authorised staff in respect of accounts where credit has been given a receipt must be given from book No. 5 and the counterfoil carefully filled up. As far as possible the Stationmaster must personally collect ledger accounts and other accounts where credit is given by the Company. He must also compare the counterfoils of the receipt books with the cash books and see that the amounts collected are duly accounted for and satisfy himself in all cases that the cash payments made by the clerks and others authorised to receive cash are correct. The train book and also the parcels cash book must be compared with the clerks' cash book and must be signed daily by the stationmaster or officer appointed to receive the cash from the clerks.

5. Stated daily times must be appointed by the Stationmaster at which he or in the case of larger stations the Chief clerk or Cashiers will receive the money collected by each person at the station and the times must be shewn in the list referred to in the first clause of this instruction. The amounts must be signed for by the Stationmaster or in the case of a larger station the chief clerk or Cashier in the subsidiary book kept by the persons receiving the money as laid down in General Manager's circular No. 957 of January 1885. After the last train on the last day of each month, the Stationmaster must make a complete settlement with each clerk and others authorised to receive cash from the public.

6. All payments by cheque, bank note, postal or post office order received from the public in respect of the business of the public must be clearly and specifically entered in the cheque and note book 278 and payments relating to goods traffic must be entered in the goods cash book No. 462 with a reference to the debit to which they relate and if from any cause the amount of a cheque does not correspond with the entry in the cash book an explanation must appear opposite each entry in the cheque and note book No. 278.

7. In order that no misapprehension may exist it must be distinctly understood that cheque, postal or P.O. orders made payable to the Great Western Railway Coy. must not be exchanged for cash under any circumstances whatever but must be paid into the Coy. in the manner described, nor must a cheque be accepted which would necessitate change being given out or cash given out in exchange for cheques.

8. The daily totals received by the Stationmaster are shown in goods cash book No. 462, parcels cash book No. 463 and booking clerks train book 1863, and are to be transferred at the close of each day's business into the daily cash account and remittance book No. 257.

9. Every person whose duty includes the handling of cash must be cautioned as to its safe custody while in his possession and must be particularly prohibited from permitting the Coy's money to become in any way mixed up with his own money or to be used for any private purpose whatever and I cannot too strongly urge upon Stationmasters the necessity of doing all in their power to prevent irregularities of this kind.

10. I must remind Stationmasters that they are personally responsible for bringing these instructions into operation and for seeing that every member of his staff is made fully acquainted with them and fully understands the same and they must satisfy themselves by constant observation and specific examination of the work that all cash received in respect of the Coy's business is duly entered in the books and accounted for.

Signed: A. E. Thomas, Officer in charge of Bilson Jcn Station.
Countersigned: T. H. Roberts, Divisional Superintendent.

SPECIAL INSTRUCTIONS

Permission to walk the Line is granted to the following:

1. To walk on line between Bilson Jcn. and Bullo Pill for purpose of repairing trucks at stations above.

Continued on page 218

BILSON YARD

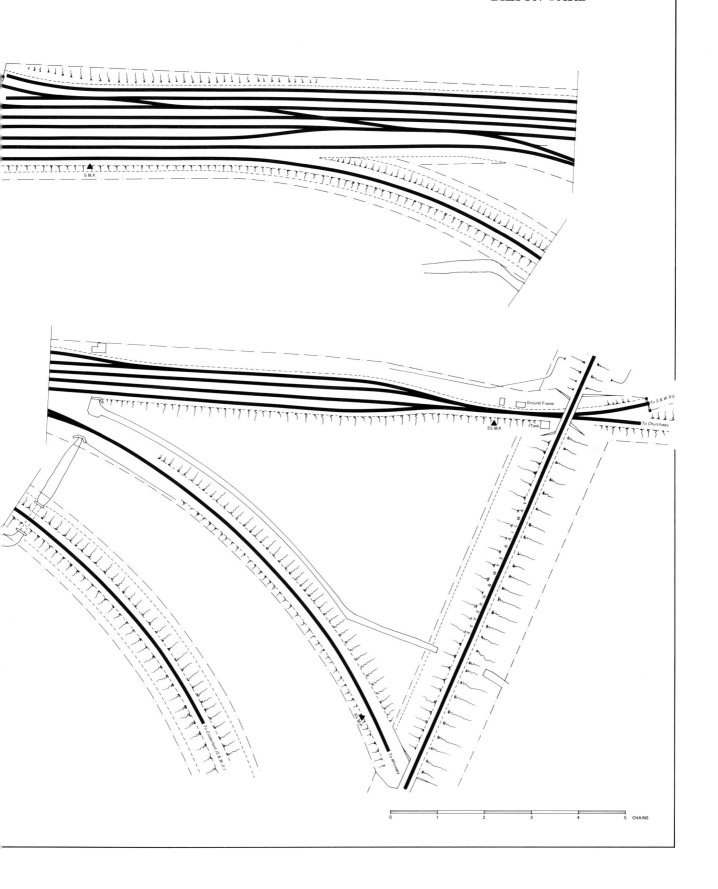

5 M.P.

Ground Frame

To S & W Riv

To Churchway

5¼ M.P.

Tank

S.B.

SEVERN & WYE JT.

To Cinderford (S & W Jt.)

5½ M.P.

To Whimsey

0   1   2   3   4   5 CHAINS

216

The Bilson signalman receiving the token for the section from Bullo (in a token carrier) and handing up the wooden train staff for the section to Cinderford Joint station, during the final years.

Derek Clayton

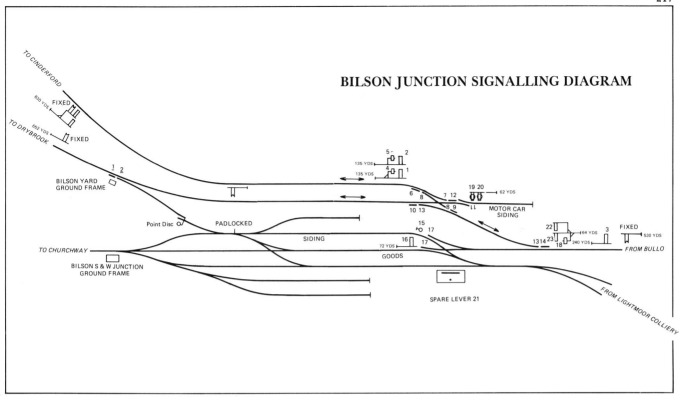

BILSON JUNCTION SIGNALLING DIAGRAM

The interior of Bilson signal box, with Len Roberts, on 16th February 1967. This box is reputed to have been the only box in the Forest area with every instrument in a single line box, including No. 6 and No. 7 Tyer's instruments, and was recorded in 1908 as having 23 levers plus 3 spare.

A. K. Pope

This view towards Letchers Bridge during the 1950s features the sleeper-built PW motor trolley sheds, the corrugated lamp shed and, in the foreground, the hand levers for local operation of the double slip. *John Norris*

2. To walk on line between Bilson Jcn. and Bullo Pill.
3. To walk on line between Bilson Jcn. and Soudley.
4. To walk on line between Bilson Jcn. and Shakemantle Siding and Bullo and halt to Ruddle Rd halts.
5. To walk on line at Brains Tramway Crossing.
6. To enter and be upon the Coy's premises in the vicinity of Bullo Cross Halt, Bullo Pill and Bilson Jcn.
7. To cross line at Eastern United Colliery.

1. W. Hurst, Wagon Repairer, Lydney & Crump Meadow Colliery.
1. Edwin Harry Fox, Wagon Repairer, Foxes Bridge.
1. Jas. Fox, Wagon Repairer, Foxes Bridge.
1. Arthur Dix, Wagon Repairer, Lightmoor.
2. Edwin Morgan, Lightmoor.
2. Harry (?) Morgan, Dean Forest Coal Co.
3. W. Meredith, Eastern United Colliery.
4. E. P. Morgan, Eastern United Colliery.
5. L. Cartwright, Trafalgar.
5. R. Cartwright, Trafalgar.
6. A. J. Dix, Wagon Repairer, Lightmoor Colliery.
4. S. Bright, Eastern United Colliery.
7. A. Adams.
7. C. Adams.
7. H. Adams.
7. F. Addis.
7. H. Addis [later deceased].
7. R. Addis.
7. W. Addis.
7. Wm. Frost.
7. J. Harris [later removed].
7. Wm. Harris [later removed].
7. F. Milliner.
7. J. Milliner.
7. Frank Davies.
7. Thos. Lusty.

One of the motorised trolleys used by the PW Department. Bilson Junction was the home station for Gang No. 117 after the introduction of the motor trolley system of maintenance on 10th April 1933. *Rev. D. A. Tipper*

Sufferance Roads & Footpaths
A crossing on the Churchway Branch to and from the neighbourhood of Trafalgar. Also a crossing on same branch near the Hawkwell Works claimed by the Crown as their right to grant permission to cross. A crossing on the Drybrook branch to and from the neighbourhood of Trafalgar. Tramway Crossing on Churchway branch is worked in accordance with printed instructions.

Custody of Cash
50/- petty cash is allowed at this station and it is kept in the safe, the key of which is always in the possession of the Stationmaster [later — and a duplicate key by the Conductor on late turn].

Wages Cash
This is delivered each Friday [later Thursday] per 2.30 p.m. car ex Newnham and the Stationmaster pays the wages of the Traffic and Engineering Dept. staffs.

Clocks
There is one eight-day clock fixed in the machine room [later crossed out], one in office and one in signal box.

Advice of Goods Traffic
Upon the receipt of any foreign wagon or important traffic a special messenger is despatched with an advice note to the consignee or telephone message is sent when practicable.

Train Staff and Regulations for working of F.O.D. Branch
This is worked in accordance with appendix to service book.

Working of Stock
A daily report is sent to Wagon Inspectors Gloucester per 4.45 p.m. car ex Bilson Jcn.

The back of the up home to main signals at Bilson Junction for the lines from Cinderford Joint and Whimsey, braced by a horizontal stay rod and by this time, 6th April 1962, with strengthening timbers at the base of the ageing wooden posts. The signals on the left-hand post applied to trains from the Whimsey line (on which the train of tank wagons is shown proceeding away from Bilson). The pair of arms on the right-hand post applied to the adjacent line from Cinderford Joint station (top arm read to main line, lower bracketed arm to the motor car siding).

A. K. Pope

Charges for Special Motor Cars & Trains
See circular book page 305.
Mr. Roberts' circular of Dec. 6th/12.

Accident & Breakdown Gang
In case of accident obstructing the working of the line, telegrams must be sent to:
1. Mr. Aldington, Paddington [later Mr. Nicholls]
2. Mr. Roberts, Gloucester [later Mr. Morris]
3. Mr. Fox, Loco Dept., Gloucester [later Mr. Dexter]
4. Mr. Perrett, Gloucester
5. Mr. Blackall, Eng. Dept., Gloucester

1 & 2 All cases of personal injury must also be telegraphed to these.
3 When Breakdown Gang is required
1 When necessary
5 [later 4] when Goods or Stock damaged
5 When necessary
To the District Engineer and Permanent Way Inspector also the District Traffic Inspector and stations where the running of any other train is likely to be affected by the accident.

Locking of Station and Custody of Keys
Signal Porter on late duty is responsible for locking up station and the custody of keys.

An earlier view taken on 27th June 1948 with the same pair of signals partially silhouetted by the strong midday sun. The subsidiary bracketed arms read to the motor car siding in which the Forest railmotors had reversed direction when travelling between Cinderford and Drybrook. At this time the facing point lock on the points in the motor car siding (essential for such a movement with a loaded passenger train) and the two ring-armed signals were still in use. By 1960 the FPL had been removed and the two siding signals replaced by one disc. The line from Cinderford is on the left and the one from Whimsey on the right.   *L. E. Copeland*

The administrative offices at Bilson, the back of which feature above, showing two generations of stone and a third very obvious brick extension. The station master was in the main office at the south end. This picture was taken on 1st October 1966.

A. K. Pope

Telegrams
Stationmaster and Goods Clerk are authorised to sign telegrams.

Engine Orders
These are signed by the Stationmaster or by the Goods Clerk for him in his absence.

F.O.D. Tramway Damhead to Ruspidge
The site of this Tramway is the Freehold property of the GWR Co. (9-8-1900).

Permissive Credits
1 month – Messrs. H. Griss & Co., Woodchester, Nr. Stroud 19/7/18.

Towels
For Stationmaster and Station Staff – 4 handtowels
For Signalboxes – 2 handtowels 15/4/16

Special Instructions for Working Sidings at Bilson Jcn Station
Invoicing Goods Traffic
All traffic forwarded from and received at the undermentioned sidings is dealt with at Bilson Jcn.

Lightmoor
Foxes Bridge
Severn & Wye Jcn
Trafalgar
Crump Meadow
Churchway
Duck [later – now called Broadmoor Brickworks and invoiced from Cinderford (Whimsey)]
New Bowson
Healey & Coy.
Addis Hill (Schofield)

The passenger service between Cinderford and Drybrook was withdrawn in 1930, leaving only the service between Cinderford and Newnham. Crump Meadow Colliery closed in 1929, Foxes Bridge Colliery in 1931 and Lightmoor in 1940, but the steady growth in output from Eastern United and Northern United ensured that Bilson yard was kept busy and often seriously congested, as mentioned on page 21.

Another view of the offices and the rail-built loading gauge spanning the 'run-round' siding. The first edition 25-inch Ordnance Survey shows what appears to be a weighing machine in front of the furthest end of the offices. This is confirmed by the 1925 track plan of Bilson yard.
A. K. Pope

Crump Meadow Colliery tip dominates the background of this view looking west across Bilson Green on 27th June 1948.

L. E. Copeland

This composite panorama of the north end of Bilson yard on 27th June 1948 provides an excellent view of the 1899/1900 embankment carrying the Cinderford Extension of the Severn & Wye Railway across the site towards the Joint station at Cinderford. It also shows the 31 chain Bilson loop line on the right climbing at 1 in 51 to join it at Cinderford Junction, the signal box of which just shows through the trees on the right. The other line, curving away behind the loop and passing through the girder bridge in the S & W embankment, led to Whimsey and Drybrook. The long crossover connecting the top end of the 'run-round' siding with the Whimsey line was controlled by Bilson North ground frame, which was operated by train crews when running in or out of the yard. The wagons on the left were empties for Northern United Colliery, the two rows on the far left were standing on the remnants of the sidings which had once served Crump Meadow and Foxes Bridge Collieries, whilst the next two rows were standing on the end of the Lightmoor empties road and the running line to Churchway respectively. Evidently with such congestion, access to and from Churchway was confined to the 'run-round'.

L. E. Copeland

Right: Bilson yard ground frame on 18th June 1933. The cover had been removed by the time the previous picture was taken, so it is not easy to spot.

L. E. Copeland

Far right: The overbridge carrying the Cinderford Loop over the site of the Forest of Dean tramroad. The overbridge in the S & W Cinderford Extension embankment can be seen in the background. By the time the loop line was opened, in 1908, the tramroad was out of use, although questions of ownership of the trackbed may have required the bridge to be built. This picture was taken on 6th October 1946.

L. E. Copeland

Cinderford Junction, shown here on 6th October 1946, dated from the opening of the loop line to Bilson Junction in April 1908, the box being a standard GWR timber-frame hipped-roof design of the period, with 8 levers plus 3 spare.

L. E. Copeland

CINDERFORD JUNCTION

A closer view of Cinderford Junction box amidst the clutter of lamp huts, tablet catcher and motor trolley huts, etc. The new loop line and junction were placed under the control of the S & T linemen stationed at Lydney. This box was regarded by the Bilson Jcn signalmen as a 'cushy number' as there was only one 8-hour shift.

J. Burrell

The loop line is shown clearly in this view, curving in from the left to join the Severn & Wye Cinderford Extension line, and controlled by the fine wooden post bracket signal containing the S & W and Bilson loop up homes and Bilson Junction fixed distant. A 15 mph speed limit was enforced in both directions. The trees on the left form the edge of Holly Hill Wood which contained the earthworks for the exchange sidings between a siding off the Whimsey branch and a tramway from Haywood Colliery detailed in Volume 2.   *L. E. Copeland*

Two postcard views of Cinderford, which grew in size and importance during the second half of the 19th century, to become an important industrial centre. The absence of a passenger service on the GWR's Forest of Dean branch prompted the town's citizens to press the Severn & Wye Railway for a station closer to the town centre than Drybrook Road. Although the first representations were made as early as 1876, the station's construction was not commenced until 1898.

Collection Ian Pope

CINDERFORD

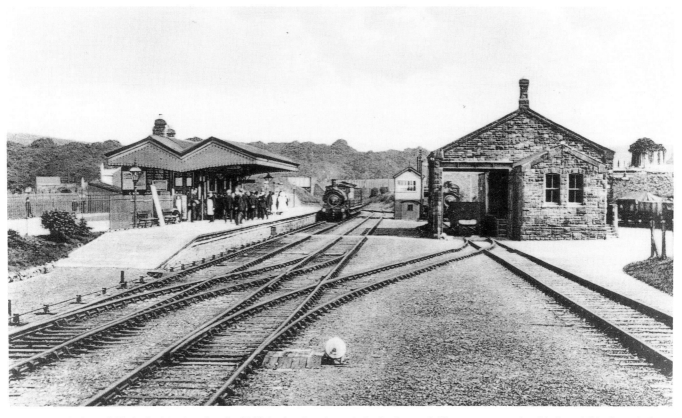

A postcard view of Cinderford station dated c.1908-9, showing the arrival of a Severn & Wye passenger train with, just visible through the goods shed door, an FoD auto train stabled behind the signal box. Both trains appear to be hauled by GWR '2021' class saddle tank locos. This is the only known view showing both services in the station at the same time, and it is likely that this arrangement may have only occurred during the early days of the FoD service. *Collection A. K. Pope*

The Cinderford extension was the last major development undertaken by the Severn & Wye Railway, albeit under joint Great Western and Midland ownership, in order to extend the S & W main line from Lydney Junction into a new station near the centre of Cinderford. The station was built by the GWR on the site of the town's fairground, the main buildings being constructed of Forest of Dean stone to the company's standard designs of the period.

Cinderford station opened to S & W passenger and local goods traffic on 2nd July 1900, the first train being an excursion to Weston-super-Mare via the Severn Bridge. Mineral traffic continued to be exchanged between the S & W and the Forest of Dean branch via the junction with the Churchway branch at the site of Cinderford Old station (see Volume 2).

As previously mentioned, the opening of the new loop line from Bilson Junction on 6th April 1908 enabled the FoD branch passenger service to reach Cinderford station, which attained joint GWR and S & W status from that date. Local goods traffic for Cinderford via the FoD branch continued to be dealt with at Whimsey (see Volume 2),

although this gradually transferred to the new station over the years.

The new service provided a much shorter route for travellers to Gloucester and this, together with increasing road transport competition after the First World War, effectively spelt the end for the Severn & Wye passenger service, which lingered on until 6th July 1929, the goods service lasting until 1949.

Cinderford signal box had already closed on 17th May 1927, the section from Cinderford Junction being worked by one engine in steam from that date. The connection with the S & W line was broken at Cinderford Junction on 31st December 1951, the junction box closing and the line between Bilson Junction and Cinderford station being worked as one block section from that date.

The history of Cinderford station has already been covered in greater detail and with more illustrations in *The Severn & Wye Railway Vol. 2*, but for the sake of completeness we have included a small selection of pictures here.

High Street

derford. 1209.

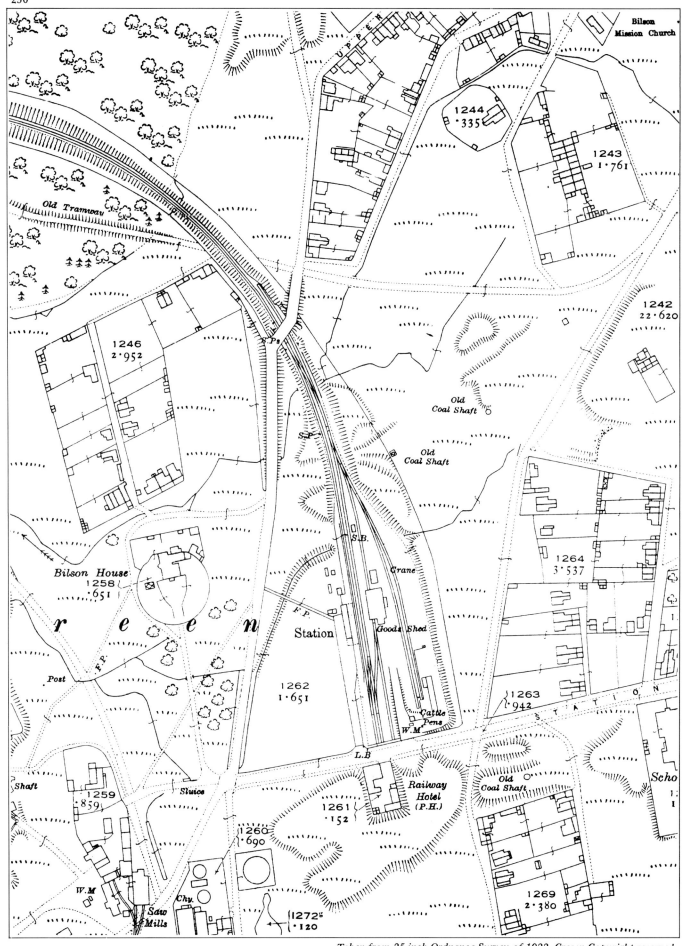

Bilson
Mission Church

1244
·335

1243
1·761

1242
22·620

Old Tramway

1246
2·952

S.P.

Old
Coal Shaft

S.P.

Old
Coal Shaft

1264
3·537

S.B.

Crane

Bilson House
1258
·651

r e e n

F.P.

Station

Goods Shed

F.P.

Post

1262
1·651

1263
·942

STATION

Cattle
Pens

W.M.

L.B.

Shaft

1259
·859

Sluice

1261
·152

Railway
Hotel
(P.H.)

Old
Coal Shaft

Scho

1260
·690

W.M.

Chy.

Saw
Mills

1272
·120

1269
2·380

Taken from 25-inch Ordnance Survey of 1922. Crown Copyright reserved.

Cinderford station goods yard throat and the redundant signal box can be seen in this view from the Valley Road overbridge on 21st June 1932. The fixed distant for Cinderford Junction replaced the former starting signal in 1929 when the box was taken out of use, and the goods yard headshunt was removed in 1941. *L. E. Copeland*

A '14XX' 0—4—2T in the loco release loop at Cinderford during shunting operations on 20th April 1933. *L. E. Copeland*

Richard Jones, seen here with his son Harry, was station master from 1924 until his retirement at the age of 61, at the end of 1932. *Courtesy Gladys Jones*

A '14XX' and auto-train can be seen in this view looking northwards over the station from behind the Station Hotel on 17th May 1948. The weighbridge office and loading bank are visible on the right while beyond these the Spero colliery site keeps the northern outskirts of Cinderford at a discreet distance. *L. E. Copeland*

A second view of the train shown earlier on page 31, this time in the more usual position next to the station building. The Station Hotel can just be seen beyond the loco.

W. A. Camwell

A Forest of Dean branch auto train at Cinderford on 7th July 1955, showing '14XX' No. 1421 at the 'Gloucester' end of trailer W30W. This is the only photo discovered showing this arrangement, which is untypical of the service and, presumably, a rare occurrence. Even so, the loco still faced 'uphill', to ensure the firebox crown was covered with water on the gradients from Bullo. *Geoffrey Oates*

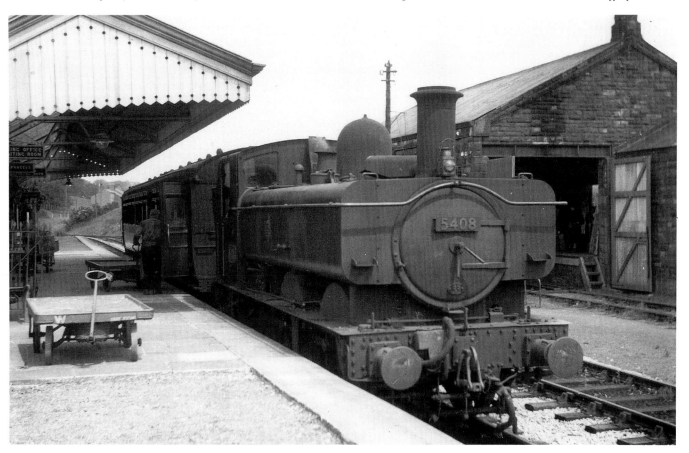

'54XX' class 0–6–0PT No. 5408 at Cinderford on 6th June 1955. The '54XX' class were a development of the '2021s' with larger wheels, dating from 1930, No. 5408 appearing regularly at Cinderford in the 1950s. *S. Fletcher*

1903			**1911**			**1918**	
1049	Feb		430	July		524	Aug
1570	Jan—Mar		1036	Jan, July, Sept—Dec		547	July—Aug
1698	Jan—Dec		1162	Nov		727	Feb—Mar, May—June
1699	Jan—Mar, May—Sept		1663	Jan—Oct, Dec		1228	June—Nov
1716	Jan—June, Aug—Dec		1665	Nov—Dec		1289	Jan—July, Aug—Dec
1848	Jan—Nov		1677	Mar—June, Aug—Dec		1613	Jan, Mar—Apl, Aug—Nov
2079	July		1690	Jan—Oct		1632	Jan—Aug, Oct—Dec
2364	Jan—Mar		1697	Jan—Feb		1673	Jan—Feb, Apl—Sept, Nov—Dec
			2082	Feb—Mar, June—July, Sept—Oct		2142	Jan—Feb, May—June
1904			2118	Jan		2160	Mar—Apl, Sept—Dec
962	Mar—Aug		2126	Apl—June, Aug, Oct—Dec			
1033	July—Oct, Dec		2155	July—Aug		**1919**	
1040	Apl—Nov					524	Feb—Mar, July—Aug
1138	July—Dec		**1912**			537	June—July, Sept—Oct
1570	Jan		1635	Oct—Nov		547	Apl
1672	Oct—Dec		1649	Sept		727	Feb, Aug—Sept, Nov—Dec
1690	Sept		1663	Jan—May		1190	May
1697	Nov—Dec		1665	Jan—Sept, Nov—Dec		1228	Mar, May
1698	Jan—June		1677	Jan—Apl		1289	Jan—Mar, June—Sept
1716	Jan—Feb, Apl		1690	Nov—Dec		1613	Apl, June—Aug
			1697	June—Dec		1632	Jan—Feb, Apl
1905			2101	June—Dec		1673	Jan—Mar, May—June, Aug—Oct
962	Sept—Oct		2126	Jan—Nov		1690	Oct—Dec
1033	Jan—Mar					2115	Aug—Sept
1138	Jan—Feb, Apl—Dec		**1913**			2140	Jan, Dec
1663	Oct—Dec		828	Apl		2160	May
1672	Feb—Oct		1566	Sept			
1690	Jan—Sept, Nov—Dec		1635	Sept—Oct		**1920**	
1697	Jan—June, Aug—Oct, Dec		1663	Apl—June, Aug—Dec		222	Oct, Dec
			1665	Jan—July, Nov—Dec		524	Sept
1906			1677	Jan		727	Jan—Feb
1138	Jan—Feb, Apl—Dec		1690	Jan—Dec		1036	Jan—Feb, Dec
1663	Jan—Apl, June—Sept, Nov—Dec		1697	Jan—May, July—Aug, Oct—Dec		1140	Feb—Mar, May—July
1672	Jan—May, Aug—Dec		2101	Jan—Apl, June, Aug—Sept, Dec		1509	Nov—Dec
1690	Jan, Mar—Dec		2126	Mar—May, July		1538	Sept—Oct
1697	Jan—Aug, Oct—Dec		2142	Sept—Dec		1539	Oct
						1673	Feb—Aug
1907			**1914**			1684	Apr, June, Aug—Dec
564	Sept, Nov		828	Aug—Sept		1690	Jan—May, July—Aug
828	Aug		1598	Feb—Mar		2082	Feb—May, Aug
962	Apl		1660	Nov—Dec		2140	Jan
964	Aug—Nov		1663	Jan		2160	July, Nov
1034	Mar		1665	Jan—May, July—Dec			
1138	Jan—May		1690	Jan—July		**1921**	
1162	Dec		1697	Jan—Oct		222	Oct
1295	Nov—Dec		2101	Mar, July, Oct—Dec		556	Jan—Feb, Apl, June
1663	Jan—Mar, May—Dec		2142	Jan—Feb, Apl—June, Sept—Oct		830	Dec
1668	July—Dec					1036	Jan—Mar
1672	Jan—Oct		**1915**			1160	Nov
1690	Dec		735	Jan—Feb, Oct—Dec		1509	Dec
1697	Jan, Mar—July		828	Jan—Feb, Apl—May		1520	Feb, May—June, Sept—Dec
2082	Oct		1660	Jan—June		1538	Mar, July—Aug
			1665	Jan—Apl, June—Aug		1684	Jan—Feb
1908			1690	July—Dec		1807	July—Nov
564	Jan—Feb		1769	Feb—Oct, Nov—Dec		2036	Jan
1162	June—Aug		2101	May, July—Sept, Oct—Dec		2082	May
1563	Feb		2142	Mar, June, Oct		2085	Aug
1580	Feb—Mar					2087	Apl
1596	Feb, Mar, June—July		**1916**			2115	July—Sept
1663	Jan		547	Sept		2140	Mar
1668	Jan—May, July—Dec		735	Feb, Apl—Dec			
1677	Feb—Dec		1228	July—Aug, Sept—Oct, Dec		**1922**	
1690	Jan—Dec		1613	Apl—July, Sept—Dec		222	Jan
1697	Jan—Dec		1660	Apl		830	May, Sept—Nov
1826	Dec		1690	Jan—Mar, May—Sept, Nov—Dec		1160	June
2082	Feb—July, Sept—Nov		1769	Jan—Feb, July—Dec		1509	Jan, Feb, Apr, June—Nov, Dec
			2101	Jan—Aug, Sept—Dec		1520	Jan, Mar—June, Sept
1909			2142	Aug		1525	Dec
1162	May					1538	June
1563	Aug—Sept		**1917**			1807	Feb, Mar, June—Dec
1596	Jan—Feb		524	Aug		2082	Feb, Aug, Dec
1668	Mar—Dec		547	Dec		2084	May
1677	Jan—Dec		727	Jan, Mar—May, Aug—Nov			
1690	Jan—Dec		743	Feb, Apl—July, Oct—Nov			
1697	Jan—Dec		1228	Apl, June, Aug—Sept, Nov—Dec			
1826	Jan, Apl—May, Oct		1289	July—Aug, Nov—Dec			
2082	Jan—June, Aug—Oct, Dec		1613	Jan—Oct			
2118	July, Nov—Dec		1632	Feb—Mar, June—Aug			
			1769	Jan—Feb, May—June			
1910			2142	June—July, Dec			
1033	Jan—May		2160	Jan—Feb, Aug—Nov			
1162	Dec						
1663	Aug—Dec						
1668	Jan—June						
1677	Jan—May						
1690	Jan, Mar—Dec						
1697	Jan—Mar, June—Dec						
2082	Jan, June—July, Sept						
2118	Jan, Feb—Aug, Oct—Nov						

The following are allocations as at 1st January.

Year	Nos.
1923	1509, 1807, 2082
1924	1509, 1520, 2115
1925	1231, 1525, 2082
1926	1026, 1807, 2142, 2146
1927	1231, 1807, 2082
1928	1161, 1525, 2069
1929	830, 1036, 1870
1930	528, 1870, 2024
1931	1429, 7700, 7741